Accession no.
36228961

Clinical Examination Skills
for Healthcare Professionals

Full the full range of M&K Publishing books please visit our website:
www.mkupdate.co.uk

Clinical Examination Skills
for
Healthcare Professionals

Edited by

Mark Ranson
Hannah Abbott

LIS - LIBRARY

Date	Fund
23/4/18	nm-WAR

Order No.

286776X

University of Chester

Clinical Examination Skills for Healthcare Professionals

Mark Ranson, Hannah Abbott (Eds.)

ISBN: 978-1-905539-76-5

First published 2014. This revised 2nd edn. published 2017

All rights reserved. No part of this publication may be reproduced, stored in a retrieval system, or transmitted in any form or by any means, electronic, mechanical, photocopying, recording or otherwise, without either the prior permission of the publishers or a licence permitting restricted copying in the United Kingdom issued by the Copyright Licensing Agency, 90 Tottenham Court Road, London, W1T 4LP. Permissions may be sought directly from M&K Publishing, phone: 01768 773030, fax: 01768 781099 or email: publishing@mkupdate.co.uk

Any person who does any unauthorised act in relation to this publication may be liable to criminal prosecution and civil claims for damages.

British Library Cataloguing in Publication Data
A catalogue record for this book is available from the British Library

Notice

Clinical practice and medical knowledge constantly evolve. Standard safety precautions must be followed, but, as knowledge is broadened by research, changes in practice, treatment and drug therapy may become necessary or appropriate. Readers must check the most current product information provided by the manufacturer of each drug to be administered and verify the dosages and correct administration, as well as contraindications. It is the responsibility of the practitioner, utilising the experience and knowledge of the patient, to determine dosages and the best treatment for each individual patient. Any brands mentioned in this book are as examples only and are not endorsed by the publisher. Neither the publisher nor the authors assume any liability for any injury and/or damage to persons or property arising from this publication.

To contact M&K Publishing write to:
M&K Update Ltd · The Old Bakery · St. John's Street
Keswick · Cumbria CA12 5AS
Tel: 01768 773030 · Fax: 01768 781099
publishing@mkupdate.co.uk
www.mkupdate.co.uk

Designed and typeset by Mary Blood
Printed in Scotland by Bell & Bain, Glasgow

Contents

Figures

Tables

Boxes

About the editors

Hannah Abbott is an Operating Department Practitioner with both clinical and academic experience, having held both teaching and senior leadership roles in Higher Education Institutes. She is currently an Associate Professor and Associate Head of School at Birmingham City University, and President of the College of Operating Department Practitioners (CODP). Hannah's current research includes non-technical skills in the perioperative environment and patient safety, in addition to her pedagogic research interests.

Mark Ranson is a Registered Nurse with some 20 years experience in healthcare practice including acute medicine, critical care, cardiology and cardiothoracic practice areas. He is currently employed as a Senior Lecturer in Acute and Critical Care at the University of Suffolk in Ipswich. Mark's main areas of interest lie in advancing healthcare practice as well as a keen interest in anatomy, physiology and pathophysiology as related to healthcare practice.

About the contributors

Susan Blainey PGCIHE, Non-medical Independent and Supplementary Prescriber, RT, BSc (Hons), RGN – Senior Lecturer (Non-medical Prescribing), University of Suffolk

Wendy Braithwaite MEd, PGCE, BSc (Hons), Dip HE, Formerly Senior Lecturer (Acute and Critical Care), University of Suffolk

Lee Cunnell PGCIHE, PG Cert Management, FHEA, BSc (Hons), Paramedic, RGN – Lecturer (Adult Nursing), University of Suffolk

James Robert Graveson BSc (Hons), PgCert – Lecturer in Paramedic Science, Birmingham City University

Esther Hosznyak BSc (Hons), MCPara – Paramedic South Western Ambulance Service, Visiting Tutor, Birmingham City University

Rachael Hosznyak BSc (Hons), GDip, PGCert, SFHEA, MCPara – Senior Lecturer in Paramedic Science, Birmingham City University

Dr Clare Laroche FRCP, MD, BSc (Hons), MBBS – Consultant in Respiratory Medicine, West Suffolk Hospitals NHS Trust

Donna Page MSc Advanced Healthcare Practice, Advanced Nurse Practitioner, Non-Medical Prescriber, Nurse Diplomate Faculty of Sexual and Reproductive Health (NDFSRH), Post-Graduate Certificate in Inter Professional Healthcare Education, BA (Hons) Psychology and French, Registered Nurse

Gareth Partington MSc, PGCIHE, BSc (Hons), RGN – Lecturer (Adult Nursing), University of Suffolk

Heather Passmore MPhil, PGCEA, BA, ADM, RM, RGN – Senior Lecturer/Education Lead (Midwifery), University of Suffolk

Dr Linda Pearce Doctorate Nursing, MSc, Nurse Practitioner, RGN – Consultant Nurse (Respiratory Medicine), West Suffolk Hospitals NHS Trust

Dr Gareth Rees MBChB, LLM, MRCPsych – Consultant Psychiatrist in Early Intervention in Psychosis Forward Thinking Birmingham

Helen Rees BA (Hons), RMN (BNurs Hons.); SCPHN (PGDip) – Teaching Fellow in Mental Health Nursing, Birmingham City University

Sooreka Wapling MSc, PGCE, BSc (Hons), RGN – Senior Lecturer (Adult Nursing), University of Suffolk

Alexander John Westaway BSc (Hons), PGCert LTHE, FHEA – Senior Lecturer in Paramedic Science, Birmingham City University

Foreword

Reflecting the increasing use of shared learning opportunities in healthcare education, the authors of this book have taken on the ambitious task of creating a reference tool suitable for a wide range of healthcare professionals who may be faced with the challenge of taking a clinical history and conducting an effective physical examination. The target audience includes nurses, midwives and members of the allied health professions, and the skills described are fundamental for any practitioner who wishes to understand their patient's specific needs and to plan appropriate care.

Recognising that readers will come from a diverse range of clinical backgrounds and roles, the opening chapter (on conducting a consultation and the skills needed to take an accurate clinical history) underpins the systems-based approach. This allows healthcare professionals to focus upon the fundamental principles of examining the system or systems that are most relevant to their specific area of practice. The use of case study examples helps readers relate the theory directly to their own areas of practice.

The authors of this book come from the same diverse range of professions for whom the book has been written, and their wealth of knowledge and experience enable them to understand the challenges facing today's healthcare professionals.

Bill Kilvington FCODP
Patient Safety Lead and Past-President, College of Operating Department Practitioners

List of abbreviations

AAGBI Association of Anaesthetists of Great Britain and Ireland

ACE Angiotensin-converting enzyme inhibitors (a type of medication to reduce hypertension)

ALP alkaline phosphatase

ALT alanine aminotransferase

APEC Action on Pre-Eclampsia

APTT measure of Albumin

ARBs angiotensin II receptor blockers (a type of medication to reduce hypertension)

ASA American Society of Anesthesiologists

AST aspartate aminotransferase

BIS bispectral Index

BMI body mass index

BP blood pressure

CMACE Centre for Maternal and Child Enquiries

CODP College of Operating Department Practitioners

COPD chronic obstructive pulmonary disease

CV cardiovascular

DAS Difficult Airway Society

DVT deep vein thrombosis

ECG electrocardiograph

EEG electroencephalogram

ENT ear, nose and throat

GI gastrointestinal

GU genitourinary

Hb haemoglobin

HCPC Health and Care Professions Council

mmHg millimeters of mercury (Hg), unit of measurement for blood pressure

IBS irritable bowel syndrome

INR international normalised ratio blood test (blood clotting)

LMA laryngeal mask airway

MAC minimum alveolar concentration

MAP mean arterial pressure

MCH mean corpuscular haemoglobin

MCV mean cell volume

mg milligrams

mmol/l millimoles per litre

μmol/L micromoles per litre

MSK musculoskeletal

MSU mid-stream urine specimen

NCCWCH National Collaborating Centre for Women's and Children's Health

NCEPOD National Confidential Enquiry into Perioperative Deaths

NIBP non-invasive blood pressure

NICE National Institute for Health and Clinical Excellence

NMC Nursing and Midwifery Council

NV neurovascular

ODP operating department practitioner

PACU post-anaesthetic care unit

Pg picograms

pH measure of acidity/alkalinity

PONV post-operative nausea and vomiting

SEQ systems enquiry

SH social history

SMS submental sign

STI sexually transmitted infection

TIVA total intravenous anaesthesia

TMD thyromental distance

ULBT upper lip bite test

VAS visual analogue scale

VDS verbal descriptive scale

VTE venous thromboembolism

WHO World Health Organisation

Chapter 1

Consultation and clinical history-taking skills

Susan Blainey

History-taking does not exist in isolation; rather it occurs in the context of a consultation. It is a competency-based activity requiring key communication skills to gather information about the patient. It can arguably be seen as the most important element in any clinical encounter. The ability to take a clinical history is certainly fundamental to developing and establishing an effective practitioner–patient relationship.

The word 'taking' suggests that this process is dominated by the clinician and this idea perhaps derives from early teaching methods, whereby medical students were taught a two-part approach to case management: firstly the interrogation of the patient; and secondly the physical examination (Armstrong 1985). Most practitioners will be familiar with the traditional concept of medical history-taking, in which the junior doctor on the ward clerks a patient by gathering information using an easily recognised standard framework. However, interrogation in medicine has long been integrated with consultation in history-taking (Neighbour 2007, Pendleton 1993), which constitutes a far more holistic approach.

Although it is often perceived as particular to medicine, where the long-established standard medical model is used (see Box 1.1, page 2), the actual *process* of history-taking is also undertaken by nursing and allied health professionals to gather information about the patient's health status.

Box 1.1: Medical model for history-taking

- Presenting complaint
- History of presenting complaint
- Past medical history
- Drug history
- Family history
- Social history
- Systems enquiry

The specific history-taking framework used by a particular professional group may vary according to the intended outcomes relating to that professional group but the *skills* required for effective history-taking are common to all healthcare professions.

Traditionally, nursing staff members take a psychosocial or humanistic approach, largely aimed at identifying patient problems and needs, as opposed to a medical diagnosis (Young *et al.* 2009). Models developed by nursing theorists as far back as 1966 (Henderson) and as recently as the 1990s (Roper *et al.* 1990, Orem 1995) have been well established for this purpose.

The modernisation agenda within the NHS Plan (2002) and Making a Difference (2002) has led to continuing policy initiatives (Department of Health 2001, 2011) to encourage new ways of working to help improve services and enhance the quality of patient care. Traditional role boundaries have been challenged and professional responsibilities have changed, enabling nurses and other allied health professions to work in different ways. Their enhanced roles require practitioners to take on responsibilities in areas that have traditionally been viewed as belonging to the medical domain. These include medical history-taking, diagnostic and physical assessment, and prescribing.

Good history-taking skills are acquired through practice, using a variety of techniques and building on past experiences. The suggestion by Tierney and Henderson (2012) that the ability to take a good history cannot be achieved by reading books rings true. It is of course an experientially acquired art, learned over time, with each patient. Through practice, a healthcare practitioner learns what to ask, what to ask next, what to emphasise, what to prioritise, what to discard and what areas to investigate. A history is more than just information gathered from the patient. Done well, it should reveal the nature and extent of the problem, the context of the problem, the impact of the problem, and the patient's concerns, ideas and expectations.

Structure *is* important and an ordered framework can be helpful in order to guide the process. But successful history-taking ultimately relies on communication skills, applied in the right manner and context to achieve a successful encounter for the patient and practitioner. It is this skill set that will enable the patient to tell the story of their illness.

The aims of history-taking

When taking a history, it is worth thinking about your overall aims. What are you trying to achieve? For example, are you trying to make a diagnosis? Are you establishing fitness for surgery? Or are you identifying risk-taking behaviour?

Goals for history-taking may alter or expand within consultations in the light of a changing context or an unfolding clinical situation. A patient history may commonly be taken to:

- establish the system(s) responsible for the symptom(s)
- make a diagnosis
- identify a differential diagnosis
- gather information about the patient's overall health status
- clarify the nature of the disease process
- establish fitness for surgery/anaesthetic
- understand the patient's individual circumstances, and their concerns, ideas, expectations and beliefs.

Effective history-taking is vital in order to arrive at an accurate diagnosis. Practitioners undertaking new roles may initially focus on mastering new physical assessment skills but equal emphasis should be placed on the ability to obtain an accurate history. The physical examination and any subsequent investigations are important but they should help to confirm or refute the differential diagnosis you have *already* made, based on the history.

Furthermore, the history should not only tell you about the likely disease process, it should also inform you about the subjective nature of the illness – in other words, the patient's experience of the disease, and its effect on their life, their concerns and ideas. In an acute or life-threatening situation, the emphasis will clearly switch to physical assessment skills, as recognising and interpreting clinical signs will take priority. Nonetheless history-taking will still be important, as key information will be required from records or relatives, for example.

The standard medical approach to history-taking

The standard framework widely used for medical history-taking provides an established seven-point credible structure. For practitioners in new roles, it offers a helpful common language that can facilitate communication across inter-professional groups. Figure 1.1 shows the complete framework, with expansion of the key areas pertinent to each of the seven components. Additionally, two parallel panels, adapted from Kurtz et al. (2003) and Bickley (2008), are embedded to demonstrate some of the key underlying factors and processes that contribute to effective history-taking.

The seven components of the comprehensive health history provide a structure for the patient's story and a standardised format for the written record. However, the order shown should not necessarily dictate the sequence of the interview. Whilst several papers and texts discuss the need to follow this approach systematically (Douglas et al. 2011, Crumbie 1999), others encourage flexibility (Shah 2005, Bickley 2008). In the *Bates' Guide to Physical Examination and History-Taking*, Lynn Bickley talks about the need for clinicians to be flexible in their interview approach to history-taking, advocating the need to change style as befits the particular or changing situation. In other words, be ready to use a focused, or problem-oriented, approach, when it best suits the patient or the situation. Like a tailor fitting a garment to an individual customer, the practitioner should adapt the scope of the health history to the individual patient. This approach will need to take into account co-factors such as the patient's perspective, concerns and problems; the practitioner's goals for assessment; the clinical setting (such as acute, inpatient or outpatient; specialist area or primary care) and the time available.

Depending on the context, you do not necessarily always have to go through all seven components. In primary care, for example, a full systems review is rarely done unless there is no clear starting point for the presenting problem. Initially, though, it may be more helpful to follow the model systematically. As you gain experience, part of the skill is having the confidence to adapt the model and approach to the specific situation.

Presenting complaint
The symptom(s) or reason(s) why the patient is seeking advice

History of presenting complaint
A continuation of the exploration of the presenting complaint, detailed area of enquiry required

Past medical history
- Four key areas: medical, surgical, obstetric and psychiatric history
- Long-term conditions
- Major operations

Drug history
- Both prescribed and over-the-counter treatments are important
- Allergies
- Recreational drug use
- Immunisations
- Contraception

Family history
- General health of other immediate family
- Illnesses that run in families, e.g. thyroid, cardiac, cancer, diabetes, asthma, TB

Social history
- Living situation
- Lifestyle habits: alcohol, smoking, diet (quality, culture, beliefs), exercise
- Occupation
- Personal relationships, sexual health, religious beliefs, leisure activities
- Pets

Systems enquiry
Head-to-toe concise review of each major system:
- cardiac
- respiratory
- gastro-intestinal
- genito-urinary
- musculoskeletal
- neurological

Key parallel factors

Identifying data:
name, age, gender, address

Consider reliability:
memory, mood, age

Identify source of history:
parent, carer, interpreter

Key parallel processes

Environment:
seating, noise distractions, computer, interruptions

Building the relationship

Establishing and maintaining rapport

Observing what you hear

Hypothesis generation

Figure 1.1: The standard medical model (adapted)

You will develop your own preferred style and, whilst each of the seven steps will be looked at individually, the actual interview will usually be more fluid and will follow the patient's leads and cues. With practice you will find that the model is simply there in the background, as a supporting framework that you draw on to fill in any gaps as the interview progresses. Your success with the patient can be measured by how far you incorporate all the separate components into one meaningful whole.

The seven components

The presenting complaint (PC)

This first step should be to establish the precise reason or reasons why the patient is seeking medical help. The specific reason the patient is seeking care should always be borne in mind, as the presenting complaint may involve a combination of physical, social or psychological problems, as demonstrated in the real-life primary care examples below.

Box 1.2: Examples of social, psychological and physical reasons for seeking care

'I need a sick note.'

'Do you think my child has autism?'

'My daughter is bullying me.'

'I want an abortion.'

'I have a cough.'

'I want to stop smoking.'

'I keep getting headaches.'

'I want to go on the pill.'

'I've got pains in my stomach.'

Remember too that social and psychological problems may initially appear in the guise of physical complaints, and the true nature of these problems may only be uncovered as the patient–practitioner relationship develops. For example, in the above case of the patient complaining of headaches, the real reason for seeking care was to get reassurance that she did not have a brain tumour. Family history revealed that her sister had recently been diagnosed with a brain tumour.

The patient's own words should be used as a basis for further exploration – for instance, the practitioner should use the phrase 'black stools' (as opposed to 'melaena') and 'sweating a lot' (as opposed to hyperhidrosis). A short sentence is all that is required here. It is important to focus on the patient's symptoms, not on the diagnosis, at this early stage in the consultation. Making an immediate diagnosis, as in the two examples given, can lead you down the wrong path, as key information regarding the *actual* symptom the patient is complaining of may be missed. In both examples, further exploration is needed to clarify the patient's meaning. The black stools may simply be due to the iron tablets the patient is taking, and excess sweating may have many causes apart from hyperhidrosis, such as menopause, anxiety, infection, and so on.

Conversely some patients present their own diagnosis – for example, 'I've got sinusitis' or 'I've got flu'. Here, it is important not to accept their diagnosis at face value but to explore and clarify the actual symptoms that have led them to this diagnosis. For instance, a friend or neighbour may have suggested it, or they may have used the Internet to search their symptoms and come up with the self-diagnosis. It is therefore important to probe a little beyond the actual complaint at this stage and try to identify the underlying *reason* why the patient is seeking medical help. For example, is it the pain, the fever, their inability to work, or a past experience with this complaint?

History of presenting complaint (HPC)

Having established the presenting complaint (or reason for seeking care), the next step is to explore in detail the history of the presenting complaint. Some detail may have been gathered as you listened to the patient's opening statement, but you will now want to apply some structure and establish the key points in a chronological and sequential order (Seidel *et al.* 2006).

The chronological pattern of events is perhaps the most important and helpful aspect to determine: When exactly did the problem start? Two weeks ago? Yesterday? If the patient struggles to clarify this, go right back and ask, for example: When did you last feel well? Then what happened? What next? Then what? Anything else?

Every aspect of each symptom needs to be explored fully. Bickley (2008) talks about the seven attributes of any symptom (see Box 1.3, page 8) and this is a useful approach to support exploration of the presenting complaint. Other acronyms in healthcare, such as the PQRST shown in Box 1.4 on page 9 (Provoke, Quality, Radiates, Severity, Time), may be equally useful as an aide mémoire when gathering information.

The PQRST, highlighted by several authors (Morton 1993, Zator Estes 2002), is an established evidence-based guide initially developed to assess the symptom of pain. Whilst some advocate using this to explore all symptoms, a note of caution should be applied, as it was primarily developed for pain assessment. It has some limitations compared with, for example, the Bates model. Nonetheless, as pain commonly triggers a patient to seek care, it is a useful tool.

Box 1.3: The seven attributes of any symptom

Location: Where is it? Does it radiate?

Quality: What does it feel like?
(E.g. sharp, dull, aching, throbbing, pressure, burning?)

Quantity: (or severity): How bad is it? (Rate on a 1–10 scale)

Timing: a. Onset – when did it start?

   b. Duration – how long has it been there? How long does it last?

   c. Frequency – how often does it occur? Is it constant/episodic?

Setting (in which it occurs): Is there an association with home/work/personal activities/emotions?

Remitting or exacerbating factors: What makes it better or worse?

Associated manifestations: Are there other symptoms associated with the main symptom?

The PQRST tool facilitates a general approach to the range of questions you need to consider. System-specific questions may require more in-depth pathophysiological knowledge as you begin to develop diagnostic hypotheses.

Using the example of abdominal pain, Box 1.4 (page 9) illustrates both generic and system-appropriate questions, applied to the PQRST, for a patient presenting with abdominal pain.

Both the symptom-questioning models highlighted here are extremely useful but largely demonstrate 'closed' questioning, inviting yes/no answers. Though useful, and certainly a necessary part of history-taking, this approach may lead to the common error of bombarding the patient with too many questions. For instance, asking 'Does the pain go through to your back?' or 'Have you seen blood in your stools?' will only lead to very brief answers. In contrast, asking 'open questions' like 'Tell me about the pain' or 'Can you tell me more about the pain?' will encourage the patient to talk.

Both types of question are needed to elicit the patient's version of events and to keep the dialogue on track. Other questioning techniques enhance the overall interview with the patient and these are expanded on in the last section of this chapter (on

'Consultation skills', page 15). Whatever technique you use, it is vital to start picking up on and following the patient's cues. Both body language and verbal cues from patients are important signs that should trigger further exploration of potential issues, concerns, ideas and expectations.

*Box 1.4: Generic and system-appropriate questions
for exploring abdominal pain using the PQRST*

Provocative or palliative – *explore provoking or relieving factors*
- Does anything make it better or worse? E.g. movement, lying down, opening bowels, passing wind, eating, drinking, painkillers, coughing?
- Do the painkillers help the pain? What type of food makes it worse?

Quality – *establish the type of pain*
- How would you describe the pain? E.g. cramping, sharp, dull, tight, throbbing, crushing, stabbing, burning?

Region or radiation – *establish the exact location of the problem
   and its extent/radiation*
- Where exactly is the pain in your stomach?
- Is it above or below the belly button? Or to the side? Which side – right or left?
- Does the pain from your stomach go through to your back? To your shoulder?
- Which one? Is the pain anywhere else?

Severity – *establish the severity of pain*
- Likert scales (1–10) can be useful to gauge the degree of pain or the progress of a symptom.
- How bad was it at first compared with how it is now? Does it vary with certain activities?

Timing – *fully explore timings*
- This includes onset, sudden, gradual, continuous or intermittent. If intermittent, how often?
- Is it worse in the morning? Does it improve throughout the day? Is it worse at night?
- Does it flare up every time you eat? Before food or after?

The following sample case demonstrates the PQRST model in action, alongside the standard medical history-taking model. The aim of history-taking in this context is to make a working diagnosis and to identify the patient's perspective on the problem. As discussed, questions relating to setting and associated symptoms (which the Bates model incorporates) are excluded in the PQRST approach. It is useful to consider whether setting and associated symptoms become relevant in the case presented.

Box 1.5: Mrs Wright's case history

Mrs Wright, aged 52, presents with abdominal pain.

The following is established:

P Sometimes worse after food; has no relationship to movement/position, passing wind.

Q Pain is burning and crampy.

R Pain is in central epigastric area and radiates through to the back.

S At its worst 8/10; lowest 5/10.

T Started 4/5 weeks ago. It comes and goes. Some days no problems; other days significant. Worse after spicy foods.

Past medical history (PMH)

The PMH includes ongoing and past medical problems. It should be tailored to the clinical needs and setting, and take into account relevance to the presenting complaint.

General questions may include: 'Do you currently have any medical conditions?' and 'Can you tell me about any medical conditions or operations that you have had in the past?'

It may be relevant to give examples of the types of conditions you mean. For instance, it is important to be aware of long-term conditions (such as asthma, diabetes, hypertension, angina, epilepsy and mental health problems) and patients may not mention these, as they don't see their relevance to the current problem. Conversely, some patients may start to list every minor illness they've had since childhood! It may be necessary to delve more purposefully and specifically into their PMH, depending on the situation. For example, you might find it useful to ask directly, with reference to the current complaint: 'Have you ever had any problems like this before?'

In someone presenting with a cough, you may wish to ask directly about history of asthma, chest infections or chronic obstructive pulmonary disease (COPD). For a patient who arrives wanting to start on the oral contraceptive pill, direct enquiry about a history of migraine would be appropriate.

Patients may not disclose past medical history voluntarily, even when directly asked about specific areas. Sensitive areas (such as sexual/reproductive health, psychiatric history, alcohol/drug abuse) may require you to give an initial explanation of your reasons for asking. You should also express understanding and acknowledgement of the sensitivity of the subject for the patient.

In Mrs Wright's case, the following PMH was ascertained.

Box 1.6: Mrs Wright's PMH

- Hysterectomy – three years ago
- Gallstones – five years ago
- Irritable bowel syndrome (IBS) – two years ago

The importance of her PMH is obvious with regard to establishing the diagnosis. The essential early question 'Have you ever had anything like this before?' is a really useful screening question that encourages symptom recall, enabling most patients to recount past problems and clearly define how they resembled or differed from the current situation.

Drug history (DH)

This is predominantly about current medications and drug allergies. Current medications include over-the-counter medicines, and asking about these may help with the diagnosis and also give an idea of the patient's perspective on the problem.

Some key general questions are:

1. Do you take any regular prescribed medicines?
2. Are you allergic to any medicines or substances?
3. Do you take any medicines not prescribed, for example from the pharmacy?
   Have you tried any over-the-counter medicines from the pharmacy for the problem?

Question 1 answers will usually provide you with a list of oral medication but not necessary topical therapies, creams/patches/suppositories/inhalers, so you may need to ask about these as well. Question 2 answers may elicit information about several allergies but these will need to be clarified, as patients often mistake medication side effects for allergies.

Depending on the particular problem, for question 3 you may need to give some examples of specific over-the-counter medicines. For instance, in the case study involving abdominal pain it would be important to enquire about the use of laxatives, antacids, analgesics, non-steroidal drugs and aspirin. Explore the use of these drugs in as much detail as is appropriate, and ascertain whether they have helped or hindered the problem.

Box 1.7: Mrs Wright's DH

- HRT – oestrogen patches
- Mebevrine 100mg TDS

Essential cues can occur at any stage during the history-taking process, and it is vital that these cues are recognised and explored. In the context of drug history, we have uncovered the possible root cause of the problem and diagnosis is becoming more certain.

Family history (FH)
It is helpful to find out whether a patient is at risk for a particular disease and to identify any current similar health problems within their family. This may also affect the patient's level of concern about their problem. A fuller family history will be appropriate in some situations. Some key questions that may be useful include:

- Are there any relatives with a similar illness to this?
- Are there any illnesses that run in your family? (Highlight as appropriate some key illnesses that can run in families such as heart disease, hypertension, diabetes, cancer, stroke, epilepsy, asthma, eczema, arthritis, thyroid and sickle cell disease.)
- Are your parents/siblings alive? If not what were their causes of death?

Box 1.8: Mrs Wright's FH

- Mother – heart attack three years ago; had presented similarly with upper abdominal pain
- Father – high blood pressure
- Grandfather – stroke aged 59

Social history (SH)

It will help you build a picture of the patient's life if you can briefly 'step into their shoes' without intruding or replacing their values with your own. This way, relevant factors affecting the person's health may be appreciated. This aspect of history-taking requires judgement, sensitivity and skill. Whilst many patients are happy to divulge all aspects of their life to you, others are not. As a general rule, you should therefore approach social issues with caution and respect. Questions must be relevant to the problem or cues you have picked up on, and you will need to use judgement and tact.

This aspect may be difficult to consider on its own, as in reality such enquiries often occur fluidly. While exploring pain, for example, it may be a good time to ask if the patient's work or hobbies have been affected. For example, have they taken time off work? This approach will naturally also lead you into asking about the type of job the patient does (or doesn't) do.

Textbooks differ widely in their interpretation of this element of history-taking. There is usually general agreement on the importance of finding out about the patient's living situation (for example, with children and pets, in a certain type of housing?), alone or with family (or significant others?), employment (their own or their partner's?), hobbies, smoking, alcohol, diet and exercise. More purposeful enquiry exploring a key area of relevance may be required, depending on the individual patient. For example, details about the living situation and significant other of an elderly person with a fractured ankle would be essential to a social history enquiry, whereas in the case study under discussion, involving Mrs Wright, different priorities are identified. The social history can sometimes yield the essential information retrospectively. It may be the final piece of the jigsaw, as it often serves to highlight the way the illness or problem affects the patient's life.

Box 1.9: Mrs Wright's SH

- Occupation – primary school teacher
- Alcohol – 8 units per week
- Smoking – never
- Diet – healthy overall; insignificant caffeine intake

Systems enquiry

This is the final area to consider within the seven-point systematic approach. A full systems enquiry addresses each physical system in detail but succinctly, through the use of closed questions. It is not always necessary to undertake a full systems review. For example, in primary care, a full systems review is not required at every consultation. Rather, it is incorporated as necessary if other aspects of history-taking have failed to illuminate the whole picture. However, in settings such as preoperative assessment a full review is usually needed. It is also useful to include a 'general' health enquiry, prior to the systems approach outlined in Table 1.1.

Table 1.1: Systems approach

System of enquiry	Key points
General health	Weight loss/fever/sweats/fatigue/skin changes
Cardiac/Respiratory	Pain/shortness of breath/cough/wheeze/ankle swelling
Gastrointestinal	Pain/indigestion/reflux/constipation/diarrhoea/nausea Swallowing difficulty/vomiting/blood in vomitus or stools
Genitourinary	Urinary – frequency/nocturia/blood/smell/pain/flow problems Genital – discharge/sores/itching Post-coital or inter-menstrual bleeding
Musculoskeletal	Joints – pain/stiffness Muscles – aches/wasting/loss of power
Neurological	Dizziness/headaches/sensory changes

Summary of history-taking structure

This chapter has outlined the seven-point history-taking model in the context of a common primary care presentation. The individual elements combine to provide a picture of the patient's problem, the context, setting and their ideas about the problem. The seven sequential components, alongside the detailed history of the complaint itself (obtained using the PQRST guide), enable the healthcare professional to make a working diagnosis of gastrointestinal reflux disease, with ibuprofen and stress as contributory factors. Key points uncovered during the history-taking process served to highlight setting and context, and the patient's beliefs, ideas and concerns. These subjective aspects could be seen as potentially sending the encounter off course. However, it is actually crucial to uncover these factors in order to be as sure as possible about the nature of the problem. The final definitive diagnosis of oesophagitis was made following endoscopy.

The history-taking model only provides the framework; the *skills* used to obtain the history ultimately dictate the success of the consultation.

Consultation skills for effective history-taking

Having looked closely at the structure of history-taking, it is important to reiterate that the approach will vary according to the clinical problem, individual patient factors and the urgency of the situation. However, the process *usually* takes the form of an interview. This section therefore aims to highlight some key communication skills that can help facilitate success in obtaining an accurate history.

The structure of history-taking (as presented here) can often be seen as clinician-centred, and the use of closed questions in several of the seven sections bears this out. Whilst these example questions are useful to guide the practitioner on the content of the enquiry, the actual question needs to be carefully constructed; *how* you say it is as important as *what* you say. The use of key communication skills, which embrace the patient perspective as well as eliciting accurate clinical information, is *key* to a successful encounter. Both perspectives are equally important, and are often referred to as 'a meeting of two experts': the clinician with the expert clinical knowledge; and the patient with the expert knowledge of themselves and their life.

For those who wish to study this in depth, there are specific textbooks looking at communication skills for practitioners. These include seminal works such as Neighbour (2007) and Hastings & Redsell (2006). There are numerous consultation models that can be dovetailed into the history-taking model (Kurtz *et al*. 2003, Helman 1981) and it is useful to develop an understanding of these approaches. They offer differing perspectives on the consultation, and a working knowledge of these strategies can be useful, as different patients may respond to different approaches.

The therapeutic impact of a clinician's consultation method should not be underestimated. There is evidence that effective history-taking involves much more than simply running through a checklist of questions (Siedel *et al*. 2003, O'Gara & Fairhurst 2004). Key skills in asking open questions, listening, noticing non-verbal behaviours, empathy and addressing patient concerns have been found to be contributory factors in obtaining accurate histories and reducing the risk of clinical errors (Fairbanks *et al*. 2007).

Practitioners use different skills, talents, ideals, knowledge, emotions and past experiences in their approach to a consultation. But it is always important to recognise the skill set you have, and to adjust and adapt to the situation. What works for one patient may not work for another. What works for the practitioner can also vary, depending on internal and external factors – including levels of patience, tolerance, fatigue, stress, workload, and so on. The skills listed in Table 1.2 (below) are universally recognised interpersonal skills that are implicitly recognised within the well-known consultation models referenced earlier.

Their desired outcomes for the patient are highlighted in Table 1.2 below.

Table 1.2: Interpersonal skills and their desired outcomes

Interpersonal skills	Desired outcomes
Listening: attentive, verbal and non-verbal	**Rapport** is developed
Conscious awareness/use of body	**Respect** is shown
Language: facial expression, tone of voice	**Partnership** is embraced
Questioning style varied • Open to closed • Clarification • Summarising • Paraphrasing • Challenging	**Empathy** is demonstrated Understanding is **checked** **Support** is provided **Cues** are picked up on **Ideas, concerns and expectations** are elicited
Time-framing	**Accurate** chronology and sequential
Signposting	**Direction for enquiry** is clear and appropriate

Summary

This chapter has briefly introduced key concepts in history-taking. Information-gathering, interpretation, clinical knowledge and interpersonal skills are all required for successful history-taking. Structure is important; systematic sequencing is helpful; and a flexible skill set acquired through practice provides the real basis for developing the art of history-taking. Several co-factors contribute to effective history-taking, and in reality practitioners are likely to have both good and bad experiences.

Finally, a few of the possible pitfalls are demonstrated in the following real-life case examples from practitioners.

Pitfalls in history-taking

Practitioner 1:
Making assumptions and putting our own values on patients

When I started out in general practice and women came in to tell me they were pregnant, I always started the consultation by congratulating them. I upset several who actually wanted a termination. I had assumed that pregnancy was a happy event (as it was for me). Now I always start by asking if the woman wishes to continue with the pregnancy, and then I congratulate if appropriate.

Practitioner 2:
Missing the psychosocial aspects of the history

Jennifer (aged 18) had been seen on several occasions by different clinicians in the past year for infected eczema on both her arms. It was treated appropriately at each visit with steroid creams and topical or oral antibiotics. The third time she saw me, I suggested that it might be helpful to get a second opinion from the dermatologist, as we were going round in circles and I couldn't understand why we were failing to manage her condition.

At this she began to cry and admitted that she was in fact deliberately causing the problem by picking at the lesions.

Practitioner 3:
The halo effect

The mother was a sister in the local intensive care unit (ITU). Her two-year-old son was ill with a high temperature and crying. The mother thought her child was seriously ill and told the GP she was an ITU sister and felt that he probably had pneumonia.

The GP sent her straight up to A&E. She repeated her explanation of her role and her assertion to the SHO in A&E and said the child needed an urgent chest x-ray. The child had a chest x-ray, which was inconclusive. The child was admitted to the paediatric ward, where the mother again stressed her work status and suggested that he might have meningitis. A lumbar puncture was performed.

The child had an ear infection.

Practitioner 4:
Not picking up on physical cues

The patient was 47 and in a women's refuge following domestic abuse. She had been referred to the mental health team as she had had a breakdown and had already been seen by a psychiatrist. She presented in a highly anxious state, accompanied by her support worker from the refuge. She had diarrhoea. She was referred urgently to the crisis team, by telephone, and an appointment with the psychiatrist was made for the following day.

She was admitted to acute care overnight with a severe exacerbation of her Crohn's disease.

References

Armstrong, D. (1985). The patient's view. *Social Science Medicine.* **18** (9), 737–44.

Bickley, L. (2008). *Bates' Guide to Physical Examination and History-taking.* Philadelphia, USA: Lippincott Williams & Wilkins.

Crumbie, A. (1999). 'History-taking' in M. Walsh, A. Crumbie & S. Reveley. *Nurse Practitioner: Clinical Skills and Professional Issues.* London: Butterworth-Heinemann.

Department of Health (2001). *Health and Social Care Act.* London: HMSO.

Department of Health (2006). *Caring for People with Long-term Conditions: An Education Framework for Community Matrons and Case Managers.* London: HMSO.

Department of Health (2011). *Healthy Lives, Healthy People.* London: HMSO.

Douglas, G., Nicol, E.F. & Robertson, C., (2011). *Macleod's Clinical Examination.* London: Elsevier.

Epstein, O., Perkin, G.D. & Cookson, J. (2008). *Clinical Examination.* Edinburgh: Mosby.

Fairbanks, R., Bisantz, A. & Sunm, M. (2007). Emergency department communication links and patterns. *Annals of Emergency Medicine.* **50** (4), 396–406.

Hastings, A. & Redsell, S. (2006). *The Good Consultation Guide for Nurses.* Oxford: Radcliffe.

Helman, C.G. (1981). Disease versus illness in general practice. *Journal of the Royal College of General Practice.* **31**, 548–62.

Henderson, V. (1966). *The Nature of Nursing: A Definition and Its Implications for Practice, Research and Education.* New York: Macmillan.

Kurtz, S., Silverman, J., Benson, J. & Draper, J. (2003). Marrying content and process in clinical method teaching, enhancing the Cambridge-Calgary guide. *Academic Medicine.* **78** (8), 802–9.

Morton, P.G. (1993). *Health Assessment in Nursing.* Philadelphia, USA: Davis.

Neighbour, R. (2007). *The Inner Consultation: How to Develop an Effective and Intuitive Consulting Style.* Oxford: Radcliffe.

Nursing and Midwifery Council (2006). *Standards of Proficiency for Nurse and Midwife Prescribers.* London: NMC.

O'Gara, P. & Fairhurst, W. (2004). Therapeutic communication part 1: General approaches that enhance the quality of the consultation. *Accident and Emergency Nursing.* **12** (3), 166–72.

Orem, D.E. (1995). *Nursing: Concepts of Practice.* St Louis, USA: Mosby.

Pendleton, D., Schofield, T., Tate, P. & Havelock, P. (2003) *The New Consultation: Developing Doctor-Patient Communication.* Oxford: OUP.

Roper, N., Logan, W.W. & Tierney, A.J. (1990). *The Elements of Nursing: A Model for Nursing based on a Model of Living.* Edinburgh: Churchill Livingstone.

Seidel, H., Ball, J., Dains, J. & Benedict, D.W. (2006). *Mosby's Guide to Physical Examination.* Philadelphia, USA: Elsevier.

Shah, N. (2005). Taking a history: Introduction and the presenting complaint. *British Medical Journal.* **13**, 309–52.

Tierney, L. & Henderson, M. (2012). *The Patient History-Evidence-Based Approach.* Columbus, USA: McGraw-Hill.

Young, K., Duggan, L. & Franklin, P. (2009). Effective consulting and history-taking skills for prescribing practice. *British Journal of Nursing.* **18** (17), 1056–61.

Zator Estes, M.E. (2002). *Health Assessment and Physical Examination.* New York, USA: Delmar Learning.

Chapter 2

Respiratory assessment

Dr Clare Laroche and Dr Linda Pearce

This chapter discusses the physical assessment skills required when examining a patient's respiratory system. To be proficient at this, you need an understanding of the structure and function of the respiratory system as well as the diseases and conditions that may affect it. The aim is to define the problem accurately (based on both subjective and objective assessments) and to develop a plan for investigation, treatment and management. Respiratory assessment consists of detailed history-taking, followed by examination, and – if possible – some simple tests of respiratory function.

History-taking: symptoms

Specific respiratory symptoms can be categorised as:

- Breathlessness (including wheeze or stridor)
- Cough (including sputum and haemoptysis)
- Chest pain or other symptoms of lung disease (including haemoptysis)

Each of these symptoms should be the subject of detailed assessment. Remember that respiratory symptoms may indicate respiratory disease or may be markers of diseases of other systems. Presenting symptoms will therefore vary according to the pathophysiology.

Breathlessness

You may observe breathlessness in the patient, or the patient may self-report it when questioned as part of the assessment. When a patient self-reports breathlessness, it is important to establish what they mean by 'breathlessness', and they must then be asked about it in detail. This questioning should be tailored to the patient's lifestyle and individual circumstances, and their responses should be compared with those that would be expected from a healthy person of the same age and sex.

You need to explore the duration of breathlessness by asking the patient a number of questions such as:

- When were you last completely well?
- When did the breathlessness start?
- How rapidly did it develop – in minutes, hours, days, weeks, months or years?
- Is it still developing?

The severity of breathlessness is also important and you can assess this by asking the patient situational questions such as:

- Does it limit your ability to carry out normal day-to-day activities or exercise? If so, to what degree?
- Can you climb stairs?
- Can you go shopping?
- Can you carry your shopping home?
- Does it affect your sleep?
- How do you sleep – propped up with pillows in bed or in a chair?

The variability of the breathlessness should also be assessed by asking questions such as:

- Is the breathlessness a constant feature of your life, both day and night?
- Is it worse at certain times or in certain seasons?
- Does it wake you when you are asleep?
- Is it worse at work or soon afterwards?
- Does it occur at rest?
- Are you aware of any precipitating factors, such as specific environments, eating certain foods or exposure to specific trigger factors?
- Are you aware of precipitating events such as stress or exercise?
- Is it affected by eating or posture?
- Are you aware of anything that improves your breathlessness, such as position, temperature changes or medication?

The patient should also be asked whether they are aware of any symptoms that are associated with their breathlessness – for example, noisy breathing, wheezing, cough, faintness, fatigue, palpitations, chest pain, general muscle pain, headache, anxiety or tingling of the fingers.

There are a number of causes of both acute and chronic breathlessness, which are shown in Table 2.1 on page 24.

Cough

Patients must be asked about their awareness of a cough, as some people – for example, smokers or those who work in certain industrial environments – may regard coughing as a normal part of life. A number of factors should be assessed.

Firstly, the duration of the cough must be determined by asking the patient how long since it first developed and whether it is getting better or worse. The severity of the cough and any impact upon their lifestyle is important, including whether it disturbs their sleep, and causes pain or urinary incontinence. In addition to severity, the variability of the cough must be considered, by asking whether it is persistent throughout the day and/ or night, whether it occurs only at night, whether it occurs upon waking and whether there are any specific triggers, such as positions or events.

Patients should be asked about the type of cough with questions such as:

- **Is it a tickly cough?**
- **Does it feel as if the cough comes from the back of your throat or deep in your chest?**
- **Does the cough produce sputum and/or blood?**
- **If so, when is the sputum produced?**
- **Is it thick and/or mucoid or frothy?**
- **Is it white or coloured?**
- **How long has it been coloured?**
- **Has there ever been blood or blood streaks in the sputum?**
- **Have you ever coughed up frank or altered blood? If so, how much?**
- **How much sputum is produced over a 24-hour period? (Useful descriptive terms are teaspoon/tablespoon/egg cup/teacup.)**
- **Has it changed in volume or purulence recently?**
- **How often do you get this type of cough? (Number of times per year.)**
- **Does it usually require a course of antibiotics to clear?**
- **Do you feel unwell when this occurs?**

Table 2.1: Causes of breathlessness

Cause	Acute	Chronic
Cardiac	• Pulmonary oedema • Acute myocardial infarction • Arrhythmias • Pericarditis • Pericardial infusion	• Left ventricular disease • Congestive cardiac disease • Valvular disease • Arrhythmias • Pericardial disease
Respiratory	• Pneumonia • Pneumothorax • Pulmonary embolism • Asthma exacerbations • Exacerbations of chronic obstructive pulmonary disease • Airway obstruction (e.g. anaphylaxis, choking, tumour) • Respiratory infections (e.g. pulmonary tuberculosis)	• Asthma • Chronic obstructive pulmonary disease • Bronchiectasis • Cystic fibrosis • Interstitial lung disease • Pleural effusion • Pulmonary hypertension • Lung malignancy
Endocrine	• Diabetic ketoacidosis • Thyroxicosis	
Neuromuscular		• Motor neurone disease • Guillain–Barré syndrome • Myasthenia gravis
Other	• Pain • Anxiety • Drugs (e.g. aspirin overdose) • Altitude sickness • Trauma	• Anaemia • Thrombo-embolic disease • Thyroid disease • Obesity • Malignancy • Psychogenic (e.g. anxiety)

(Adapted from Borton 2010)

Chest pain

Chest pain may be associated with respiratory and cardiac disease as well as other disorders. The lungs themselves do not have pain receptors (Guyton & Hall 2010) and, for this reason, many serious respiratory diseases may not present with pain. Chest pain may be associated with pleural or chest wall disease, pressure on other thoracic organs or infiltration of lung disease into other areas. It may also be a cardinal sign of cardiac disease. The patient must therefore describe the pain as carefully and completely as possible.

Patients should be asked about the type of pain and what this feels like – for example, whether the pain is sharp, heavy or crushing, burning or sore, or stabbing. The practitioner should also determine whether the pain is worse on inspiration (pleuritic) or is associated with any area of tenderness over the chest wall. The site of the pain should be explored with questions such as:

- Is the pain localised in one part of the chest or is it generalised?
- Where is it worst?
- Does it radiate to other parts of the chest or body?

It is also important to ask about the duration and frequency of the pain with questions such as:

- How long have you had the pain?
- Was the onset sudden?
- How often do you experience the pain?
- How long do these episodes last?
- Is the pain improving or worsening?

Considering the pain in the context of the patient's daily life can help you assess its severity and variability. Ask the patient to describe how bad the pain is, whether it limits any of their daily activities or sleep and whether any activity triggers the pain or makes it worse (such as moving, breathing or coughing) or whether it is postural. The patient should be asked if anything eases the pain, including whether painkillers are required. They should also be asked whether the pain is constant or varies in severity and whether it is associated with any other symptoms, like breathlessness or palpitations.

Other symptoms of lung disease

Enquiry may elicit general symptoms or local symptoms in other parts of the body that may indicate disease in the respiratory system. These may include:

- Fevers or night sweats, which can be associated with acute respiratory infections such as pneumonia or exacerbations of bronchiectasis, chronic infections such as tuberculosis, or other disorders such as lymphoma or inflammatory lung diseases.

- Hoarseness, which may indicate local disease affecting the larynx, lung cancer, psychological disease, side effects of medication or secondary effects of lung disease.

- Neurological symptoms, which may indicate the presence of secondary effects of respiratory disease such as lung cancer, or may be secondary to polycythaemia due to hypoxia.

- Generalised muscle weakness, which may be secondary to respiratory insufficiency, such as is found in COPD, or may be because of debility due to malignant or other chronic disease.

- Bone pain, which may be associated with secondary spread of malignant disease. For instance, when a tumour compresses the surrounding nerves it can cause pain, numbness, or tingling, and if the surrounding blood vessels are compressed, it can affect the blood flow. If bone pain is reported, further assessment may include checking muscle strength, sensation to touch, and reflexes.

- Weight loss (with or without anorexia), which may be associated with many respiratory diseases.

- Psychological disorders, for example depression and anxiety, which may be caused by chronic respiratory disease and affect response to treatment *(Cross & Rimmer 2007).*

Physical examination

An initial inspection of the patient should include a number of general observations, which should be recorded:

- Level of consciousness
- Rate, rhythm, depth and effort of breathing
- Facial expression
- Scarring, especially scars that may relate to operations carried out on the thorax

- Lesions on the chest wall, such as swellings and tumours
- Localised prominences
- The condition and colour of the skin
- Vascular abnormalities
- The presence of venous congestion

Identifying cyanosis by observation may often be difficult, especially in artificial light. Central cyanosis can be recognised if the tongue, lips and nails have a blue discoloration, and is due to hypoxia. Common causes include acute severe asthma, severe pneumonia, pulmonary embolus, left ventricular failure, chronic airflow obstruction and pulmonary fibrosis.

Peripheral cyanosis due to impaired circulation in the extremities may be observed in the nail beds only or generally in the hands and feet. It is caused by slow movement of blood through the capillaries due to causes such as cold weather, Reynaud's disease or peripheral vascular disease, and does not signify the presence of hypoxia.

Expiratory lip pursing, when the patient purses their lips on expiration, may be a sign of severe airflow obstruction and is most commonly seen in severe COPD and emphysema. Nasal flaring (involving the use of the alae nasae muscles) may be associated with the use of other accessory muscles of respiration in respiratory distress.

Clubbing is defined as a loss of the angle between the nail and the nail bed, in association with increased curvature of the nails. The nail bed becomes spongy and the ends of the fingers become bulbous. The pathogenesis of finger clubbing is unknown and many conditions are associated with it. Respiratory causes of clubbing include bronchial carcinoma, lung fibrosis and chronic pulmonary sepsis. Clubbing may be congenital or familial.

Signs of superior vena caval obstruction (SVCO) are engorged non-pulsatile jugular veins, dilated veins on the anterior chest wall and, depending on severity, oedema of the face, neck and conjunctiva. The cause is usually bronchial carcinoma, with the collateral circulation bypassing the obstruction and using the azygous and intercostal systems to return blood to the heart.

The lymphatic system should be examined for enlarged glands, which may be indicators of secondary disease from primary respiratory causes. Enlarged glands in the supraclavicular fossa may be associated with bronchial or gastric carcinoma, tuberculosis, sarcoidosis or lymphoma (Rawles et al. 2010).

Examination of the chest

Examination of the chest should always be carried out in a respectful, gentle manner. In order to gain experience in examination, it is necessary to practise these techniques in the normal chest. This will enable you to correctly identify any deviations from normality. An appropriate format for chest examination is:

- Inspection
- Palpation
- Percussion
- Auscultation

These assessments should be carried out separately for the anterior and posterior chest.

The anterior thorax and lungs are best examined in a supine position. This position has an added advantage in women, as the breasts are less likely to be in the way. The posterior thorax and lungs may be examined with the patient in the sitting position. The patient's arms should be folded across their chest, with their hands resting on the opposite shoulders. This helps to ensure the scapulae are moved partly out of the way, increasing access to the lung fields. If appropriate and more comfortable for the person, both the posterior and the anterior chest may be examined in the sitting or standing position.

To examine the posterior thorax, if the patient is unable to sit up (even with help), it will be necessary to examine them lying down, and roll them first to one side and then to the other. This will enable you to carry out all parts of the examination of each part of the chest in each position.

The general shape of the chest should be noted. In a normal adult, the ratio of anteroposterior to lateral diameter is 1:2. This ratio is 1:1 in children and the elderly. The presence of structural deformities or abnormalities should be noted:

- **A barrel-shaped chest (increased AP diameter) may indicate chronic hyperinflation, possibly as a result of reversible or irreversible obstructive disease.**
- **The chest may be funnel-shaped (pectus excavatus) or keel-shaped (pectus carinatus, 'pigeon chest'). Or Harrison's sulcus (a horizontal indrawing of the lower ribs) may be present. These may signify congenital disease or obstructive disease during the development of the chest in infancy and childhood.**

- Other abnormalities of the shape of the chest may be congenital, or associated with abnormalities of the spine such as kyphosis and kyphoscoliosis.

Movement on respiration

General observation of the chest movement upon respiration will help you build up an overall picture of the patient's respiratory function. Discreetly observe the patient from the front while they are breathing quietly. The rate, pattern and distribution of movement of the chest wall should all be observed carefully, as important diagnostic indicators may be noted.

Check whether:

- Undressing for the examination has caused the patient to become breathless
- Their breathing is deep or shallow
- There is equal, bilateral chest movement
- Respiration is obviously restricted by pain
- The patient is using accessory muscles of respiration (sternocleidomastoid, scalenus, trapezius and alae nasae muscles) or using their arms to support their chest while breathing
- There is any intercostal recession, which is most easily seen in the lower lateral chest wall
- Changes in patient position affect respiration, for example the rate, pattern or ease.

You should then examine the posterior chest in the same way.

Palpation

Palpation of the thorax may reveal abnormalities of the skin and underlying structures, asymmetry and also areas of localised or generalised tenderness. It may also be used to further assess respiratory excursion. The trachea should lie in the midline. To assess its position, place the tips of the index and middle fingers at the suprasternal notch, gently move them upwards and separate them until they lie on each side of the trachea, where it emerges from the thorax. The fingertips should be equidistant from the midline.

The palpation should, like all examinations, take place in a structured way to avoid omitting any part of the thorax. It may be carried out with the fingers or with the palmar areas, as appropriate. Lymph nodes in the cervical superficial, posterior and deep supraclavicular fossae should be assessed. For the anterior chest the palpation should commence in the supraclavicular region, progressing to the infraclavicular, sternal, rib and axillary areas. The posterior chest is then examined in a similar way, commencing in the supraclavicular region, progressing to the suprascapular and infrascapular regions, and then to the lateral walls of the thorax.

The depth and symmetry of respiratory movements may be noted by spreading the hands over the lower posterior chest wall so that the thumbs touch in the midline over the thoracic spine and the fingers spread towards the lateral walls of the thorax. As the patient breathes in and out, any inequalities in movement between the two sides of the chest wall will be revealed by the relative movement of the thumbs away from and towards the midline. Asking the patient to take deep breaths may highlight these differences. This procedure should be repeated by placing the hands on the upper part of the back with the fingertips resting just below the shoulders. A pneumothorax (especially spontaneous) will most commonly occur in the upper lobe and may be missed if only lower chest symmetry is assessed (Jarvis 2011).

Structural abnormalities or asymmetries may be further noted, as should the presence and location of swellings, which may not always be apparent on observation. If there are any areas of tenderness, their location and extent, as well as their association with respiration or movement, should be observed. The sensation of crackling under the fingers on palpating the chest wall (surgical emphysema) should also be noted.

Tactile vocal fremitus can help you assess the condition of the underlying lung and pleura. Place the ulnar (small finger) aspects of both hands on the part of the chest to be assessed and ask the patient to say something (usually the words 'ninety-nine' or 'one hundred and one'). A vibration (fremitus) may be felt through the chest wall. If the vibration is difficult to feel, you can ask the patient to speak louder. Where the vibration is obstructed (for instance, by a pleural effusion), the fremitus is reduced.

Percussion

The purpose of percussion is to set up a vibration that is audible. It is used to help assess areas of varying density within the lungs. The presence of fluids, solids and air will produce different resonances. A normal, air-filled lung will produce a resonant note, while a collapsed or consolidated lung will produce a dull sound. If the cavity is filled with fluid (effusion), a stony dull sound will be heard. If there is air in the bulla or pleura space, the percussion will be hyper-resonant.

In order to conduct this assessment, the middle finger of the non-dominant hand is placed on the chest wall, with the distal interphalangeal joint firmly pressed against the chest; the finger should be extended at this joint. The tip of the middle finger of the dominant hand is then brought sharply down on the distal interphalangeal joint. The movement of the percussing hand should be from the wrist, and the percussing finger should be in contact with the distal interphalangeal joint for as short a time as possible, to avoid damping the vibration. The clavicles are percussed directly with the percussing finger.

The percussion should then proceed down the anterior, posterior and lateral chest; and normal areas of dullness over the liver and heart should be noted. When percussing, it is especially important to compare one side with the other. Each percussion note should be evaluated for resonance and be noted as resonant, hyper-resonant, dull or stony dull. The presence of morbid obesity makes percussion more difficult.

Auscultation

Auscultation is the evaluation of breath sounds with or without the aid of a device such as a stethoscope. In a healthy person, breath sounds should not be audible to the naked ear. If there is an element of upper airway obstruction, breath sounds may be audible (for example, stridor).

The stethoscope amplifies breath sounds, which may be listened to through the bell (better for low-frequency sounds) or diaphragm (better for high-frequency sounds). The bell may produce better results in the very thin or those with hairy chests. The patient should be asked to breathe in and out deeply through an open mouth, to reduce added sounds from the oral cavity. It is important to understand how the lobes of each lung lie within the thoracic cavity; the middle lobe can only be heard from the anterior (see Figure 2.1).

The examination should begin on the anterior chest at the upper lobes and move down over the chest wall. The examination should be at least 2.5cm from the midline, to exclude the sounds transmitted from the central airways. The two sides of the chest should be directly compared at each position of auscultation. One full inspiration and expiration should be evaluated in each position. The examination should proceed from the anterior to the posterior chest, again progressing from the upper to the lower lobes (see Figures 2.2 and 2.3, pages 32 and 33).

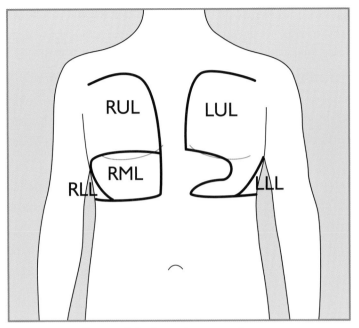

Figure 2.1: Anterior auscultation

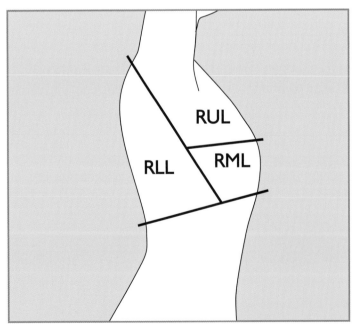

Figure 2.2: Lateral auscultation

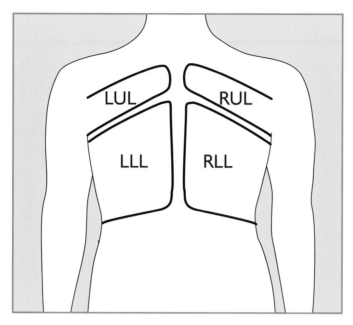

Figure 2.3: Posterior auscultation

The presence and timing of normal and added sounds should be noted. Normal sounds increase throughout inspiration, fading away quickly during expiration. Turbulent airflow in the central airways produces the tracheal and bronchial sounds and the vesicular breath sounds occur somewhere between the trachea and the alveoli. Tracheal and bronchial breath sounds are not transmitted well through air-filled lungs; therefore, vesicular breath sounds predominate in the normal lung.

The different added sounds may be described as:

1 Crackles (formally known as Crepitations)

Fine crackles are produced by small airways popping open during inspiration or the passage of air through areas of secretion. They may be caused by inflammation or small amounts of fluid in the airways and, depending on the cause and site of origin, may be heard at any time during respiration. Early inspiratory crackles originate mainly from the proximal airways and are often fewer in number and much coarser: causes include asthma, chronic bronchitis or localised bronchiectasis. Late inspiratory crackles originate from the alveoli and continue into late inspiration. Usually they first appear at the base of the lungs and spread as the condition worsens. Causes include fibrosis, pneumonia and pulmonary oedema due to left ventricular failure.

2 Coarse crackles (formally known as Rales)

Coarse crackles are caused by secretions (such as bronchiectasis) in the airways and, depending on the cause, may be heard at any time during respiration. They often clear on coughing.

3 Wheeze (formally known as Rhonchi)

Wheezing sounds are caused by narrowing of the airways. They may vary in intensity and volume and, depending on the cause, may be heard at any time during respiration. Generalised continuous sounds are associated with asthma, chronic bronchitis and congestive cardiac failure. In chronic bronchitis, the wheeze often clears after coughing. In asthma, the wheeze is more commonly heard on expiration but may occur in both phases of the respiratory cycle. A persistent localised (usually mainly inspiratory) wheeze would suggest partial obstruction of a proximal bronchus, caused either by a foreign body or a tumour. An inspiratory 'squeak' is characteristic of bronchiolitis, either due to acute infection or acute or chronic inflammation of the bronchioles. When a wheeze is observed, possible causes may include asthma, COPD, congestive heart failure or left ventricular failure.

4 Pleural rub

Normal pleura move soundlessly. Creaking or grating noises throughout the respiratory cycle (occasionally only during inspiration) may indicate pleural inflammation or infection.

5 Stridor

Stridor is a wheeze that occurs predominantly or completely during the inspiratory cycle; it tends to be louder in the neck than over the chest wall. Stridor signifies major obstruction of the trachea or large airways, and possible causes may include tumour or inhaled foreign body.

The absence of breath sounds either locally or generally may be an important marker of chest disease, such as a pleural effusion. If no additional sounds are heard, you may consider anaemia, pulmonary emboli, neuromuscular disorders or anxiety (Rimmer & Cross 2007). All findings should be documented in a logical sequence.

Summary

Taking a comprehensive history, observing and assessing the breathless patient can provide valuable insights into the possible causes of breathlessness. The findings should not be reviewed in isolation, but should inform your decisions on further investigations and treatment options.

Case study 1

Presenting condition

The patient is a 50-year-old lady who presents with shortness of breath and chest pain.

History of presenting condition

She has been getting increasingly short of breath for two to three years. She has to stop for a rest on her way to the shops (about half a mile on the flat), but can manage stairs. She has some wheezing on exertion. For the past ten years, she has normally coughed up clear sputum in the morning. About a month ago, the shortness of breath became worse and she started to cough up green sputum (about an eggcup per day). She has never coughed up blood.

Her doctor gave her a course of antibiotics (amoxicillin) and the sputum became clear again. Over the past week she has again been getting 'bad'. Her sputum has again turned green and she has a fever. She has no pain/nausea/vomiting/heartburn/dizziness/palpitations/abdominal pain/skin rashes. She has not injured her chest. She has never had chest pain on exertion. Her appetite has been normal, but she thinks that she has lost 7–8 kg over the past month even though she hasn't been dieting.

Previous medical history

She takes a non-steroidal anti-inflammatory drug (NSAID) for arthritis in her hips (prescribed by her GP). She was also prescribed a steroid inhaler for breathlessness, but it did not help so she does not take it now. She has had no lung function tests. She has no allergies, and takes no other medicines.

Family history

Her father is alive and well, but he has a smoker's cough. Her mother died of breast cancer aged 52 and her older sister also died of breast cancer. She has two younger sisters. There is no other relevant family history. Her husband died six years ago of chest disease. He smoked but the doctor said it was because he had worked at the docks all his life.

Social history

She lives in a three-bedroom house, and has worked at the checkout in a local supermarket for the past six years. Before that she was a housewife. She has three children, who are all well. She has no pets. She has smoked 20 to 25 cigarettes per day for the past 30 years. She does not drink and has not travelled recently.

Results of examination

The patient is a pale lady, not breathless at rest but breathless on mild exertion. She is alert and well orientated. She has come for a review of systems. All is otherwise normal.

At rest her respiration rate is slightly raised (18/min) but the rhythm is normal. She purses her lips on expiration. She is not using accessory muscles of respiration. Her pulse is raised at 90/min, and she is apyrexial.

She is neither cyanosed, nor obviously anaemic. She has no nail abnormalities.

- **Inspection: Chest shape normal, movements apparently normal and equal**
- **Palpation: Expansion appears equal; tactile vocal fremitus (TVF) increased right lower lobe, no enlarged glands detected**
- **Percussion: Dull right base, otherwise normal**
- **Auscultation: Widespread crackles and wheeze, apart from the right base where breath sounds are absent, vocal resonance increased right base**

Summary

This lady presents with breathlessness, and purulent sputum. She has a long history of tobacco consumption and is therefore at risk of COPD. In view of her weight loss, which may be related purely to COPD, malignant disease should be considered. She is clearly at risk of bronchial carcinoma. However, it should be noted that her husband died of respiratory disease, having worked in the docks. (He may have died from asbestosis or even mesothelioma.) She will have been in contact with the asbestos fibres (for example, when washing clothes) and is therefore at risk of both asbestosis and mesothelioma. Whatever the diagnosis, she would appear to have a super-added respiratory infection. Note: non-steroidal anti-inflammatory drugs can cause bronchospasm.

Differential diagnosis

- Exacerbation of COPD?
- Respiratory tract infection?
- Underlying malignancy (weight loss)?
- Bronchial carcinoma?
- Asbestosis?
- Mesothelioma?

The patient needs investigation by means of blood tests, lung function tests, chest x-ray, possibly high-resolution computed tomography (HRCT) and bronchoscopy.

Also to be considered: Regular breast checks for patient and her sisters, because of family history of breast cancer.

Conclusion

Taking a logical approach to respiratory examination will help you arrive at a differential or provisional diagnosis for any underlying conditions. It is important to remember that any number of extra pulmonary conditions can affect the respiratory system. A comprehensive holistic history is essential, in addition to the physical assessment, in order to provide a detailed picture of the patient's current health status. Summarising and discussing the findings of the assessment will provide an opportunity for clarification and will lead on to a discussion of the most appropriate medical investigations.

References

Borton, C. (2010). *Breathlessness* [online] Available from: http://www.www.patient.co.uk/doctor/breathlessness. htm (Accessed 18/02/13).

Cross, S. & Rimmer, M. (2007). *Nurse Practitioner Manual of Clinical Skills*. Oxford, UK: Baillière Tindall, Elsevier Science.

Guyton, A.C. & Hall, J.E. (2010). *Textbook of Medical Physiology*. Philadelphia, USA: Saunders, Elsevier.

Jarvis, C. (2011). *Physical Examination and Health Assessment*. Philadelphia, USA: Saunders, Elsevier.

Rawles, Z., Griffiths, B. & Alexander, T. (2010). *Physical Examination Procedures for Advanced Nurses and Independent Prescribers – Evidence and Rationale*. London: Hodder Arnold.

Rimmer, V. & Cross, S. (2007) *Nurse Practitioner Manual of Clinical Skills*. Philadelphia USA: Saunders.

Chapter 3

Cardiovascular assessment

Mark Ranson and Wendy Braithwaite

Despite a continued fall in the mortality rates directly attributable to coronary heart disease (CHD), diseases of the heart and circulatory system also known as cardiovascular disease (CVD) remain the main cause of death in the UK, accounting for some 191,000 deaths each year – or one in three of all deaths (British Heart Foundation 2015).

The main forms of CVD are CHD and stroke. Almost half (46%) of all deaths from CVD are directly linked to CHD and nearly a quarter (23%) are due to stroke. It can therefore be seen that CHD, by itself, is the most common cause of death in the UK (British Heart Foundation 2015). Indeed, the National Institute for Health and Clinical Excellence (NICE 2010) asserts that individuals suffering from acute coronary syndromes (ACS), encompassing unstable angina, non-ST elevation myocardial infarction (NSTEMI) and ST elevation myocardial infarction (STEMI), have a poor prognosis and high mortality rate if left untreated.

Clearly, comprehensive and systematic assessment of patients with CHD is necessary in order to aid early detection and promote early intervention, which will facilitate ongoing reduction in associated mortality rates. Traditionally, doctors undertook physical examination of the cardiovascular system, with other healthcare professionals participating in some elements of history-taking and observations. However, many healthcare professionals are now taking on advanced roles, which include physical examination of body systems (Department of Health 2010, Royal College of Nursing 2010). The aim of this chapter is therefore to take a systematic approach to appraising the relevant aspects of the cardiovascular system in a patient with suspected CHD. To inform this process, the content of this chapter will be based on a case study.

Box 3.1: Case study – presenting condition

John is a 45-year-old man who has presented to his GP with recurrent episodes of central chest pain for the last two weeks. John was referred to his local NHS Trust for urgent assessment in the Rapid Access Chest Pain Clinic (Wood & Timmins 2001). This service is organised and led by a range of healthcare practitioners from a variety of non-medical healthcare backgrounds.

Patient history

On attendance at the rapid access chest pain clinic, the first step would be to obtain a history from the patient. As history-taking has been discussed in Chapter 1, discussion here will focus on the elements that are relevant to John's presentation with recurrent episodes of chest pain. The history taken in this scenario would need to include an exploration of symptoms, together with past medical history, medications, family and social history and a risk assessment for CHD. As discussed in Chapter 1, the history taken will help to ascertain a potential diagnosis, with subsequent physical examination and tests being used to confirm the probable cause.

Symptom assessment

Whilst John presented with perhaps the most obvious and common cardiac symptom of chest pain, patients with cardiac disease may also present with palpitations, breathlessness, oedema, syncope and fatigue (Gleadle 2003).

Chest pain

When the myocardium is deprived of oxygen due to an insufficient blood supply, ischaemic pain will occur. In CHD this ischaemic pain is a consequence of thickening and hardening of the vessel walls (arteriosclerosis) and the deposit of plaques containing cholesterol, lipids and fibrin in the inner walls of the vessels (atherosclerosis).

On questioning, John described the classic presentation for ischaemic chest pain. The pain was described as occurring in the centre of his chest, with some radiation to both arms. Patients may also commonly describe radiation to the jaw or back. John described his pain as 'heaviness in the centre of his chest that felt like pressure and led on to an aching pain centrally'. The pain was usually associated with exertion and would have a sudden onset. When questioned about how he had relieved the pain, John stated that the only way to get it to abate was to rest completely for a period of time. Other symptoms commonly associated with cardiac chest pain are nausea, vomiting and sweating, though John did not report any of these associated symptoms. Assessment of John's symptoms suggested that he was indeed experiencing cardiac chest pain.

In contrast, patients presenting with inflammatory-type chest pain related to conditions such as pericarditis will often describe sharp central pain, which is unrelated to exercise but made worse by inspiration and/or coughing. Relief from these symptoms is often achieved by sitting forward. Other causes of chest pain not related to CHD may include chest infections, musculoskeletal causes, indigestion, acid reflux and aortic dissection. It is therefore crucial that a thorough assessment of chest pain is made, in addition to the patient history and physical examination.

Past medical history and assessment of cardiac risk factors

During the history-taking process, practitioners review previous medical records in order to establish any previous acute or chronic medical conditions. Of particular importance to John's case would be the presence of existing CHD, as evidenced by previous angina or myocardial infarction as well as by any congenital cardiac abnormalities or previous cardiac surgery. There was no evidence in John's history or notes to indicate pre-existing CHD, nor were the risk factors associated with CHD noted. These could include hypertension, hypercholesterolaemia, cerebrovascular accident (CVA) or diabetes mellitus (DM).

In addition, John had not suffered from rheumatic fever (RF) as a child. A history of RF during childhood may mean that the heart valves have been damaged. This places the patient at a higher risk of developing endocarditis, an infective, inflammatory disease affecting the valves of the heart (Jowett & Thompson 2007).

Drug history

Whilst John was not currently taking any medication, a review of medications (including prescription, over-the-counter and herbal medications) should be carried out, as there may be some effects on cardiac function or potential interactions with medication that may be subsequently prescribed. Recreational drug use should also be explored, due to its potential impact on cardiac rhythm, but John denied such drug use. It is also crucial to explore any drug allergies that may be present during this discussion.

Family and social history

Given the known genetic and hereditary links in CHD, John was also asked about the incidence of CHD, DM, CVA, familial hypercholesterolaemia, hypertension and congenital heart disease in his close family such as parents and siblings. It was noted that John's father had died suddenly at the age of 60, but that a cause of death was never established. This finding raised the suspicion of a family cardiac history, given that sudden death is often associated with CHD and cardiomyopathy.

Assessment of social history explored John's lifestyle and its potential effects on his health. In a patient with suspected CHD, the identifiable risk factors may include smoking, lack of exercise, excessive alcohol consumption, a diet high in saturated fats and stress.

John's social history was largely unremarkable, although it did emerge that his job was under threat and he was at risk of being made redundant. Whilst he did not feel stressed, he acknowledged that this had probably been putting him under strain for the past month. Foxton (2004) suggests that it may be beneficial to use a risk calculator to establish a patient's risk status, based on age, gender, cholesterol levels and other risk factors. As well as indicating the individual's level of risk, this can also help the practitioner to focus on specific and relevant health promotion needs following the initial consultation.

Vital signs

To ascertain John's clinical condition and underpin the physical examination, his vital signs were recorded. Pulse and blood pressure are seen to relate directly to the cardiovascular system, but it is important to record and document *all* vital signs. For example, changes in respiratory rate may be an early indication of deterioration in the patient's condition (Ryan *et al.* 2004), whilst a raised body temperature may point to an infective element in the presentation and subsequent diagnosis (Timmis & Mills 2006).

In John's case, it was particularly relevant to note the rate as well as the character of the pulse. Pulse character can give vital clues when arriving at a final diagnosis. For instance, it may be weak and thready in a shocked state, bounding in an infective scenario or due to valve abnormalities, and show decreased force if there is vessel narrowing or occlusion present.

In the context of cardiovascular assessment, it is also considered good practice to palpate both radial pulses at the same time. Any delay between the transmission of impulses on either side can be indicative of an aortic compromise such as aneurysm. Mean blood pressure may be the most useful indicator of perfusion, with a pressure of 60mmHg needed to perfuse the coronary arteries, the brain and kidneys. Whilst a systolic and diastolic blood pressure should be recorded and documented to assess for hypertension or hypotension, a mean pressure can be easily approximated from the usual reading by using the following formula:

$$\text{Diastolic BP} + (\text{Systolic BP} - \text{Diastolic BP})/3$$

Introduction to physical examination

To facilitate a thorough physical examination of the cardiovascular system, the patient's chest needs to be fully exposed. This can lead to embarrassment and apprehension in some patients, which can have an adverse effect on the findings of the examination, particularly in relation to heart rate and blood pressure. The environment selected must therefore be appropriate for the examination, the individual's privacy and dignity must be respected at all times, and the examination must be handled sensitively by the practitioner (Epstein *et al.* 2008).

The four principles of physical examination can be applied to cardiovascular system assessment (as they can be to most body systems). The four principles are as follows:

1. **Inspection**: observation of the person as a whole, followed by more focused examination of particular areas
2. **Palpation**: using the technique of touch to assess temperature, texture, moisture and size of organs
3. **Percussion**: the practitioner places a finger firmly over a particular organ and taps another finger with short, sharp strokes against the first finger to assess transmission of sound (NB: this technique is not integral to cardiovascular assessment)
4. **Auscultation**: listening to sounds produced by internal organs, using the bell and the diaphragm of a stethoscope

In John's case, the practitioner carrying out the assessment had been performing general inspection during the history-taking and recording of vital signs. Bickley (2008) explains that observation of the person as a whole during this time can enable the practitioner to detect signs of distress (e.g. non-verbal signs of pain), breathlessness, obvious skin colour changes (e.g. cyanosis or paleness) and general physique (e.g. whether they are overweight or underweight).

Certain genetic conditions (such as Down's syndrome and Marfan's syndrome) predispose the individual to cardiovascular abnormalities, and the clinical characteristics of these conditions can be easily observed during general inspection. The practitioner should also be looking out for any obvious chest deformities, signs of previous surgery and visible pulsations due to aneurysm of underlying vessels. Having noted the findings of the general inspection, detailed examination of the cardiovascular system can now proceed. Whilst individual practitioners develop their own order in which to carry out the examination, it is important to be consistent and logical in the order, thus minimising the number of position changes for the patient. Most practitioners will commence the cardiovascular examination with the hands.

Hands

John's hands were inspected for signs of blue discolouration, which would indicate peripheral cyanosis. Whilst this may give an indirect indication of reduced cardiac output, the same sign will be evident in a patient with cold hands, so it must be considered in context.

Compressing the distal phalanx of the middle finger for 5 seconds assesses capillary refill. Once the pressure is released, the capillaries should refill and colour should return in 2 seconds or less (although this can increase to 4 seconds in the elderly as a normal variant). Again, a delay in capillary refill may indicate a reduced cardiac output (Epstein et al. 2008).

General inspection also allows the practitioner to look for signs of nicotine staining to indicate a history of smoking and nail clubbing. Clubbing of the nails is observed by obliteration of the angle between the nail bed and the adjoining skin. A thickening of the tissues at the nail bed and curving of the nail may also be observed. Bickley (2008) points out that the exact underlying cause of nail clubbing is not known but may be related to increased vascularity and increased tissue fluid. In the context of cardiovascular examination, this could be related to cyanotic heart disease or endocarditis. A more detailed examination across the hands allows the practitioner to look for more specific cardiovascular signs, together with their potential clinical significance, as outlined in Table 3.1 opposite.

Table 3.1: Clinical signs in the hand

Sign	Description	Potential clinical significance
Splinter haemorrhages (See Figure 3.1a)	Small, splinter-like lesions observed under the finger nails	May be linked with endocarditis
Osler's nodes (See Figure 3.1b)	Painful, palpable lesions most often found on the pads of the fingers and/or toes	May be linked with endocarditis
Janeway lesions (See Figure 3.1b)	Non-tender macular lesions most often found on the palms of the hands (or soles of the feet)	May be linked with endocarditis
Palmar xanthomas (See Figure 3.1c)	Non-tender, yellow coloured maculo-papular lesions found on the palms of the hands	May be linked with hypercholesterolaemia
Tendon xanthomas	Yellow-coloured deposits around the tendons of the hand, commonly noted on the knuckles	May be linked with hypercholesterolaemia

LIBRARY, UNIVERSITY OF CHESTER

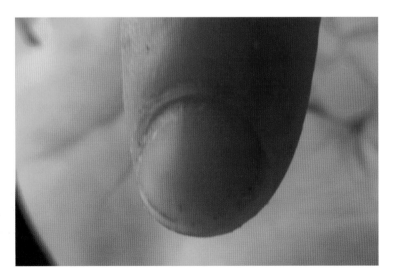

Figure 3.1a: Splinter haemorrhages

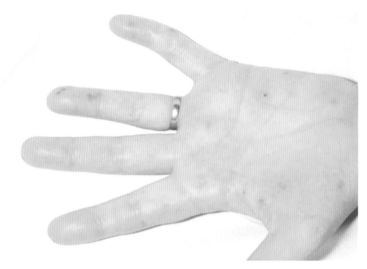

Figure 3.1b: Osler's nodes and Janeway lesions

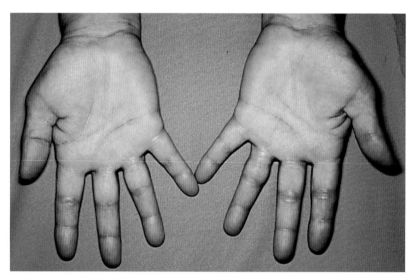

Figure 3.1c: Palmar xanthoma

Face

John's face was assessed in terms of general colour. Some types of cardiac valve disease can produce a characteristic discolouration of the cheeks known as a malar flush. This is best described as the appearance of cyanotic changes in the area of the cheeks.

The eyes require particularly careful examination. The conjunctiva of John's eye was observed by gently pulling down the lower eyelid and noting the colour of the conjunctival membrane. A conjunctiva that appears pale may be linked with underlying anaemia. The eyes can also provide signs of underlying hypercholesterolaemia, which can result in a greyish ring at the periphery of the cornea (called an arcus – see Figure 3.2a) and yellow lesions above or below the eyes (known as xanthelasma – see Figure 3.2b), which may indicate lipid deposits under the skin. However, as Rushforth (2009) explains, these signs can be normal variants and may not be clinically significant beyond the age of 50. Indeed, an arcus observed in an individual over the age of 50 will often be described as 'arcus senilis' to indicate its likely association with age rather than a clinical condition.

The mucosal membranes inside John's mouth were also examined to check for central cyanosis, which is an indicator of reduced oxygenation of the blood.

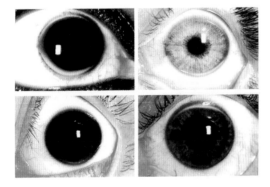

Figure 3.2a: Corneal arcus

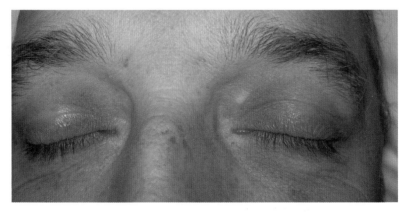

Figure 3.2b: Xanthelasma

Jugular venous pressure

John was positioned lying down at an approximately 45-degree angle. A pillow was used to flex his head slightly, with John looking straight ahead in order to relax the sternomastoid muscle. The practitioner was then able to observe the internal jugular vein while looking for transmission of pulsations just above the clavicle.

In normal physiology, the vertical height of the pulsations estimated from the sternal angle should be below 4cm. This measurement gives an indirect assessment of central venous pressure (CVP) and is associated with right atrial pressure. Approximation of this measurement gives the practitioner an indication of the patient's blood volume state and cardiac function (see Figure 3.3). An elevated JVP may be associated with underlying heart failure, tamponade (excessive accumulation of pericardial fluid), hypervolaemia, pulmonary embolism and superior vena cava obstruction (Bickley 2012).

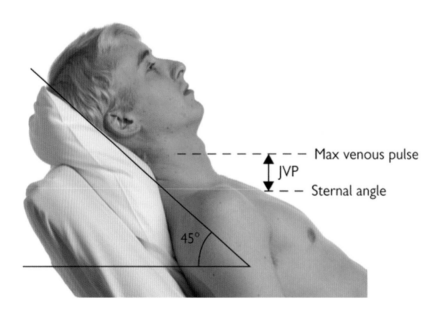

Figure 3.3: Measuring a patient's JVP

Carotid pulses

John's carotid pulses were examined by means of carotid palpation, noting the character of the pulse in order to assess left ventricular function. Whilst both carotid pulses were assessed, the practitioner took care not to palpate both pulses at once and avoided stimulation of the carotid sinus. Both these actions can result in a reflex drop in heart rate and blood pressure, leading to reduced cerebral perfusion, causing syncope. Auscultation over both carotid arteries with a stethoscope allowed the practitioner to assess for the sounds of turbulent blood flow (termed bruits), which could indicate atherosclerosis in the carotid arteries.

The precordium

Inspection

A general inspection of John's chest wall allowed the practitioner to observe any abnormalities in the chest shape, unusual pulsations that would not usually be seen with the naked eye, and any scars indicating previous thoracic surgery for either cardiac or pulmonary reasons.

Palpation

By placing a hand flat on John's chest, pointing away from the left of the sternum, the practitioner was able to begin locating the apical impulse or apex beat. Identified by feeling for the most lateral site of impulse on the chest wall, this assessment correlates to the contraction of the left ventricle, and can give an indirect assessment of the condition of this chamber. In John's case the apical impulse was located in the mid-clavicular line at the fifth intercostal space, which is the normal location for an adult.

The main clinical cause of displacement of the apical impulse is hypertrophy of one or more of the chambers of the heart. It is worth noting at this point that in patients who are obese or have a muscular chest wall or those with barrel-shape deformities of the chest, the apical impulse may be undetectable (Turner *et al.* 2009). In John's case, the practitioner was also able to assess whether their placed hand was lifted with each heartbeat (known as a heave). This could indicate enlargement of the chambers of the heart, resulting in an abnormal degree of excursion with each heartbeat, or if any murmurs were palpable through the chest wall (termed a thrill), and often described as feeling the same as placing a hand on the chest wall of a purring cat.

Percussion

This is not routinely performed in cardiovascular assessment.

Auscultation

The practitioner then proceeded to auscultate the precordium in order to assess whether the heart sounds were normal and if any additional sounds were present. To assess all cardiac sounds at high and low pitch, the precordium should be auscultated, first using the diaphragm of the stethoscope to detect high-pitched sounds and then using the bell of the stethoscope to detect low-pitched sounds. The landmarks for positioning of the stethoscope during auscultation are shown in Figure 3.4.

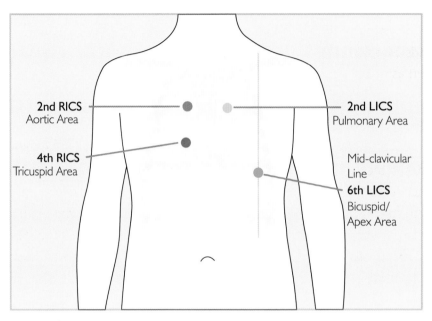

Figure 3.4: Stethoscope positions for auscultation

When auscultating using a stethoscope, the resonance of one cardiac cycle corresponds to two heart sounds often described as 'lub dub', indicating the closure of valves during the cardiac cycle.

S1 (lub)
The atria fill with blood and then contract, pushing the blood into the ventricles. This is the onset of systole. To prevent backflow during ventricular contraction, the valves between the atria and ventricles should close securely. In this way the first heart sound or S1 (lub) occurs as a result of the closure of the tricuspid and bicuspid valves.

S2 (dub)
Systole continues and blood leaves the ventricles through the open aortic and pulmonary valves. As systole completes and these valves close, the second heart sound, S2 (dub), is produced. This denotes the end of systole and there is a short pause before the onset of the next set of heart sounds. The short period between S2 and the next S1 is known as diastole, and allows the ventricles time to fill adequately before the next systole.

Physiological splitting

As a result of pressure changes during inspiration, valve closure on the right side occurs slightly later than valve closure on the left side. Whilst this slight variation is not usually heard, it is sometimes possible to distinguish two components for each heart sound. This is a normal variant and would not be considered clinically significant. In John's case, only heart sounds S1 and S2 were audible, indicating normal valve function. This is usually documented as:

HS I + II + Nil Added

Abnormal heart sounds

An early sign of heart failure (caused by pressure on the valve by the steadily increasing fluid volume) is the appearance of a third heart sound occurring early in diastole as a dull low-pitched sound. This finding is considered abnormal in patients over 30 years of age. A fourth heart sound may also appear in patients with pulmonary valve disease or reduced left ventricular compliance. This sound manifests itself late in diastole and is dull and low-pitched in character. It is often very soft and difficult to hear. These abnormal sounds are termed S3 and S4 respectively.

Murmurs

During auscultation, the practitioner also listens for any abnormal sounds (commonly described as 'whooshing' sounds) that could be associated with abnormal turbulent blood flow across the valves of the heart when the valve is not functioning normally. There are two main types of damage and malfunction of the valves:

1. Incompetent valve
2. Stenotic valve

An incompetent valve does not close properly, due to damage or disease. The abnormal sound of blood flow produced results from the blood being regurgitated backwards when the chamber contracts.

A stenotic valve does not open properly, due to damage, disease or, in John's case, the ageing process. The abnormal sound of blood flow produced results from the blood being forced across a valve that has not opened completely.

If the murmur is heard between the two heart sounds, it is known as a systolic murmur. However, if it is heard after both heart sounds it is called a diastolic murmur. Once a murmur has been identified as systolic or diastolic, it will usually be given a grade to describe its intensity, as follows:

- **Grade 1** – a quiet murmur that can only be heard after careful auscultation over a localised area
- **Grade 2** – a quiet murmur that is heard immediately once the stethoscope is placed over the relevant localised area
- **Grade 3** – a moderately loud murmur
- **Grade 4** – a loud murmur heard over a widespread area with no thrill palpable
- **Grade 5** – a loud murmur with associated precordial thrill
- **Grade 6** – a murmur sufficiently loud that it can be heard with the stethoscope raised just off the chest surface

Generally, loud murmurs are more likely to be significant than quiet murmurs. However, some murmurs are not associated with a large volume of abnormal blood flow but can still be very loud, usually due to vibration of the surrounding structures caused by the jet of abnormal blood flow. As with all aspects of physical examination, the practitioner develops skill in distinguishing these abnormalities from the normal heart sounds through practice and exposure to patients with relevant conditions. A more detailed description of the types of murmurs and their associated conditions is given in Table 3.2 on page 53.

Further examination

During the physical examination, all John's major arteries were assessed in order to ascertain that pulses were present and to detect the presence of bruits and aneurysms. John's lower limbs were examined for signs of varicose veins, ulceration and oedema, all of which could be signs of systemic cardiovascular disease.

Depending on the skill of the practitioner undertaking the assessment, the retina may be examined to check for clinical changes that can be caused by conditions such as hypertension or hypercholesterolaemia.

Finally, all information must be accurately and legibly documented. Not only is this a professional requirement (Health Professions Council 2008, Nursing and Midwifery Council 2009); it also provides a record of the signs detected and the actions and investigations undertaken, as well as establishing a baseline against which improvements or deterioration can be measured, thus facilitating continuity of care.

In summary, John underwent a thorough, systematic cardiovascular review in order to assess the likelihood of his chest pain being cardiac in origin. Although the findings of his physical examination were largely unremarkable, this assessment would need to be supplemented by further diagnostic, functional tests and investigations, coupled with a top-to-toe assessment to explore other potential causes for his chest pain.

Table 3.2: Types of murmur and associated clinical conditions

Sound	Where is it most audible?	What you will hear and what it implies
Systolic murmurs		
Aortic stenosis	Second right intercostal space; sound may radiate to neck or left sternal border	Medium-pitched, often harsh, grating sound occurring at mid-systole. Most often with rheumatic heart disease and congenital valve disorders.
Pulmonary stenosis	Second or third left intercostal space; sound radiates towards the shoulder and neck	Medium-pitched, mid-systolic. Harsh sound, louder on inspiration and when patient is supine. Generally heard in congenital valve disease.
Mitral regurgitation	Apex, fifth intercostal space, left mid-clavicular line; sound may radiate to left axilla or back	High-pitched blowing sound occurring throughout systole, common in rheumatic heart disease and after rupture of ventricular papillary muscle; worsens during expiration and when patient is supine.
Tricuspid regurgitation	Lower left sternal border; sound may radiate to right sternum	High-pitched, blowing sound occurring throughout systole; heard in right ventricular failure and rheumatic heart disease; intensifies on inspiration and when patient is supine.

Diastolic murmurs		
Aortic regurgitation	Second right intercostal space; sound may radiate to left or right sternal border	High-pitched blowing sound that increases when patient leans forward and holds breath; most often heard in rheumatic and congenital valve disease, Marfan's syndrome.
Pulmonary regurgitation	Second left intercostal space; sound may radiate to left lower sternal border	High-pitched, blowing sound increases with inspiration; most often heard with pulmonary hypertension.
Mitral stenosis	Apex, fifth intercostal space, left mid-clavicular line; sound gets louder with patient on left side; does not radiate	Low-pitched, rumbling sound that increases with exercise, inspiration and left lateral position; most often heard with rheumatic heart disease.
Tricuspid stenosis	Fourth left intercostal space at sternal border	Low-pitched, rumbling sound that increases with inspiration; most often heard with rheumatic heart disease and often in combination with other valve abnormalities.

References

Bickley, L.S. (2012). *Bates' Guide to Physical Examination and History-Taking.* Philadelphia, USA: Lippincott, Williams & Wilkins.

British Heart Foundation (2015). *Heart Disease Statistics.* Oxford, UK: Department of Public Health.

Department of Health (2010). *Advanced Level Nursing: A Position Statement.* London: DoH.

Epstein, O., Perkin, D.G., Cookson, J., Watt, I.S., Rakhit, R., Robins, R.W. & Hornett, G.A.W. (2008). *Clinical Examination.* London: Mosby.

Foxton, J. (2004). Coronary heart disease: Risk factor management. *Nursing Standard.* **19** (13), 47–54.

Gleadle, J. (2003). *History and Examination at a Glance.* Oxford, UK: Blackwell Science.

Health Professions Council (2008). *Standards of Conduct, Performance and Ethics.* London: HPC.

Jowett, N.I. & Thompson, D.R. (2007). *Comprehensive Coronary Care.* Oxford, UK: Baillière Tindall, Elsevier Science.

National Institute for Health and Clinical Excellence (2010). *Unstable Angina and NSTEMI.* London: NICE.

Nursing and Midwifery Council (2009). *Record Keeping: Guidance for Nurses and Midwives.* London: NMC.

Royal College of Nursing (2010). *Advanced Nurse Practitioners: An RCN Guide to the Advanced Nurse Practitioner Role, Competences and Programme Accreditation.* London: RCN.

Rushworth, H. (2009). *Assessment made Incredibly Easy.* (UK edition) London: Lippincott, Williams & Wilkins.

Ryan, H., Cadman, C. & Hann, L. (2004). Setting standards for assessment of ward patients at risk of deterioration. *British Journal of Nursing.* **13** (20), 1186–90.

Timmis, A. & Mills, P. (2006). 'The cardiovascular system' in Swash, M. (ed.) *Hutchinson's Clinical Methods.* London: W.B. Saunders, 79–124.

Turner, R., Angus, B., Handa, A. & Hatton, C. (2009). *Clinical Skills and Examination: The Core Curriculum.* Oxford, UK: Wiley-Blackwell.

Wood, G.G. & Timmins, A. (2001). Rapid assessment of chest pain: The rationale is clear but evidence is needed. *British Medical Journal.* **323** (7313), 586–7.

Chapter 4

Gastrointestinal assessment

Mark Ranson

Abdominal pain is a common presentation and healthcare professionals need to be confident about dealing with it. Patients can present with a variety of symptoms and complaints so it is important to have an understanding of the underlying problems that can lead to abdominal pain (Bickley & Szilaygi 2007). The ability to undertake and document a clear, concise and systematic assessment of the gastrointestinal system is therefore an important skill, particularly for those healthcare professionals working in areas associated with this specialty. Many healthcare professionals are now taking on advanced roles, which include physical examination of body systems (National Practitioner Programme 2006, Royal College of Nursing 2010). The aim of this chapter is therefore to take a systematic approach to appraising the relevant aspects of the gastrointestinal system. To inform this process, the content of this chapter will be based on a case study.

Box 4.1: Case study – presenting condition

Jane was a 35-year-old woman who presented with a three-day history of generalised abdominal pain associated with episodes of nausea and vomiting. Her medical history was unremarkable and she was usually fit and well.

Patient history

The first step in Jane's examination would be to obtain a history from the patient. As history-taking has been discussed in Chapter 1, discussion here will focus on the elements that are relevant to Jane's presentation with a three-day history of abdominal pain. In practice, acronyms can help the healthcare practitioner to take a structured history as well as acting as an aide mémoire to ensure that all the vital questions are asked. Jane was first asked some open questions to establish the main symptom and presenting complaint. More specific questioning was guided by the use of the O, P, Q, R, S, T, U, V, W acronym (adapted from Kumar & Clark 2016, Epstein et al. 2009).

Table 4.1: Abdominal pain history-taking questions

O	Onset/Are other systems affected?
P	Precipitating factors/pattern/progression/periods/pregnancy/recent foreign holiday/recent antibiotic use?
Q	Quality/quantity of pain (using a scale of 0–5)? Quantity of blood/vomit/stool produced?
R	Relieving factors – heat, cool, massage, rest, medications? Red flag symptoms such as weight loss?
S	Severity/difficulty swallowing? Systemic symptoms? Stools? Sexual history?
T	Timing of symptoms?
U	Urinary symptoms?
V	Vomiting? Voice changes?
W	Any recent weight change?

The history taken from Jane also included questions about past medical history, drug history (prescribed, over-the-counter and recreational), family history particularly focused on bowel and other gastrointestinal disorders, allergies and social history particularly in relation to gastrointestinal-related risk factors such as diet, alcohol intake and smoking (Kumar & Clark 2016).

Introduction to physical examination

Having completed the history-taking, the need for a physical examination of the abdomen was explained to Jane. As with any procedure, the practitioner should allow time for the patient to ask questions and give informed consent to continue (Department of Health 2000). This helps to alleviate any apprehensions about the physical examination, which is particularly important – given that anxiety and embarrassment can have a physiological effect on body function, thus altering the findings during the examination. Jane's dignity was maintained throughout by only exposing the area being examined at the time, and ensuring that this area was covered again following the examination. Each part of the examination was explained to Jane as it happened, in order to avoid overloading her with too much information at once, which can provoke anxiety.

Table 4.2: Non-abdominal elements of the examination

Location	Sign	Can be associated with
Hands	• Clubbing of nails • Leukonychia (white patches on nails) • Koilonychia (spoon-shaped nails) • Palmar erythema (reddening of the palms)	Chronic liver disease
	• Dupuytren's contracture (one or more fingers bending in towards the palm)	Alcohol abuse
Tongue	• Smooth tongue	Iron deficiency
	• Beef steak tongue (bright red colour)	B_{12} or folate deficiency
	• Dry tongue	Dehydration

Lips	• Angular stomatitis (corners of mouth, pale tongue)	Anaemia
	• Cyanosed lips	Chronic liver disease (pulmonary-arterio shunting)
Mouth	• Ulcers, candida, gingivitis	General dental hygiene
	• Brown freckles around mouth and on lips (Peutz Jegher's syndrome)	Small bowel polyps
Teeth	• Erosions posterior aspect of teeth	Excessive vomiting
	• (Breath: ketosis, alcohol)	
Skin	• Spider naevi (large arteriole with smaller vessels radiating from it)	Chronic liver disease
	• Telangiectasia (small dilated blood vessels on face)	
	• Blue discolouration	Acute haemorrhagic pancreatitis
	• Flanks (Grey Turner's sign)	
	• Peri-umbilical area (Cullen's sign)	
	• Jaundice	Liver disease
Torso	• Gynaecomastia (enlarged male breasts) and/or testicular atrophy	Chronic liver failure
Lymph nodes	• Behind left sternoclavicular joint (Virchow's node)	Abdominal neoplasm

General survey

The practitioner noted Jane's overall appearance as she entered the room in order to elicit initial clues that could be used to guide the history-taking and physical examination. Observations made included her gait, co-ordination, level of consciousness, facial expression, tone of voice, grooming, clothing, height, weight, build, posture and any obvious odours. Given Jane's presentation with abdominal pain, the focus of the physical examination was the abdomen. However, it is important to acknowledge and assess for signs elsewhere on the body that may be related to gastrointestinal conditions.

Abdominal examination

The four principles of physical examination can be applied to abdominal examination (as indeed they can be to the physical examination of other body systems). However, the order in which these four principles were carried out in Jane's examination was changed, as the examination was focused on the abdomen. The four principles and their order in abdominal examination are as follows:

1. **Inspection**: visual inspection of the abdomen as a whole
2. **Auscultation**: listening to the sounds produced by internal organs using the bell and the diaphragm of a stethoscope (NB: this is performed earlier in an abdominal examination, as palpation and percussion may cause increased bowel sounds and mask problems)
3. **Palpation**: using the technique of touch to assess temperature, texture, moisture and size of organs
4. **Percussion**: placing a finger firmly over a particular area or organ and tapping another finger with short, sharp strokes against the first finger to assess transmission of sound

Abdominal inspection

Jane was given the opportunity to use the toilet before the examination – in order to ease progress and maximise comfort. She was asked to lie flat on an examination couch, with one pillow under her head and her hands by her side. Having positioned Jane comfortably, the practitioner exposed the abdomen and took a step back to perform a general inspection of the abdomen, looking mainly for symmetry whilst remembering the presenting symptoms and complaints. Any asymmetry observed in the abdomen could be due to one of the 'Five Fs':

- Flatus
- Foetus
- Fat
- Faeces
- Fluid

During the visual inspection, the practitioner also checked Jane's skin for rashes or lesions, spider naevi (see Table 4.2, page 59), striae (stretch marks) and dilated veins, particularly over the abdominal wall. These findings can suggest other abnormalities that may require further investigation, though they were not present in Jane's case. In addition the practitioner should use the inspection to note any evidence of issues that might not have arisen during the history-taking (such as scars indicating previous injury or surgery and swellings indicating hernias or masses) and should question the patient about them. Abdominal inspection is also an opportunity to observe any abnormal movement within the abdomen on respiration, peristalsis or the presence of any unexpected pulsations (Bickley 2012). The abdominal inspection proved unremarkable in Jane's case.

Boundaries of the abdomen

Having completed the general inspection of the abdomen, the practitioner prepared to move on to the next three principles of physical examination – auscultation, palpation and percussion. In order to provide some useful boundaries to begin the examination, the abdomen can be imagined as being divided up into four quadrants, right upper, right lower, left upper and left lower (see Figure 4.1).

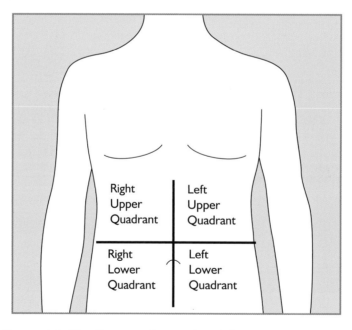

Figure 4.1: The four quadrants for abdominal examination

Whilst these imaginary boundaries can be useful in the early stages of the examination, more specific anatomical boundaries are required to facilitate examination and documentation of findings. It is therefore possible to further divide the abdomen into nine segments. The nine segments and their related anatomical structures are detailed in Table 4.3 below.

Table 4.3:
The nine abdominal divisions and associated anatomical structures

Segment	Associated anatomical structures
Right hypochondria	Liver
Epigastric	Stomach
Left hypochondria	Spleen
Right lumbar	Kidney
Umbilical	Bowel
Left lumbar	Kidney
Right iliac fossa	Ovary and appendix
Suprapubic	Bladder
Left iliac fossa	Ovary and descending colon

Auscultation

The practitioner explained to Jane that the next part of the examination involved listening to the abdomen. The main objective at this stage is to listen to bowel sounds. All four of the main quadrants described above were auscultated for bowel sounds. The practitioner should note that an increase in bowel sounds is often associated with abdominal obstruction or laxative abuse and may be commonly described as a 'tinkling' sound. A decrease or absence of bowel sounds is often associated with a paralytic ileus (paralysis of the intestinal muscles) and generalised peritonitis (inflammation of the peritoneum).

After listening with the diaphragm of the stethoscope, the practitioner switched to the bell of the stethoscope, listening in all four quadrants and the epigastric region for vascular sounds and bruits in the aortic, renal, iliac and femoral arteries to assess for signs of obstruction and atherosclerosis in blood vessels. Jane was found to have normal bowel sounds and no evidence of excess vascular sounds or bruits present in all four of the main quadrants and the epigastric region. Table 4.4 highlights some abnormal sounds that may be heard on auscultation.

Table 4.4: Abnormal auscultation sounds

Sound	Location	Possible Indication
Bowel sounds: hyperactive or hypoactive sounds created by air and fluid movement through the bowel	All four quadrants	• Hyperactive = diarrhoea or early intestinal obstruction • Hypoactive/then absent sounds = paralytic ileus or peritonitis • High-pitched/tinkling = intestinal fluid and air under tension in a distended bowel • High-pitched/rushing with abdominal cramp = obstruction
Systolic bruits: continuous, medium-pitched sound caused by blood flow in a large vascular organ	Abdominal aorta; renal artery/iliac artery	• Partial arterial obstruction or dissecting abdominal aneurysm • Renal artery stenosis • Hepatomegaly
Venous hum: continuous, medium-pitched sound caused by blood flow in a large vascular organ	Epigastric or umbilical	• Hepatic cirrhosis
Friction rub: harsh grating sound that sounds like two pieces of leather being rubbed together	Hepatic and spleen	• Inflammation of the peritoneal surface of an organ • Liver tumour

Abdominal palpation and percussion

Jane was informed that palpation (touch) was the next stage of the examination (see Table 4.5, page 66). The practitioner ensured that their hands were warmed, as sudden contact on the abdomen with cold hands can elicit an abnormal response from the patient. Jane was also asked to identify the site of her pain so that the examination could be commenced away from that site, with the practitioner working towards the identified painful area.

Using one flat hand, the practitioner first performed light palpation over all four quadrants whilst observing Jane's face for signs of discomfort and noting if pain occurred on removal of the pressure (rebound). Deeper palpation was then performed over all four quadrants, using both hands on top of each other. In this way, the practitioner was able to assess whether pressure caused discomfort, identify the region of the discomfort and find out whether the discomfort was caused by superficial palpation, deep palpation or rebound. The practitioner was also feeling and assessing for the following:

- **Guarding – voluntary muscle spasm to protect from pain**
- **Rigidity – fixed and tense muscles caused by involuntary spasm which can suggest generalised peritonitis**

No masses were palpable in Jane's abdomen. But if a mass is felt, the practitioner needs to describe the mass in terms of its:

1. Site
2. Size
3. Shape
4. Consistency
5. Fixed or mobile?
6. Tenderness
7. Pulsatility

Palpation in the midline, just above the umbilicus, allowed the practitioner to assess Jane's abdominal aorta. In some slim people the aorta is palpable and insignificant, but in others an easily palpable aorta could raise suspicion of aortic aneurysm.

Percussion performed across all four quadrants of the abdomen and the epigastric region should reveal mostly tympanic sounds. However, there are likely to be some areas of dullness, indicating the presence of faeces and fluid. Table 4.6 (page 66) gives an overview of some of the sounds that may be heard during percussion of the abdomen.

Table 4.5: Areas of the hand used in palpation

Area of hand	Used to assess
Palmar surface of the hand and finger pads	Size, consistency, texture, fluid, surgical emphysema Texture and form of a mass or structure
Ulnar surface of the hand and fingers	Vibration
Dorsal surface of the hands	Temperature

Table 4.6: Percussion sounds of the abdomen

Sound	Description	Location
Tympany	Musical sound/high pitch, little resonance	Air-filled viscera
Hyper-resonance	Pitch sounds between tympany and resonance	Base of left lung
Resonance	Sustained sound of moderate pitch	Vesicular lung tissue or the abdomen
Dullness	Short, high-pitched sound with little resonance	Solid organs

Groin palpation

The use of one hand on each side allowed the practitioner to gently palpate the groin area, checking for hernias in the inguinal and femoral regions. Lymph nodes are also palpable in the groin area and can be checked for enlargement, with or without associated tenderness (lymphadenopathy). No abnormalities were detected during Jane's examination. But had enlarged and tender lymph nodes been palpable, the practitioner would have been prompted to make a thorough check of the spleen in the later examination, as these can be associated with conditions such as lymphoma or leukaemia.

Liver percussion and palpation

In order to check for tenderness, firmness, rounding or irregularity of the edge of the liver, the practitioner began to percuss from 10cm below the lower rib on the right side in the mid-clavicular line, slowly working upwards towards the ribcage. The practitioner noted when the sound from percussion started to become dull, and used this position to indicate the lower edge of the liver.

Percussion was then moved up to the third intercostal space, with the practitioner systematically percussing down between each intercostal space until the sound began to dull. This indicates the upper border of the liver and should typically be found around the sixth intercostal space. Hurley (2011) suggests that a normal liver span is 8–10cm in women and 10–12cm in men.

Having established that Jane's liver span falls within acceptable parameters, it was now possible for the practitioner to palpate the lower edge of the liver. Jane was asked to breathe in whilst the practitioner gently inserted the tips of the fingers under the lower costal margin to palpate the lower border of the liver. If the liver edge is felt, the practitioner should note whether it is smooth or irregular, soft, firm or hard and tender (a healthy liver is not usually tender).

Spleen palpation and percussion

The spleen is not usually palpable unless it is enlarged (doubled in size). In order to assess for an enlarged spleen (splenomegaly), the practitioner began palpation in Jane's umbilical area and proceeded to palpate in a diagonal line across to the lower left costal margin. Jane was then asked to take a deep breath whilst the fingers were pushed gently but firmly under the ribcage, attempting to palpate the spleen.

Splenomegaly, which was not present in Jane's case, would prompt the examiner to consider conditions such as chronic myeloid leukaemia, portal hypertension, haemolytic anaemia or infections such as tuberculosis. Percussion was performed in the ninth intercostal space anterior to the axillary line (Traub's Space) to assess further for splenomegaly. In Jane's case the sounds produced were resonant. This suggested an absence of splenomegaly, as the sounds become dull if the spleen is enlarged.

Kidney palpation

It should be noted that palpation of the kidneys is quite difficult and can be uncomfortable for the patient. The practitioner cupped one hand behind Jane's back and pressed firmly under the anterior costal margin in an attempt to catch the lower pole of the kidney between the fingers as the organ moved up and down with respiration. By placing the flat of the hand over the posterior renal area and using the other hand to briefly 'thump' over the renal angle, the practitioner can check for costovertebral angle tenderness. Tenderness in the kidney area would lead to suspicions of an underlying infective or obstructive pathology.

Summary

The examination of Jane's abdomen proved unremarkable up to this point. However, it is important to point out here some specific manoeuvres that may be required in the presence of certain pathologies in order to confirm a diagnosis.

Psoas sign

Asking the patient to raise their right thigh against pressure, or asking the patient to lie on their left side while extending their right leg behind them, will stretch the Psoas muscle. If this causes pain, it can be indicative of appendicitis.

Obturator sign

Flexing the right thigh at the hip, bending the knee up and rolling the flexed knee internally assesses this sign. If this causes pain in the right upper quadrant it can be indicative of appendicitis, due to irritation of the obturator muscle.

Murphy's sign

Pressing the fingers under the right costal margin and asking the patient to take a deep breath in as the practitioner pushes inwards and upwards may cause the patient to experience an increase in tenderness and to stop inspiring. This is known as a positive Murphy's sign and is indicative of acute cholecystitis.

Rovsing's sign

If the patient experiences pain in the right lower quadrant whilst pressure is being applied in the left lower quadrant (either on palpation or as rebound tenderness), then a positive Rovsing's sign is present, suggesting peritoneal irritation.

(Above adapted from Longmore & Wilkinson 2014)

Is there a need for vaginal and/or rectal examination?

At this stage in Jane's abdominal examination, the practitioner needs to consider the need for vaginal (PV) and/or rectal (PR) examination. Indications for PV examination would be to rule out differential diagnoses such as ovarian cyst, ovarian torsion, ectopic pregnancy or pelvic inflammatory disease. Nothing in Jane's examination so far would produce a differential diagnosis of one of these conditions. PV examination would therefore not be deemed necessary in her case.

However, PR examination should be part of an abdominal assessment and will be discussed in more detail. It is also worth pointing out that all healthcare areas should have 'a for alarm' symptoms that would result in an urgent referral for investigation for cancer. The common alarm symptoms cited here are as follows:

- Evidence of GI bleeding
- Dysphagia (difficulty swallowing)
- Unexplained and unintentional weight loss over a short period of time
- Persistent vomiting
- Iron deficiency anaemia with no obvious cause
- Palpable mass – rectal, epigastric or abdominal
- Change in bowel habit
- Persistent rectal or abdominal pain
- Tenesmus (a feeling of constantly needing to pass stools)

(National Institute for Health and Clinical Excellence 2005)

Digital rectal examination (DRE)

As with abdominal complaints, patients may present with a range of rectal symptoms and complaints. Whilst this is not readily apparent within Jane's presentation, it is important to consider the implications of these in the context of gastrointestinal examination as a whole. For many patients, undergoing DRE is an embarrassing experience. It is therefore vital that the examination is undertaken empathically, ensuring the patient's privacy and dignity (Royal College of Nursing 2003).

DRE can be used to assess anal sphincter function, tone and sensation, the presence of faecal matter and its consistency, as well as the effects of rectal medication and other interventions designed to ease evacuation of the rectum and the need for manual removal of faeces (Royal College of Nursing 2003). In the context of abdominal examination, it is used to aid in the diagnosis of rectal and prostate tumours and should always be performed in individuals who have experienced a change in urinary flow or bowel habit.

There are various positions that the patient can adopt for DRE, depending on their mobility and comfort (Swartz 2014).

Table 4.7: Patient positions for DRE

Position	Indications
Standing	Often used when examining men – allows thorough inspection of the anus and palpation of the rectum.
Left lateral (Sim's position)	Patient lies on their left side with their knees drawn up to their chest. Patients who are weak and confined to bed are often examined in this position.
Knee–elbow position	Patient kneels on the examination couch, resting on their elbows.
Dorsal (Lithotomy) position	Patient lies on their back with knees flexed. Can be used when the patient has difficulty standing, is in severe pain or where mobility is restricted.

History before DRE

Whilst history-taking for abdominal assessment has already been discussed earlier in this chapter, there are some additional questions that may be pertinent prior to undertaking DRE. These include:

- How often do you have your bowels open?
- What are your stools like?
- Is the anus sore or itchy? If so, when? What relieves this?
- Any incontinence – passive or urgent in nature?
- Do you feel you have to strain to pass a stool?
- Do you ever feel you cannot empty your bowels fully?
- Do you ever notice blood mixed with a stool or on the tissue when you wipe?
- If so, what colour is it? Bright red or a darker red?
- Sexual history – any anal sex or sexually transmitted infections in the past?

Inspection

Visual inspection of the anus is the first step in the examination, with the practitioner looking for:

1. Inflammation
2. Excoriation – linear abrasions of the epidermis
3. Nodules
4. Scars
5. Tumours
6. Skin tags – hypertrophied folds of skin
7. Pilonidal sinuses – small pits in the skin that can become infected
8. Anal warts – overgrowth of skin with typical warty appearance
9. External haemorrhoids – swollen, blueish veins that are tender to touch
10. Rectal prolapse – folds of red mucosa protruding from the anus
11. Anal fissure – a painful crack in the anal wall
12. Gaping anus – reduced or absent internal and external anal tone

(Adapted from Marsh 2006, Swartz 2014)

Rectal examination

Palpation

Having explained to the patient that the lubricant may feel cold, the practitioner (using a gloved lubricated finger) should sweep superficially around the anus and perianal region, checking for tenderness, firmness, induration, fistula tracts, lesions or any other abnormalities.

Insertion

Start by applying slight pressure on the anus. It has been suggested that getting the patient to talk or take slow deep breaths can aid insertion. It is worth noting here that if anal fissures are seen during inspection, the practitioner needs to proceed with caution, as insertion may be too painful. It may be necessary to delay the insertion phase of the examination until the fissures have been treated. Ask the patient to take a deep breath in and insert the finger into the rectum.

The examination finger should be moved around the rectum, from posterior to anterior and lateral to medial. The ischial spines, coccyx and lower sacrum should be felt easily. In a normal rectum, the mucosa should feel smooth and flexible. Rectal tumours may be felt as a shelf-like protrusion into the rectum (Talley & O'Connor 2013). Infiltration of the Pouch of Douglas by neoplastic cells from intraperitoneal metastases often project into the anterior wall of the rectum and are known as Blumer's Shelf (Swartz 2014).

The walls of the rectum should be felt for polyps, which may be sessile (attached by a base) or pedunculated (attached by a stalk). During the ongoing examination, there are some specific areas that should be examined, depending on whether the patient is male or female.

Male patient

The prostate gland can be felt towards the ventral-abdominal surface of the body as it lies anterior to the wall of the rectum. The size, consistency, sensitivity and shape of the gland should be assessed. There is a mid-line groove called the sulcus that divides the lobes of the prostate. A healthy prostate feels smooth and the lobes are the same size. In prostate enlargement, one or both lobes may feel enlarged. The practitioner should note any tenderness, nodules or masses. In prostatitis, the gland will feel 'boggy' and the patient may experience tenderness on palpation. If a cancerous tumour is present it may feel hard or have a 'woody' feel to it, or a discrete lump may be felt. Cancer of the prostate frequently involves the posterior lobe, although only T3 and T4 (locally advanced prostate cancer) tumours are easily palpated. T1 and T2 (early localised prostate cancer) tumours may be missed, as they are too small to be detected through DRE.

Female patient

In the female patient, it is important to ascertain whether any vaginal tampons or pessaries are present, as these can affect the findings of the examination. Rectovaginal palpation should be undertaken in women. This examination permits better evaluation of the posterior portion of the pelvis and the cul-de-sac than bimanual examination via the vagina alone. The recto-vaginal septum is palpated, assessing for tenderness and signs of thickening. Digital examination in this area can also allow detection of the presence of nodules or masses. It should be noted that the cervix and a retroverted uterus may also be palpable in this region.

Removal

Before removing the examining digit, the practitioner should ask the patient to squeeze the anus together around their finger. This gives an indication of anal tone and the condition of the rectal muscles. Once confident that the examination is complete, the examining digit can be slowly removed from the anus. The examination finger should be inspected for stool, blood, pus or malaena. The final step is to remove the excess gel from the anus and ensure that the patient is comfortable. The findings of all examinations undertaken should be recorded accurately and legibly in the patient's records.

Conclusion

Following a systematic approach to abdominal assessment will help you reach a diagnosis and ultimately work out an appropriate treatment plan. It is important to ensure that a full history is taken prior to any physical examination, as this allows the physical examination to be better focused. Assessment must begin as soon as the patient walks into the room, with their physical appearance providing important clues.

The systematic process of abdominal inspection, auscultation, palpation and percussion will allow further steps towards diagnosis to be taken. Specific tests for identified pathology may then be required to narrow differential diagnosis still further. Abdominal examination should be followed by rectal or vaginal examination if indicated, which will again aid diagnosis. You should conclude the gastrointestinal system examination by explaining to the patient the findings of the examination and any further investigations that may be required. This should be followed by accurate and legible documentation of the findings of the examinations in the patient's clinical records.

References

Bickley, L.S. (2012). *Bates' Guide to Physical Examination and History-Taking.* Philadelphia, USA: Lippincott, Williams & Wilkins.

Bickley, L. & Szilagyi, P. (2007). *Bates' Guide to Physical Examination.* Philadelphia, USA: Lippincott, Williams & Wilkins.

Department of Health (2000). *Good Practice in Consent: Achieving the NHS Plan Commitment to Patient-centered Consent Practice.* London: Department of Health.

Epstein, O., Perking, G.D., DeBono, D.P.E. & Cookson, J. (2009). *Clinical Examination.* London: Mosby.

Hurley, K.F. (2011). *OSCE and Clinical Skills Handbook.* Toronto, Canada: Elsevier Saunders.

Kumar, P. & Clark, M. (2016). *Clinical Medicine.* London: W.B. Saunders.

Longmore, M. & Wilkinson, I. (2014). *Oxford Handbook of Clinical Medicine.* Oxford: Oxford University Press.

Marsh, A. (2006). *History and Examination. Abdominal Examination.* Edinburgh, Scotland: Mosby.

National Institute for Health and Clinical Excellence (2005). *Referral Guidelines for Suspected Cancer.* London: NICE.

National Practitioner Programme (2006). *Optimising the Contribution of Non-medical Healthcare Practitioners Within the Multi-professional Team: A Good Practice Checklist.* London: Department of Health.

Royal College of Nursing (2003). *Digital Rectal Examination and Manual Removal of Faeces: Guidance for Nurses.* London: RCN.

Royal College of Nursing (2010). *Advanced Nurse Practitioners: An RCN Guide to the Advanced Nurse Practitioner Role, Competences and Programme Accreditation.* London: Royal College of Nursing.

Swartz, M. (2014). *Textbook of Physical Diagnosis: History and Examination.* London: W.B. Saunders.

Talley, N. & O'Connor, S. (2013). *Clinical Examination: A Systematic Guide to Physical Diagnosis.* Sydney, Australia: Churchill Livingstone.

Chapter 5

Neurological assessment

Sooreka Wapling

The nervous system is the most highly developed and complex system in the body. Its function is to coordinate and control the many activities of the organism. Rapid communication between the various parts, the effective, integrated activity of different organs and tissues and the coordinated contraction of muscle are almost entirely dependent upon the nervous system, although some degree of coordination results from the action of hormones (Tortora & Derrickson 2011).

Many patients may suffer from a nervous system disorder and the symptoms will depend on which area of the nervous system is involved and what is causing the problem. Nervous system disorders may occur slowly and cause a gradual loss of function (degenerative) or they may occur suddenly and cause acute (life-threatening) problems. Symptoms may be mild or severe.

The following are the most common general signs and symptoms of a nervous system disorder:

- Persistent or sudden onset of a headache
- A headache that changes or is different
- Loss of feeling or tingling
- Weakness or loss of muscle strength
- Sudden loss of sight or double vision
- Memory loss

- Impaired mental ability
- Anxiety

To perform a reliable assessment, it is necessary to take a logical and systematic approach to neurological assessment, as the signs and symptoms will provide important clues to the nature of the underlying pathology (Scadding & Losseff 2012). It is also important to remember that many patients may not have any obvious abnormal signs on examination or may experience symptoms differently from others.

Introduction to neurological assessment

Physical assessment remains the starting point. The neurological assessment aims to determine:

- Presence or absence of malfunction
- Location, type and extent of nervous system lesions
- Status of neurological deficits
- Potential threat to survival
- Highest degree of functional ability
- Influence of disability on individual's lifestyle

The following case study will encourage critical thinking regarding some of the assessments that will be needed and further tests that may be necessary to inform the decision-making process.

Box 5.1: Case study – presenting condition

Tim was a 55-year-old who was admitted to the ward via Accident and Emergency, following a fall. He had no previous medical history. On questioning, he stated that he was out walking his dog when he noticed that he frequently stumbled for no apparent reason and his grip on the lead was not as tight as was needed. He also noticed that his left eye became blurred at times.

Observations

The ABCD2 algorithm predicts a patient's very early risk of stroke following a transient ischemic attack (TIA). The score is calculated according to five important clinical risk predictors (see Table 5.1 below). Following the national Stroke Association (2006) guidelines, risk factors ABCD2 (age, blood pressure, clinical features, duration, diabetes) = stroke risk score.

Table 5.1: National stroke strategy (Department of Health 2007)

Risk factor	Criterion	Points	Score
A – Age	>/= 60 years	1	
B – Blood pressure	>/= 140/90 mm Hg at initial evaluation	1	
C – Clinical features	Unilateral weakness Speech disturbance No symptoms	2 1 0	
D1 – Duration of symptoms	> 60 mins 10–59 mins < 10 mins	2 1 0	
D2 – Diabetes	History No history	1 0	
Total score: 1–7			

Low risk: 1–3

Moderate risk: 4–5

High risk: 6–7

Table 5.2: Results of Tim's ABCD2 assessment

What we know	What we think we know	What we want to find out
55 years	< 60 yrs	Does age contribute to symptoms?
BP 140/90	BP 140/90	Use of ABCD2 score?
Stumbles	Symptoms have resolved/ weakness on one side	Has he been advised to take or been prescribed aspirin?
Blood glucose = 6 mmols	Not diabetic	Can we exclude hypoglycaemia?
Total ABCD2 score = 3	Score < 4	Low/moderate/high risk?

History

Presenting complaint

Ask how long he has noticed these symptoms for.

Ask about any associated symptoms – does he suffer from any of the following?

- Headache
- Twitches, tremors, weakness, numbness, paraesthesia
- Nausea and vomiting
- Visual disturbances

Past medical history

- Enquire about any medical problems he may have.
- Is he taking any prescribed medications? If so, what are they?

Systematic assessment

- Loss of weight?
- Loss of appetite?

Social history

- Lifestyle – smoking, drinking, prescribed/non-prescribed drugs?

- Work – degree of stress?
- Hobbies?

Family history

AVPU – rapid assessment of level of consciousness

Assessing the level of consciousness is a vital part of the examination. Using the acronym 'AVPU' (alert, responsive to voice, responsive to pain and unresponsive) can help the practitioner make a rapid assessment of a patient's mental state.

All the above will be manifested in a change in mental state, ranging from altered personality to confusion or loss of consciousness. For Tim, some of these changes may be temporary or permanent (Adam *et al.* 2010).

Consciousness requires both arousal and mental content (Brust 2012) but confusion and disorientation may not be immediately apparent. Tim's level of consciousness is the earliest and most sensitive indicator that his mental status has changed.

The examination proceeds in steps, from higher to lower levels of integration. A conclusive diagnosis should not be made on the basis of the neurological examination alone but also based on the physical examination and the results of other specialised investigations such as a CT scan or MRI.

The tests for cerebral function are divided into three types:

1. Evaluation of general cerebral function, such as disturbances of intellect, memory and disorders of speech (these all relate to problems of the cerebral cortex)
2. Appraisal of specific malfunctions
3. General behaviour of the patient

Assessing speech

During your initial conversation with Tim, his speech will probably be one of the first things you notice about him, albeit unconsciously. Words and sentences are controlled by speech centres in the brain's dominant hemisphere (Brust 2012).

Assessing perception, action and reaction

Observe Tim's behaviour, body language, moods and emotions. Note whether he is cooperative. A patient's mood and insight may be demonstrated by their reaction and the degree to which they cope with the illness. The clarity with which a patient presents their story and answers questions will give an indication of their intellectual capacity, their personality and their mood (Scadding & Losseff 2012).

Assessing general behaviour

Observe Tim's manner, his ability to think, reason and make judgements. Consider how he reacts to others and his surroundings, noticing whether he expresses any anxiety, anger, hostility, euphoria or indifference, as changes in mental state are a major sign of deterioration.

Look for evidence of self-neglect. Poor hygiene and lack of concern with his appearance may indicate anxiety, depression or dementia.

The presence of persistent headache and a stiff neck, and any resistance to movement, could suggest arthritis, cervical spondylosis; and passive neck flexion may be indicative of meningitis or subarachnoid haemorrhage (Brust 2012).

Observe whether Tim screws his eyes when you are testing his pupils' responses to light. This is called photophobia (avoidance of light). Pupil responses to light are the most important guide to the cause of coma (Scadding & Losseff 2012).

- **Phonophobia (avoidance of noise) could be due to headache, or brain/head injury.**
- **Dizziness, tingling, numbness, tremors, weakness or paralysis are all signs to look out for during a neurological assessment.**

Coma scale – additional assessment

The Glasgow Coma Scale (GCS) of Teasdale & Jennett (1974) is the most widely used tool to measure the level of consciousness following any neurological disorders.

This tool assesses the function of the cerebral cortex and the brain stem. It looks at behavioural responses in three categories:

1. **Eye opening**: degree of stimulation required to elicit this, as this indicates that the reticular activating system (RAS) in the brain stem is active.
2. **Verbal response**: quality and type of vocalisation, as the ability to use language is one of the highest functions of the brain and it also indicates that the patient has an intact airway.
3. **Best motor response**: the patient should be able to obey simple commands.

The GCS scale consists of 15 items with a total score of 15 points. A score of 15 points indicates a fully orientated and alert person, which is the optimal level of consciousness. Deep coma is indicated by 3, the lowest score. The model involves assessing the patient at specified time intervals and recording the best response on each subscale. It is common practice to sum across all scores (e.g. GCS 10). However, more information is yielded by keeping subscale scores separate (e.g. E3, V3, M4), as it is useful to observe trends or alterations in neurological function (Macintosh & Moore 2011).

Table 5.3:

Glasgow Coma Scale (Adapted from Teasdale & Jennett 1974)

Eye opening (E)	Spontaneous	4
	To voice	3
	To pain	2
	None	1
Verbal response (V)	Orientated	5
	Confused	4
	Inappropriate words	3
	Incomprehensible sounds	2
	None	1
Best motor response (M)	Obeys commands	6
	Localises	5
	Withdraws	4
	Abnormal flexion	3
	Extension	2
	None	1

Whilst this scale is useful for many conditions (such as dysphasia, oral dyspraxia and tracheostomy), dysarthria may preclude vocalisation or meaningful responses on the verbal scale.

Examination of the cranial nerves

The cranial nerves are so named because they arise from the brain or brain stem and they are part of the peripheral nervous system assessment. There are 12 pairs of cranial nerves, each of which is responsible for a distinct activity (Macintosh & Moore 2011).

Cranial nerve I (olfactory)

After assessing the patency of both nares, have Tim close his eyes, obstruct one nare, and sniff. Use common, easily identifiable substances, such as coffee, toothpaste, orange, vanilla, soap, or peppermint. Use different substances for each side. Bilateral decreased sense of smell occurs with age, tobacco smoking, allergic rhinitis and cocaine use. Unilateral loss of sense of smell (neurologic anosmia) can indicate a frontal lobe lesion.

Cranial nerve II (optic)

To check visual acuity, have Tim read newspaper print and check the visual fields for each eye. Unilateral blindness can indicate a lesion or pressure in the globe or optic nerve. Loss of the same half of the visual field in both eyes (homonymous hemianopsia) can indicate a lesion of the opposite-side optic tract, as in a stroke.

Cranial nerve III (oculomotor)

Assess pupil size and light reflex. A unilaterally dilated pupil with unilateral absent light reflex and/or if the eye will not turn upwards could indicate an internal carotid aneurysm or uncal herniation with increased intracranial pressure.

Cranial nerve IV (trochlear) and cranial nerve VI (abducens)

Have Tim turn his eyes downward, temporally and nasally. If the eyes will not do this, the patient may have a fracture of the eye orbit or a brain stem tumour. (Note: cranial nerves III, IV and VI are examined together because they control eyelid elevation, eye movement, and pupillary constriction.)

Cranial nerve V (trigeminal)

- Motor – palpate jaws and temples while Tim clenches his teeth.
- Sensory – have Tim close eyes and touch cotton ball to all areas of face.

Unilateral cranial nerve deficit is seen with trauma and tumours.

Cranial nerve VII (facial)

- Motor – check symmetry and mobility of face by having Tim frown, close his eyes, lift eyebrows, and puff cheeks.
- Sensory – assess Tim's ability to identify taste (sugar, salt, lemon juice).

An asymmetrical cranial nerve deficit can be found in trauma, Bell's palsy, stroke, tumour and inflammation.

Cranial nerve VIII (acoustic or vestibulocochlear)

This tests hearing acuity. Impairment indicates inflammation or occlusion of the ear canal, drug toxicity, or a possible tumour.

Cranial nerve IX (glossopharyngeal) and X (vagus)

- Motor – depress the tongue with a tongue blade and have Tim say 'ahh' or yawn. The uvula and soft palate should rise. Gag reflex should be present and the voice should sound smooth.

Deficits can indicate a brain stem tumour or neck injury.

Cranial nerve XI (spinal accessory)

Have the patient rotate the head and shrug shoulders against resistance. If the patient is unable to do this, it may indicate a neck injury.

Cranial nerve XII (hypoglossal)

- Motor – Assess tongue control. Wasting of the tongue, deviation to one side, tremors, and an inability to distinctly say l, t, d and n sounds can indicate a lower or upper motor neurone lesion.

Cerebellar function

The cerebellum controls balance and coordination and this is evident if you observe whether Tim can perform smooth and accurate movements. Ask him if he suffers from vertigo, as this is an illusion of movement and occurs when there is damage to the vestibular system or its brain stem connections.

Examination of gait

Ask Tim to stand up and observe whether he is steady on his feet. Note that his posture is erect, with feet together. Ask him to walk to the end of the room and to turn round and walk back.

Test for balance and coordination

Ask Tim to walk in tandem fashion (heel to toe) along a straight line.

Romberg's test

Ask Tim to stand erect with feet together, first with his eyes open and then with his eyes closed. If he sways, the test is said to be positive, suggesting he has problems with his balance.

Test coordination

With his eyes open, ask Tim to touch his nose with his finger, first with one hand and then with the other. Repeat this test with his eyes closed. Check for any intention tremor.

Ask Tim to pat his knees with his palms and then alternate with the back of the hands by pronating and supinating his hands. Resting tremor is a sign of Parkinson's disease.

Fine finger movements

Ask Tim to touch the thumb with each finger of the same hand. Repeat same action for each hand.

Motor system assessment – muscle strength, coordination and balance

It is important to be able to detect patterns of weakness, as Tim has some problems with his balance but no problems walking.

Muscles of the arms

Inspect and palpate, then check for size, consistency and possible atrophy. Using a tape measure, compare corresponding parts of the upper arms. Then examine and compare the fine muscles of each hand, looking for wasting and fine tremors of the hand. This will indicate whether Tim has Parkinson's disease, myopathy or lower motor neurone weakness.

Muscles of the legs – tone and strength

Inspect and palpate, then check for size, consistency and muscle bulk for possible atrophy. Using a tape measure, compare corresponding parts of the thighs and calves for size.

- Muscle tone – muscles are palpated at rest and the assessor moves the limb for resistance to passive movement to check for any abnormalities, such as spasticity, rigidity/flaccidity. Some patients may find it hard to relax while they are being examined, which can artificially increase stiffness in their limbs.

- Muscle strength – assess normal strength of the muscles. First, without resistance, test the major joints for flexion and extension, and observe for any muscle weakness. Then repeat the test with resistance. This will allow you to recognise patterns of sensory loss associated with damage to the spinal cord. For example, a stroke patient carries one arm held to the side, with elbow, wrist and fingers flexed. Please also remember to take into account the age and physique of the patient.

Sensory pathways

Examine the legs and ask Tim if he is experiencing any pain in them.

Sensory impulses give rise to conscious sensation and adjust body position in space, while sensory fibres transmit sensations of touch, pain, temperature and position (Bickley & Szilagyi 2003). It is important to recognise patterns of sensory loss associated with damage to the spinal cord or to individual nerve roots.

Ask Tim to close his eyes and apply a light touch of a piece of cotton wool to each leg. Then ask him if the sensitivity to cotton wool on one side of his body compares with that on a corresponding area on the opposite side (all the way from the upper arms to the feet).

Follow the same procedure using a blunt pin. Also ask Tim if he can distinguish between hot and cold sensations.

Hold a vibrating tuning fork to the bony prominences, starting from the wrist, and moving to the elbow, shoulder, hip, knee, shin and ankle. Test Tim's ability to feel when the vibration stops, comparing sensitivity side to side. Move the fingers and toes passively and ask Tim to indicate the direction of movement and the final position of the digit.

Reflex testing

Assessment of reflex and reaction time is important in order to evaluate afferent nerves, synaptic connections, efferent nerves and pathways.

Test deep tendon reflexes (including the biceps, triceps, patella and ankle jerks) with a tendon hammer by briskly tapping onto the tendon directly or onto a finger placed over the tendon.

Biceps reflex

- Rest Tim's elbow in your hand.
- Position your thumb over his biceps tendon.
- Percuss your thumbnail and observe for forearm flexion.

Any lesion will make the biceps weak and cause a lot of jerking

Triceps reflex

- Flex Tim's arm slightly, using your hand to steady his arm.
- Percuss the tendon right above the back of his elbow.
- Observe for elbow extension.

Patella reflex

- Ask Tim to sit on a chair and ask him to cross his legs so that the leg is dangling freely.
- Percuss the tendon right below his patella.
- Observe for leg extension at the knee.

Achilles reflex

- Support Tim's foot in your hand.
- Rotate his foot and leg outward.
- Percuss the Achilles tendon.
- Observe his ankle for plantar flexion.

There are three main types of postural reflexes:

- Static reflexes – concerned with maintaining the position of the body and its parts at rest. These are simple reflexes confined to one limb, as in the extended limb of a standing man.
- Righting reflexes – normal attitude in relation to gravity is called posture. The automatic reactions always tend to maintain the position of the head, ears and eyes in space. The reflex centres involved are situated at all levels of the spinal cord and brain stem but are, to some extent, under the overriding control of the cerebral hemispheres.
- Stato-kinetic reflexes – producing the smooth, balanced progressive movements and posture characteristic of the healthy individual (such as the coordinated movements required for walking and running).

Conclusion

Finally, all information must be accurately and legibly documented. Not only is this a professional requirement (Health Professions Council 2008, Nursing and Midwifery Council 2009); it also provides a record of the signs detected and the actions and investigations undertaken, as well as establishing a baseline against which improvements or deterioration can be measured, thus facilitating continuity of care.

References

Adam, S., Odell, M. & Welch, J. (2010). *Rapid assessment of the acutely ill patient: essential skills for nurses.* Oxford, UK: Wiley Blackwell.

Bickley, L.S. & Szilagyi, P. (2003). *Guide to Physical Examination and History-Taking.* Philadelphia, USA: Lippincott Williams & Wilkins.

Brust, J.C.M. (2012). *Coma: Current Diagnosis on Treatment.* New York, USA: McGraw Hill.

Burton, N. (2009). *Clinical Skills for OSCEs.* Banbury, Oxfordshire, UK: Scion Publishing Limited.

Health Professions Council (2008). *Standards of Conduct, Performance and Ethics.* London: HPC.

Macintosh, M. & Moore, T. (2011). *Caring for the Seriously Ill Patient.* London: Hodder Arnold.

Nursing and Midwifery Council (2009). *Record Keeping: Guidance for Nurses and Midwives.* London: NMC.

Rushforth, H. (2012). *Assessment Made Incredibly Easy.* Philadelphia, USA: Lippincott Williams & Wilkins.

Scadding, J.M. & Losseff, N.A. (2012). *Clinical Neurology.* London: Hodder Arnold. Chapter 3.

Teasdale, G. & Jennett, B. (1974). *Trauma Scores* [online] available from http://www.trauma.org/archive/scores/gcs (Accessed 18/03/13).

Tortora, J. & Derrickson, B. (2011). *Principles of Anatomy and Physiology.* Singapore: John Wiley & Sons (Asia).

Chapter 6

Genitourinary assessment

Donna Page

The World Health Organisation defines sexual health as:

> …*a state of physical, emotional, mental and social well-being in relation to sexuality; it is not merely the absence of disease, dysfunction or infirmity. Sexual health requires a positive and respectful approach to sexuality and sexual relationships, as well as the possibility of having pleasurable and safe sexual experiences, free of coercion, discrimination and violence. For sexual health to be attained and maintained, the sexual rights of all persons must be respected, protected and fulfilled.*
> (WHO 2006)

Good sexual health is thus more than the absence of sexually transmitted infections or unwanted pregnancies. It is a question of rights, including the right to make one's own choices and, as stated by the Faculty of Sexual and Reproductive Health, the right to 'holistic sexual and reproductive healthcare which operates around the needs of the individual, rather than professional silos' (FSRH 2015a).

Overview of sexual and reproductive health in the UK

Contraceptive and sexual health (CASH) services in the UK are commissioned by local authorities in addition to GP-provided services. There is wide variation in how services are delivered, from small, community-based clinics to fully integrated sexual health community clinics, because of differing commissioning arrangements (Department of

Health 2013). The government recognises that this variation in provision may lead to fragmented services and states that there should be an emphasis on joined-up working to prevent sexual ill-health as one of the key principles of best practice in commissioning (Department of Health 2013, p. 41).

These key principles are outlined in the *Framework for Sexual Health Improvement in England*, published by the Department of Health in 2013. This sets out 'a comprehensive package of evidence, interventions and actions to improve sexual health outcomes', including quantitative measures such as a reduction in unwanted pregnancies and an increase in the uptake of HIV testing. The document also recognises the World Health Organisation's holistic approach to sexual health and contains qualitative outcomes, such as having the knowledge and ability to prevent sexually transmitted infections and to make responsible and informed choices about relationships and sex.

The move to primary care

Historically, sexual well-being has been seen as an aspect of health that is dealt with by specialist services, such as genitourinary medicine clinics (GUMs). However, as part of the government's drive to improve sexual health outcomes through joined-up provision, community services are increasingly being expected to address the sexual health needs of their patients. NICE (2007) recommends that healthcare professionals should assess a person's risk of acquiring a sexually transmitted infection when they present for other reasons such as a cervical smear, requesting contraception or travel advice and immunisation.

Furthermore, HIV testing in community settings has been proposed since 2008 (BHIVA/BASHH/BIS 2008) in order to decrease the number of late diagnoses (associated with increased morbidity and mortality). This has been shown to be both feasible and acceptable to staff and patients (HPA 2011). An increasing emphasis on community services actively assessing and testing for sexually transmitted infections (STIs), with appropriately robust pathways leading to specialist services, therefore means a community healthcare practitioner needs to be able to carry out basic sexual history-taking and genitourinary assessment.

Skills needed for sexual health interventions

Discussing a person's sexual health may present a challenge for many clinicians, both ethically and personally. For instance, some reported sexual practices may be outside the scope of their knowledge and understanding. It is imperative that the clinician embarking on caring for a patient's sexual health has had the opportunity to reflect on the limitations of their understanding and any assumptions they may hold. This can be done alone, or with colleagues, and can be a useful process to guide further training needs. Every clinician must feel able to approach a client's sexual health with the same non-judgemental attitude as they would any other area of practice.

Box 6.1: Case study

Karl is a 21-year-old gay man who attends his GP's surgery because he is worried about his risk of catching an STI. The Practice Nurse seems uncomfortable during the consultation. She asks very few questions and it is clear that she assumes Karl is heterosexual. The result is that Karl feels unable to disclose the fact that he regularly has unprotected anal sex with male partners. The nurse takes a first-catch urine sample and a blood test for HIV and syphilis but fails to take a rectal swab, thus missing a potential site of infection. He should also have been tested for and vaccinated against hepatitis B.

The following guidance is intended to equip non-specialist clinicians with an understanding of how to take a sexual health history, including suggestions on how to phrase the questions and advice on ways to create an environment that facilitates openness and trust.

Sexual history-taking

Careful assessment is vital in managing the care of a patient with a sexual health problem and can ultimately save time and make your consultation more effective. There are a number of reasons to take a full sexual history. These include:

- Identifying any symptoms of infection
- Assessing the possibility of pregnancy or need for emergency contraception
- Identifying anatomical sites of exposure to infection
- Assessing any risk-taking behaviour in order to tailor health promotion and risk reduction discussions to the individual
- Assessing exposure to HIV and hepatitis B and C in order to test and prevent infection
- Identifying other sexual health issues, such as psychosexual problems.

(Adapted from Brook et al. 2013)

It is useful to warn the patient beforehand that you will be asking them some intimate questions. Reassure them that you ask all patients the same questions and that you are not there to judge but to get an accurate understanding of the problem. Be clear that all information will be treated confidentially (with the usual caveats). It is best to start with questions that may cause less anxiety, such as the patient's medical history and allergies (Brook *et al.* 2013). Always introduce the sexual history section of the consultation with a short sentence such as 'So now I'd like to ask you some questions to assess your sexual health if that's OK.' Allow the patient to answer before proceeding.

Patients generally respond well to this approach because they understand the purpose and level of questioning and feel that they have some control of the conversation. This can be an empowering experience for the patient, leading to disclosure of sexual issues they may not have felt able to talk about before.

In addition to the usual components of history-taking, the following should be elicited as a minimum when assessing a patient's sexual history, according to the British Association for Sexual Health and HIV (Brook *et al.* 2013). Suggested phrases are given which may be useful to those who are new to this form of questioning. It is helpful to draw up a local template to guide your sexual history-taking, particularly if you will not be taking sexual histories on a regular basis. The rationale for each question is given in Table 6.1 below.

Table 6.1: Sexual history-taking template

	Suggested phrase	Rationale
Confirm whether symptomatic or asymptomatic	*Do you have any symptoms or problems?*	Differential diagnoses may include urinary tract infections, dermatological issues or cancer. Patients with symptoms suggestive of a sexually transmitted infection may need examination and empirical treatment that day. Women may present with vaginal discharge, dysuria, deep dyspareunia, vulval skin problems, post-coital bleeding or inter-menstrual bleeding. Men may present with dysuria, urethral discharge, testicular pain or swelling or peri-anal or anal symptoms (Brook *et al.* 2013).
For women, menstrual cycle, contraceptive use and cervical cytology history	*When was your last period?* *Did it come on time?* *Was it a normal period?*	Pregnancy should be considered in both pre- and peri-menopausal women. The Faculty of Sexual and Reproductive Health provides clear guidance on methods used to exclude pregnancy.

cont.	*What contraceptive method do you use?* *Do you have any problems with it?* *When was your last smear test?* *Have you ever had an abnormal smear test?*	Healthcare professionals can be 'reasonably certain' that a woman is not currently pregnant if any one or more of the following criteria are met and there are no symptoms or signs of pregnancy: • She has not had intercourse since her last normal menses • She has been correctly and consistently using a reliable method of contraception • She is within the first 7 days of the onset of a normal menstrual period • She is within 4 weeks postpartum for non-lactating women • She is within the first 7 days post-abortion or miscarriage • She is fully or almost fully breastfeeding, amenorrhoeic, and less than 6 months postpartum. A pregnancy test, if available, adds weight to the exclusion of pregnancy, but only if ≥3 weeks since the last episode of unprotected sexual intercourse (UPSI). NB: Healthcare professionals should also consider whether a woman is at risk of becoming pregnant as a result of UPSI within the last 7 days (FSRH 2015b). If the patient is overdue for a smear test, offer cervical screening or, as a minimum, encourage her to attend for cervical screening. If there are signs consistent with cervical cancer, such as inter-menstrual bleeding, post-coital bleeding or post-menopausal bleeding, and if the cervix is abnormal on examination (with inflammation, contact bleeding, visible ulcerating or fungating lesion, or foul-smelling serosanguinous vaginal discharge), cervical screening is not appropriate and the patient should be referred via the suspected cancer referral pathway (NICE 2014).
For women, pregnancy and gynaecological history	*Do you have children?* *If yes, what kind of deliveries did you have?*	

cont.	Have you had any other pregnancies? If no, have you ever been pregnant? Have you ever been seen by a gynaecologist because of problems with your womb, ovaries or fallopian tubes?	These questions may reveal a history of ectopic pregnancy, recurrent miscarriage or multiple terminations and diagnoses such as endometriosis or fibroids.
Previous STIs	Have you ever had a sexually transmitted infection? If so, what and when? Did you complete the treatment?	This affords an opportunity to record the last HIV test that was carried out and the result, as well as identifying ongoing untreated infection.
Last episode of sexual intercourse (LSI)	When did you last have sex?	This helps ascertain whether a patient has been exposed to STIs during the 'window period'. This is currently 2 weeks for chlamydia (Nwokolo et al. 2015) and gonorrhoea (Bignall & Fitzgerald 2011), 90 days for syphilis (Lazaro 2013) and 4 weeks for HIV or 8 weeks following an event classified as high-risk (BASHH 2014). Post-exposure prophylaxis for HIV can be initiated within 72 hours via referral to sexual health or the Emergency Department. For women, this question is important in order to ascertain the possible need for emergency contraception.
Gender of partner	Was that with a male or female partner? For men, if this is a heterosexual contact, ask the follow-up question: Have you ever had sex with a man?	To identify men who have sex with men (MSM) in order to offer hepatitis B testing and vaccination.
Anatomical site of exposure	What kind of sex do you have, vaginal, oral, anal, or all three? For a man who tells you he has oral and/or anal sex with a man, ask the follow-up questions: Do you give or receive oral sex, or both?	In order to ensure the correct anatomical sites are sampled. For example, a man who carries out penetrative anal sex but has never been receptive would not need rectal screening.
Condom use	Did you use a condom? For which type of sex?	To assess the level of risk.

Suspected infection in partners	*Did this partner have any lumps, bumps, sore parts or anything else that worried you?*	Empirical treatment may be required as a contact of someone with an STI.
Previous sexual partner details for the past three months	*How many different people have you had sex with in the past three months?* Ask the same questions above for each partner.	To assess the level of risk.
Blood-borne virus risk assessment	*Have you ever been vaccinated for hepatitis B?* *Have you ever had sex with someone from abroad or while you've been abroad?* *Have you ever paid for or been paid for sex?* *Have you ever injected drugs or had sex with someone who does?* *Have you ever had sex with someone with hepatitis or HIV?* *Has anyone ever forced you to have sex or to do anything you didn't want to sexually?*	To assess the need for hepatitis B and C screening and vaccination. Non-consensual sex is thought to occur in 1 in 10 women and 1 in 71 men in the UK (Mercer *et al.* 2013). Support services should be made available if the patient indicates they would appreciate this, although not all survivors will.
This is also a good time to carry out a safeguarding assessment according to your usual protocols and to ask about intimate partner violence.	*Do you ever have any problems with controlling, threatening or violent behaviour?* *Have you ever been scared of a partner?*	Domestic abuse support services contact details should be made available to the patient.
For men, time of last micturition.	*When did you last pass urine?*	Men should hold their urine for at least 1 hour in order to achieve the most reliable result (Nwokolo *et al.* 2015).

Asymptomatic screening

Sexual health screening to prevent transmission in people with no symptoms suggestive of STIs is a key part of the Department of Health's strategy (Department of Health 2013). As a minimum, patients should be tested for chlamydia, gonorrhoea, HIV and syphilis and

93

the patient will not need a physical examination. A good sexual history will identify those needing additional hepatitis B and hepatitis C screening.

Chlamydia and gonorrhoea

For women practising vaginal sex, a self-taken vulvovaginal swab should be taken and a self-taken rectal swab for those receiving anal sex. Pharyngeal swabs are not routinely taken in asymptomatic women (Lazaro 2013). For men, a first-catch urine sample (the first 20ml of urine passed) should be taken, plus self-taken pharyngeal and rectal swabs in men who perform fellatio and/or receive anal sex.

HIV and syphilis

Take 10ml of clotted blood. There is no need for pre-test counselling although informed consent should of course be obtained. Discuss with the patient the fact that HIV is managed as a long-term condition and that early diagnosis leads to better outcomes. All practitioners should play their role in destigmatising HIV – regular testing should be promoted as an integral part of keeping healthy.

Hepatitis B and C

The following patients should be tested for hepatitis B:

- Men who have sex with men (MSMs)
- Commercial sex workers (CSWs)
- Injection drug users (IDUs)
- Persons infected with hepatitis C or HIV
- Sexual assault victims
- Anyone born in (or who has had a sexual partner born in) a country with a high prevalence of hepatitis B infection (i.e. outside Western Europe, North America and Australasia)
- Anyone who has had a sexual partner who was infected with hepatitis B or who was at high risk of HBV infection
- Anyone born to a mother infected with hepatitis B.

The following patients should be tested for hepatitis C:

- IDUs
- HIV-infected MSMs (and their sex partners)
- Anyone exposed to potentially contaminated needles (e.g. needlestick victims)
- Anyone born to a mother infected with hepatitis C.

All patients should be offered re-testing if sexual contact has occurred within the window period of 60 days.

Physical examination

If the patient reports symptoms, physical examination should be undertaken.

A chaperone should be available and should be offered to both male and female patients for any intimate examination (Brook *et al.* 2013).

It is very likely that a patient will have some degree of anxiety about any physical examination of the genitourinary system. The clinician can do a great deal to minimise this as much as possible by ensuring that the patient maintains a degree of control over the situation. Explain the procedure to the patient so there are no surprises and gain informed consent before starting. Although time is usually at a premium, approach the examination in a calm and unhurried manner. Advise patients that they can ask you to stop the examination at any time. Be aware that patients may have had negative sexual experiences in the past, which may impact on their ability to tolerate an intimate examination.

Ask the patient if they would like to empty their bladder before starting.

Box 6.2: Gender-specific questions

MALES

- Examine the external genitalia, including the penis, scrotum and scrotal contents. This should be done in a supine, then standing position. Keep the patient covered as much as possible.

- Note any pubic infestations.

- Note whether circumcised or not and assess how easily the prepuce can be retracted.

- Examine the skin, including beneath the prepuce, for ulcers or lesions.

- Examine the urethra for discharge.

- Palpate for inguinal lymphadenopathy.

- Palpate the corpus cavernosum and corpus spongiosum for masses, induration or tenderness.

- If any scrotal mass is found, assess for translucency to determine whether the mass is cystic or solid.
- If necessary, assess the prostate by rectal examination for size, swelling and tenderness.

FEMALES

- Examine the patient ideally lying supine on a couch with legs raised on supports. If leg supports are not available, the woman should flex her hips and knees, with feet together or apart, whichever is more comfortable for her. Keep the patient covered as much as possible.
- Examine the vulva for any ulcers, lesions or discharge. Gently part the labia and retract the clitoral hood to enable examination of the urethra and clitoris.
- Note any pubic infestations.
- Examine the anogenital area for ulcers, lesions and discharge.
- Palpate for inguinal lymphadenopathy.
- Examine the vagina and cervix. Choose an appropriately sized speculum. Lubricate the speculum with warm water in preference to lubricants. Position an examination lamp appropriately to facilitate full visualisation of the cervix.
- Inspect the vaginal wall for inflammation, lesions, varicosities, prolapse and foreign bodies.
- Observe the cervix for discharge, inflammation, masses and lesions. Note any friability or contact bleeding.
- Swabs can be taken at this stage.
- Remove speculum and proceed to bimanual examination. Remind the patient of the procedure and ensure she gives consent to proceed.
- Insert lubricated and gloved index and middle fingers into the vagina. Locate the cervix between the two fingers and move gently, assessing mobility and any cervical excitation, a sign of inflammation.

- Palpate the adnexae by moving the fingers of the vaginal hand to each lateral fornix and applying pressure on the abdomen with the abdominal hand to the corresponding abdominal quadrant. Note any tenderness or masses.
- Palpate the position of the fallopian tubes; these are not usually palpable. Palpate the ovaries, which should be smooth and firm if palpable but not tender.

Following examination, provide privacy for the patient to dress. Provide tissues and hand-washing facilities. Women may need a sanitary pad.

Once dressed and seated, discuss your findings with the patient and negotiate a treatment plan. Avoid having discussions while the patient remains undressed and on the examination couch.

It is good practice to take the opportunity to ask the patient if they have any other concerns that have not yet been discussed. If you have been able to facilitate trust and openness, the patient may want to talk to you about issues such as psychosexual problems or safety in relationships.

Further issues to be discussed

- Treatment – empirical or once swab results are available
- How results will be communicated
- Need for emergency contraception and ongoing contraception
- Bloods for HIV and syphilis plus hepatitis B and C if indicated
- Discussion of risk-taking behaviour and provision of condoms
- Referrals – to specialist sexual health services, such as gynaecology or urology. The following symptomatic patients should be referred to the specialist sexual health service – men with dysuria and/or genital discharge, patients with symptoms at extra-genital sites (e.g. rectal or pharyngeal), pregnant women, genital ulceration other than uncomplicated genital herpes, patients with gonorrhoea (BASHH/MEDFASH 2014)
- Further investigations, such as ultrasound scan for suspected uterine pathology

- Contact tracing – a useful guide to this for practitioners working outside specialist services is available in the 'Further resources' section at the end of this chapter
- Advise any patient with a confirmed or suspected STI to abstain from sex until they have completed treatment and their sexual partners have been screened and treated
- Contact details for sexual assault or domestic abuse support services if necessary.

Conclusion

Everyone has the right to expect good sexual and reproductive healthcare throughout their lives. In order to achieve this, healthcare practitioners need to possess the skills to assess and examine the genitourinary tract in a way that enables and empowers people to care for their own sexual health and seek help and advice when needed. This responsibility means that we must critically examine our own attitudes and knowledge about sex, as well as the way we carry out consultations, assessments and examinations. Gaining greater insight into the approaches we take, including the language we use, will enable us to become more skilled, empathetic and effective practitioners.

References

Bignall, C. & Fitzgerald, M. (2011). *UK national guideline for the management of gonorrhoea in adults, 2011.* Available from: https://www.bashhguidelines.org/media/1044/gc-2011.pdf (Accessed 23/12/2016).

British HIV Association, British Association for Sexual Health and HIV, British Infection Society (2008). *UK National Guidelines for HIV Testing.* Available at: http://www.bashh.org/documents/Sexual%20History%20Guidelines%20 2013%20final.pdf (Accessed 23/12/2016).

British Association for Sexual Health and HIV (2014). *BASHH/EAGA statement on HIV window period.* Available at: https://www.bashhguidelines.org/media/1069/bashh-eaga-statement-on-hiv-wp-nov-14.pdf (Accessed 23/12/2016).

British Association for Sexual Health and HIV/MEDFASH (2014). *Standards for the Management of Sexually Transmitted Infections.* Available at: http://www.medfash.org.uk/uploads/files/p18dtqli811626lrv19i6lrh9n2k4.pdf (Accessed 23/12/2016).

Brook, G., Bacon, L., Evans, C. *et al.* (2013). 2013 UK national guideline for consultations requiring sexual history taking. *International Journal of STD and AIDS.* **25**(6), 391–404

Department of Health (2013). *A Framework for Sexual Health Improvement in England.* Available at: https://www.gov.uk/government/uploads/system/uploads/attachment_data/file/142592/9287-2900714-TSO-SexualHealthPolicyNW_ACCESSIBLE.pdf (Accessed 23/12/2016).

Faculty of Reproductive and Sexual Health (FRSH) (2015a). *Better care, a better future: a new vision for sexual and reproductive health care in the UK.* Available at: https://www.fsrh.org/documents/fsrh-vision/ (Accessed 23/12/2016).

Faculty of Reproductive and Sexual Health (FRSH) (2015b). *Intrauterine Contraception.* Available at: https://www.fsrh.org/standards-and-guidance/documents/ceuguidance intrauterinecontraception/ (Accessed 23/12/2016).

Health Protection Agency (HPA) (2011). *Time to test for HIV: Expanding HIV testing in healthcare and community services in England.* Available at: http://www.bhiva.org/documents/Publications/Time_to_test_final_report__ Sept_2011.pdf (Accessed 23/12/2016).

Kingston, M., French, P., Higgins, S. *et al.* (2015). *UK national guidelines on the management of syphilis 2015.* Available at: https://www.bashhguidelines.org/media/1053/syphilis-2015.pdf (Accessed 23/12/2016).

Lazaro, N. (2013). *Sexually transmitted infections in primary care.* Available at: https://www.bashhguidelines.org/media/1089/sexually-transmitted-infections-in-primary-care-2013.pdf (Accessed 23/12/2016).

Mercer, C.H., Tanton, C., Prah, P. *et al.* (2013). Changes in sexual attitudes and lifestyles in Britain through the life course and over time: findings from the National Surveys of Sexual Attitudes and Lifestyles (Natsal). *Lancet Online.* **382**, 1781–94.

NICE (2007). *Sexually transmitted infections and under-18 conceptions: prevention.* Available at: https://www.nice.org.uk/guidance/ph3/chapter/1-Recommendations (Accessed 23/12/2016).

NICE (2014). *Cervical Cancer and HPV.* Available at: https://cks.nice.org.uk/cervical-cancer-and-hpv#!diagnosissub (Accessed 23/12/2016).

Nwokolo, N.C., Dragovic, B., Patel, S., *et al.* (2015). *2015 UK national guideline for the management of infection with Chlamydia trachomatis.* Available at: https://www.bashhguidelines.org/media/1045/chlamydia-2015.pdf (Accessed 23/12/2016).

World Health Organisation (WHO) (2006). *Defining Sexual Health.* Available at: http://www.who.int/reproductivehealth/topics/sexual_health/sh_definitions/en/ (Accessed 23/12/2016).

Further resources

RCN genital examination in women – a resource for skills development and assessment. Available at: https://www2.rcn.org.uk/__data/assets/pdf_file/0004/512734/004_368.pdf (Accessed 27/2/2017).

Sexual Health in Practice (SHIP) interactive training for GPs and Practice Nurses. Available at: http://www.medfash.org.uk/ship-training (Accessed 27/2/2017).

Sexually Transmitted Infections in Primary Care – a practical guide on the management of STIs for GPs. https://www.bashhguidelines.org/media/1089/sexually-transmitted-infections-in-primary-care-2013.pdf (Accessed 27/2/2017).

Chapter 7

Musculoskeletal assessment

Lee Cunnell and Gareth Partington

The ability to articulate the human skeleton allows us to perform the everyday activities of living. Any disruption in this ability can lead someone to seek help from a healthcare practitioner. In the United Kingdom, 3.5 million patients attend hospital with musculoskeletal conditions, of which the majority are self-limiting or predictable in their effects (Wardrope & English 2003). Musculoskeletal disorders are common in primary as well as secondary care, but it is generally recognised that patients are inadequately assessed for these presentations (Lillicrap *et al.* 2003, Roche *et al.* 2009). It is important to remember that complaints of the musculoskeletal system are sometimes surprisingly complex and they require effective assessment and management (Doherty *et al.* 1992, Moncrieff & Pomerleau 2000).

This chapter will discuss the principles needed to assess a patient presenting with musculoskeletal system symptoms. It will also consider a case study involving a middle-aged female netball player, who fell and injured her ankle.

An accurate assessment requires both the subjective history of the injury or condition, and the objective findings of the examination. Whilst a good history should give you most of the information you need, what you see, feel, move and even hear will add vital detail to complete the assessment.

Global overview of the patient

The global overview of the patient assumes that there may be potential systemic and life-threatening injuries or conditions as part of the patient's presentation. Integral to your global overview of the patient is the ABCDE (Airway, Breathing, Circulation, Disability, Exposure) mnemonic. The very nature of the musculoskeletal system could mean significant life-threatening trauma, with or without fracture, and its exclusion should be a priority.

Assessment begins the instant you see the patient. Watch when they walk (if they are able to do so). Observe their gait as well as posture; this will give you information about their muscle strength, any obvious deformity, abnormal movement or asymmetry of body shape. Always compare the affected with the unaffected side. Assess coordination and balance. Ask to see their shoes; uneven wear could indicate long-term gait imbalance. Do they need a walking aid? Are they wearing any splints? Can they remove their coat? Always keep in mind that altered motor function may have non-musculoskeletal causes. For example, abnormal gaits may have a neurological origin. Importantly, is the patient's behaviour consistent with the presentation? An overly anxious patient may raise concerns about the significance of the condition or whether this is a non-accidental injury (NAI).

As part of the initial assessment, try to establish whether the presentation is traumatic or non-traumatic (Judge 2007). If injury is the reason, consider the cause and/or mechanism of the insult. The mechanism and forces involved in the injury (the kinematics) should give you valuable clues as to the likely extent of the damage. 'I just tripped on the way to the shops and hurt my ankle' has a different mechanism of injury, with different bio-mechanical forces involved, than 'I fell three feet off a ladder and landed on my ankle.' Finally, consider any possible distracting injuries that may mask the real problem. Bear in mind that the patient may not realise they have other injuries at initial presentation.

History-taking and musculoskeletal assessment

Despite injury being a common reason for the patient to seek help, not all musculoskeletal presentations are the result of injury. Consider possible underlying pathological, pharmacological and/or medical causes in your questioning. Musculoskeletal conditions can cause severe systemic illness, such as septicaemia from joint infection and acute kidney injury from rhabdomyolysis. Systemic diseases can also manifest with musculoskeletal symptoms. If inflammation is present, venous thromboembolism should be considered as a possible cause, especially if it is unilateral and with no history of injury. Other symptoms (such as fever, weight loss and general feelings of malaise) can be related to a variety of articular disorders, such as rheumatoid arthritis.

Table 7.1:
Examples of conditions that affect the musculoskeletal system

Degenerative	Osteoarthritis
Tumour	Primary and metastatic
Crystal formation	Gout
Infective	Rubella, mumps, bacterial, e.g. Staphylococci
Post-infective	Rheumatic fever
Trauma	Sprains, fractures
Tendinitis	Such as Achilles tendinitis
Nerve entrapment	Carpal tunnel syndrome

Patients with musculoskeletal problems present when they experience pain and/or a loss or decrease of function (Walsh 2006). Pain and functional ability should be central considerations in the history-taking and subsequent examination. Pain assessment is important not only so that adequate treatment can be administered but also because the type of pain described can give clues to the problem.

Two *aides mémoires* (see Tables 7.2 and 7.3 on page 104) are the SOCRATES and the PQRST mnemonics (Douglas *et al.* 2009). Both allow objective qualification of pain reported by the patient. A simple pain scale (0 = no pain, 10 = the worst pain experienced) may also be useful as a baseline and to measure the effect of any treatment or change in condition. Ask the patient to pinpoint exactly where the pain is. Identify whether the pain is new or recurrent, made worse on initial movement or after protracted use. You also need to remember that joint pain may be referred from other joints or be extra-articular in origin.

Table 7.2: PQRST

P	Provokes – does anything make the problem better or worse?
Q	Quality – how does the patient describe the pain?
R	Region and radiation – where is the pain and does it radiate elsewhere?
S	Severity – there are various scales available. How does the patient rate the pain experienced?
T	Time – the history of the pain. How long has it been there? Has it improved or got worse? When did it start? How long did it last? How often has it occurred?

Table 7.3: SOCRATES

S	Site – where is the pain?
O	Onset – when did the pain start and was it sudden or gradual?
C	Character – what is the pain like now?
R	Radiation – does the pain radiate anywhere?
A	Associations – are any other signs or symptoms associated with the pain?
T	Time course – does the pain follow any pattern?
E	Exacerbating or relieving factors – does anything change the pain?
S	Severity – how bad is the pain now?

Functional assessment

Functional assessment is a simple way to establish the impact of an injury or disease on the patient's ability to carry out everyday activities. It gives clues as to the extent and cause of the condition and success of any treatment (Monk 2006). It allows for the use of simple language and assessment techniques that patients will understand and be able to respond to. For the novice healthcare professional, it also offers a means of assessment and screening that introduces the skills needed for more advanced diagnostic examination. The GALS (Gait, Arms, Legs and Spine) screening method (Doherty *et al.*

1992) can be used to assess musculoskeletal disability (Walsh 2006). It includes functional elements – both in the questions asked and examinations performed.

The GALS screening questions include:

- **Do you have any pain or stiffness in your muscles, joints or back?**
- **Can you dress yourself completely without any difficulty?**
- **Can you walk up and down the stairs without any difficulty?**

(Arthritis Research UK 2011).

History of the presenting complaint

Taking a history of the presenting complaint involves establishing the reason for the patient seeking help and the contributing factors. This may or may not be their only or worst problem. As discussed earlier, consider whether the patient has presented for reasons of injury or disease. Consider whether the presentation is systemic or local in nature and if it is acute, chronic, or acute on chronic? Is it a joint, bone or muscle problem, or a combination of all three?

Does the condition or injury appear to be progressive? If so, what are the exacerbating factors? If injury is the cause, enquire about pain, decrease in function and range of movement (ROM). Ask whether this is the first time that they have injured this joint or limb. Has there been any swelling and, if so, how quickly did it occur? Was there any noise at the time of the injury, such as a cracking or popping sound? Did the injury cause breaks in the skin? This is important if systemic infection is suspected.

Consideration should be given to pain, paraesthesia, paralysis, pallor and pulse. Joint stiffness is also an important musculoskeletal symptom for enquiry. Stiffness may result in weakness, fatigue and/or limited mobility. The nature of the stiffness, in combination with other symptoms, may suggest certain types of disease. For example, severe and prolonged joint stiffness, especially in the morning, may indicate inflammatory disease. Stiffness when standing, after sitting for a period of time, is common in osteoarthritis. Other symptoms that may be present include redness, deformity, weakness and instability.

Past medical history

Note any previous disorders or indeed injuries that may affect the presenting complaint. In particular, ask about known orthopaedic disease, including arthritis, osteoporosis, and other associated rheumatoid diseases. You should also enquire about skeletal deformity, and trauma (Walsh 2006), surgery, treatments or systemic disease, as mentioned previously.

Medications and previous treatment

Find out what medications the patient is taking, including prescription, complementary and over-the-counter preparations. Certain medications may induce musculoskeletal symptoms – for example, diuretics can precipitate gout; corticosteroids can cause osteoporosis; angiotensin-converting-enzyme (ACE) inhibitors can lead to myalgia; and immunosuppressants may result in problems with infections (Douglas *et al.* 2009). The commonly taken non-steroidal anti-inflammatory drugs (NSAIDs), used for musculoskeletal pain, have been associated with gastrointestinal bleeding, renal failure, increased risk of pulmonary embolism and atrial fibrillation (Schmidt *et al.* 2011).

Establish which medications the patient may have tried in order to alleviate their symptoms. These may mask the severity of the presentation but give clues to the effectiveness of the treatment tried hitherto. You should also ask whether the patient has had any previous treatment for the condition. For instance, have they seen a physiotherapist and, if so, what kind of therapy have they been given? If walking is the concern, have they tried orthotics or walking aids? If so, what kind and for how long?

Family history

Musculoskeletal conditions that are familial in nature should form part of your enquiry. Gout, arthritis, osteoporosis, muscle wasting and weakening diseases are such examples. Asking about family members and if they have had any musculoskeletal injury or disease may be key to diagnosis and should not be overlooked.

Social and occupational history

Ask about the patient's occupation and whether anything in their employment exacerbates or has caused the problem. Musculoskeletal injuries are common in manual workers, for example. In non-manual workers, the patient's problem could be attributed to poor office ergonomics – for instance, repetitive strain injuries (RSIs) are common within both groups.

Ask whether the patient participates in dangerous hobbies or sporting activities. Consider diet and lifestyle and the age of the patient. Vitamin D deficiency would be a consideration in cases where sun avoidance has been promoted. Lower levels of vitamin D have been linked to arthritis as well as rickets. In post-menopausal patients, oestrogen deficiency contributes to osteoporosis, which can lead to a higher risk of fractures (Forsbald & Jochems 2008). The social and occupational history is vital, both to establish the potential cause or exacerbating factors, and also because the nature of the musculoskeletal injury or disease may limit the patient's ability to return to work or resume their sport or recreational activities. In this age of increased litigation, the practitioner's assessment (and judgement) may have both legal and occupational consequences for the patient and possibly their employer.

Systemic enquiry

Systemic enquiry has already been covered in Chapter 1 but it is important for the practitioner to ensure that there are no further underlying diseases or conditions manifesting or affecting the musculoskeletal presentation. This is also a good time to summarise the information obtained thus far and to seek clarification if required.

Table 7.4: History overview

Global overview	ABCDE Assess for life-threatening conditions
Injury or non-traumatic presentation?	Consider the mechanism of injury, or with non-injury presentations try to establish the likely underlying cause
Pain?	PQRST and simple pain scale
Function?	How has the condition affected the ability to carry out everyday activities? (Use GALS screening questions.)
Acute or chronic or acute-on-chronic?	Is this the first time this has happened? If not investigate previous presentations.
Other associated musculoskeletal symptoms?	Stiffness, swelling, deformity
Medications and treatment?	What has been tried so far and did it work?
Family, work and leisure?	Any history of musculoskeletal injury or disease in the family? How does the patient's condition affect their work or leisure activities, or vice versa?

Clinical examination

A clinical examination of the musculoskeletal system is a systematic process to ensure that nothing is overlooked. Patients presenting with new injuries can make this difficult. They may be bleeding, generally feeling unwell or unable to walk. If required, reassess them using the ABCDE approach (see page 102). When completing the examination, maximise the patient's comfort. Painful joints in particular may require support; the patient may cradle or 'protect' their injured limb, and the simple use of pillows may be helpful.

An injured patient may present with pain, swelling, bruising and disability. A more specific sign is an irregular angle of a bone that is broken. Generally, it may not be clear whether the patient has injured bone or soft tissue. The diagnosis is reached by exclusion, beginning with a fracture. If necessary, continue to ask questions during the examination until you know as much as the patient knows about events before and after the injury. Your questions may include:

- Was the joint forced into an abnormal position?
- Was the patient able to weight-bear immediately after the injury or 15–20 minutes after, and has walking improved or become worse?
- If there was swelling, was the swelling noticed immediately (haemarthrosis) or has it increased over time (inflammatory)?
- What, if anything, limits the movement? Is it pain or the thought of pain? Or is it not possible to move?

The Ottawa ankle rules may help the practitioner distinguish a fracture from a soft tissue injury, or at least help them decide whether there is a need for further investigations (Bachmann *et al.* 2003). Additional questions during the examination also allow for further confirmation of the information gleaned during the history. As the practitioner becomes more experienced, they will be able to take a history and examine in a more simultaneous manner, making the whole process more efficient.

Musculoskeletal examination should involve:
1. Inspection (looking)
2. Feel (palpation and neurovascular observations)
3. Movement
4. Function

You will require good uninterrupted light to complete these steps accurately. Ask the patient to reveal the part of the body that needs to be examined. Expose the area of concern, whilst maintaining the patient's dignity at all times. Examination will normally be from the joint above the affected area, which will need to be exposed along with the healthy side for comparison. This may prove more difficult if both sides are affected, so having a good knowledge of normal anatomy and biomechanics is important.

1. Inspection (looking)

Observe for any physical deformities or abnormalities that may affect normal function. Look at physical appearance, checking for symmetry and compare both sides of the body, observing the patient's gait. If possible, ask your patient to walk away from you and then return.

- **Do you notice any balance or coordination concerns?**
- **Is there muscle wasting?**
- **Consider the gait cycle. Is it symmetrical? Does any part of the cycle cause the patient pain?**

In practice, this examination would be completed as part of your initial assessment, following the global overview and prior to taking the history.

Table 7.5: Types of gait

Antalgic gait	This is adopted to avoid bearing weight on a painful limb (hip, knee, ankle) and presents as a limp.
Ataxic gait	Unbalanced, uncoordinated walk, with a wide base of support. Often due to cerebellar disease.
Festinating gait	Short accelerating steps are used to move forward; often seen in people with Parkinson's disease.
Hemiplegic gait	Flexion of the hip because of inability to clear the toes from the floor at the ankle and circumduction at the hip.
Spastic gait	The legs are held close together and moved in a stiff manner, often due to central nervous system injuries.
Step/gait/foot drop	Characterised by high lifting of the legs with the toes pointing downwards and bending of the knee; associated with neurological disorders and (rarely) diseased muscle.

Look at the area(s) or joint(s) to be examined and the surrounding region(s). Look for swelling, bruising, redness, skin changes or wounds. Compare this with the expected normal anatomy.

2. Feel (palpation)

Along with movement, this stage of assessment is the most difficult for the patient, and it is important to obtain their trust and confidence. Skilled, competent and careful handling on the part of the practitioner will ensure that the patient is relaxed and the observations are accurate, rather than distorted by their anxiety or tension.

Palpation is also a systematic and structured process, using touch to assess all the structures relating to the injury or affected area. This will include the area from the joint proximal to the injury, and assessment of circulation and neurological function of the area distal to the injury. Crepitus, clicking and other interruptions to normal movement in the joint or tendon sheath will only be felt by moving the part. Elicit these signs gently but *do not* assess for crepitus from a suspected fracture.

The finger pads are more sensitive than the tips, and you should use single digit palpation as this is more precise and will help you pinpoint any areas of pain or tenderness. Explore the anatomical landmarks in order, feeling each layer of tissue from skin down to bone. A tender area should not be directly palpated. It is helpful to palpate proximal to the tender area and then move distally until the patient complains of pain. Repeat this from the other three directions (observing a rectangle of tenderness), thus reducing the need to create more discomfort. Palpation will also allow you to gain further information on any deformities that you may have seen, as well as feeling for localised heat that may indicate inflammation or bleeding.

3. Movement

Joint movement is measured precisely with a goniometer. This level of accuracy is not required for a minor injury but it is important for the practitioner to know the 'normal' type and range of movement for each joint to allow for comparison. Assessment of movement is carried out in stages, each with a distinct technique and objective:

- Active movement
- Passive movement
- Resisted movement
- +/- Stress testing (Walsh 2006)

Active movement

To measure active movement, the patient performs movement unassisted, utilising their own muscle power. Each joint has a different full range of movement and this is measured, following a sequence of articulations. This enables the practitioner to assess the muscles that move the joint and the joint itself. Any restrictions should be noted, and the patient should be asked to describe what is preventing the movement. Assess whether movement is normal and symmetrical and, importantly, whether this causes the patient pain. Observing their facial expressions can assist you in this.

Passive movement

Passive movement aims to remove the muscle, tendon and the tenoperiosteal junction from the test, and to stress tissues such as ligament and cartilage. It is important to explain to the patient that they should relax their muscles and allow the practitioner to make the movements on their behalf. The practitioner should lift the injured part and take the joint through the same movements that have been tested actively, giving reassurance that it will be performed gently and that the patient's responses to these movements will guide the extent of assessment.

If there is no improvement in the range of movement when compared with the active movement, and other symptoms remain, then inert tissue (such as ligament and tendon) is the likely cause of the problem. If the range of movement is increased, and the symptoms reduced, then it is most likely muscular in origin (Meadows 1999). Once again, be considerate and take into account any pain that the patient may be experiencing.

Passive movement elicits symptoms from the tendons and ligaments of the joint. However, muscle or tendon damage can be detected by stretching the muscle. Only resisted movement, with no movement of the joint, isolates the contractile tissue. Each joint has a resting position, where the joint capsule is at its most relaxed. This position is recommended (Meadows 1999).

Resisted movement

To measure resisted movement, stabilise the patient using one hand. With the other hand, oppose the direction of movement offered by the patient.

* **A weak, painful muscle suggests a major problem such as fracture or metastases.**
* **A weak painless muscle may have a complete tear of the tendon or possibly a nerve lesion.**
* **A strong painful muscle has a partial injury that hurts but does not reduce function.**
* **A strong pain-free muscle is normal.**

Stress testing

Passive tests of the joint, creating movements that the patient cannot perform naturally, can aid in the diagnostic process (Fujii et al. 2000). Two examples of these are the talar tilt and the drawer tests which help the practitioner assess ankle stability. Talar tilt should be performed with the patient seated and the ankle/foot unsupported in 10 to 20 degrees of plantar flexion. The examiner should stabilise the medial aspect of the distal part of the leg, just proximal to the medial malleolus, with one hand, and apply inversion force slowly to the hind foot with the other hand. The lateral aspect of the talus should be palpated during inversion of the hind foot to determine if tilting is occurring at the ankle joint. Whilst talar tilt can range from 0 to 23 degrees, most normal ankles will show a tilt of 5 degrees or less.

The drawer tests are used to detect rupture of the cruciate ligaments in the knee. The patient should be supine, with the hips flexed to 45 degrees, the knees flexed to 90 degrees and the feet flat on the table. The examiner sits on the patient's feet and grasps the patient's tibia and pulls it forward (anterior drawer test) or backward (posterior drawer test). If the tibia pulls forward or backward more than expected, the test is considered positive. Excessive displacement of the tibia anteriorly indicates that the anterior cruciate ligament is likely to be torn, whereas excessive displacement posteriorly indicates that the posterior cruciate ligament is likely to be torn.

4. Function

Assessing function of the affected area or joint will give valuable clues as to how the condition impacts on the patient's daily life. As we have seen, reduced function (as well as pain) is the most common reason for initial presentation to the healthcare practitioner. Simple everyday activities can made very difficult by seemingly minor limitations. For example, the inability to flex an elbow sufficiently can affect a patient's ability to brush their teeth or feed themselves. Function of the lower limbs can be assessed by watching the patient's gait, or how easily they can stand up from a sitting position.

As suggested earlier, the GALS assessment is a sound basis on which to quickly assess the individual's musculoskeletal system (Doherty et al. 1992, Arthritis Research UK 2011). A summary of the GALS examination follows.

Gait

Ask the patient to walk away from you and then towards you. Look at the symmetry and smoothness of their gait. Then ask the patient to stand in the anatomical position. Observe them from the front, back and both sides. Look for muscle bulk, symmetry of the joints and limb alignment. You should also check whether they can extend their elbows fully.

Arms

Observe movement of the shoulders by asking the patient to put their hands behind their head. Ask them to hold their arms out straight, and look at the back and palms of the hands. Assess for grip strength and fine motor movement by asking them to make a fist, squeezing your fingers and asking them to touch their thumbs with each finger. Finally squeeze their metacarpo-phalangeal joints. Here, you are assessing for inflammation.

Legs

Ask the patient to lie on the examining couch. Assess flexion and extension of the hips and knees. Perform a patella tap, by holding the top of the thigh, and then slide your hand down to just above the patella. By doing this, you have forced any possible fluid behind the patella. With your other hand, tap the patella. If it bounces back, there is fluid behind the patella. Next, look at the patient's feet, checking for any deformities, calluses and/or swelling. Finally, squeeze the metatarsophalangeal joints, again checking for inflammation.

Spine

Ask the patient to stand, and observe them from the front and back, looking for any scoliosis. Assess them from the sides, looking for any abnormal lordosis and/or kyphosis. Check for lateral flexion of the neck by asking the patient to tilt their head towards their shoulders. Finally, ask the patient to bend to touch their toes. If you place two fingers on their lumbar spine, your fingers should move apart on flexion (moving forward) and come together on extension (moving back).

Table 7.6: Examination summary

Repeat global overview if required	The nature of musculoskeletal presentations means that patient condition may deteriorate. Reassess ABCDE if unsure.
Comfort and dignity	Ensure that the patient is comfortable. This will facilitate the examination.
Additional questions	Reconfirm and clarify history as well as potential new information.
Inspect	Check gait, bruising, swelling, wounds. Compare bad with good.

continued overleaf

Feel	Check anatomy, structures, lumps, bumps, heat and neurovascular observations.
Movement	Active, Passive, Resisted, +/- Stress testing
Function	Watch to see how the injury or condition is affecting the ability to carry out everyday activities of daily living.
GALS	

Regional examination of the musculoskeletal system (REMS)

This assessment is a more detailed set of examination techniques, which should be carried out once an abnormality has been detected (Arthritis UK 2011). It applies the principles previously described to specific joints.

The head, neck and jaw

Examine for normal cervical lordosis. Inspect the head, neck and jaw for signs of deformity, lack of symmetry, swelling and signs of trauma, surgical scars and/or muscle wasting. Palpate for bony steps in the cervical midline. Ask the patient to turn their head from side to side and palpate for any lumps, tender areas, crepitus or resisted movement as you flex the neck forwards and extend the neck backwards.

Check full range of movement by asking the patient to touch their right ear to their right shoulder, and do the same for the left. Ask the patient to touch their chin to their chest and then look up towards the ceiling. With shoulders parallel, they should be able to turn their head to the left and right to achieve alignment with the shoulders. Palpate for clicks and observe for abnormal jaw movement at the temporomandibular joint. The patient should achieve 45 degrees neck extension, flexion and lateral movement, and 70 degrees rotation.

The spine

Exclude the need for in-line stabilisation and/or immobilisation from the mechanism of injury, and carry out a global overview. Even if the patient is ambulant, there may be an occult injury that will require immediate immobilisation. Consider the kinematics and the potential for injury. Observe the patient in a standing position. Check for scoliosis (uneven shoulder height and shoulder blade prominence close) and kyphosis (abnormally rounded thoracic curve).

Ask the patient to walk away from you, stop, turn around and walk back towards you. Observe for symmetry of movement, symmetrical gait and pedal clearance as they step. Measure the distance from the nape of the patient's neck to their waist. Ask the patient to bend forward at the waist, noting the increase in this measurement. An increase of less than 5cm could indicate reduced spinal mobility. Palpation of the spinal processes should follow, noting any pain, swelling or deformity.

The shoulder

Examine the neck to ensure that there is no restriction of movement or associated discomfort. Where there is no history of trauma, shoulder examination should always begin with an examination of the neck in order to rule out a referred pathology.

Watch the patient remove their clothing and observe any restricted range of movement (Rawles *et al.* 2010, Purcell 2010). Then observe the shoulders, anteriorly, laterally and posteriorly for any lack of symmetry, deformity, inflammation and/or muscle wasting.

Consider signs of focal trauma, swelling, bruising, redness and fine muscle tremors.

Check symmetry with uninjured side. Observe for signs of a 'step' over the acromioclavicular joint (ACJ), sternoclavicular joint (SCJ), scapulothoracic and sub-acromial joints.

Gently palpate the major shoulder landmarks, including the sternoclavicular joint, the clavicle, humeral head, scapula, and (laterally) the deltoid muscle. Feel for muscle wasting, inflammation and pain.

The shoulder normally has a noticeably wide range of movement so you should ask the patient to move their arm through the range of movements expected. Demonstration by the practitioner may be helpful. Observe for capsular pattern and arcs of pain. Capsular pattern refers to a pain or restriction in range of movement specific to the injury, while arcs of pain refers to the characteristic discomfort felt on moving the joint.

If the pain is transient depending on range of movement, ask yourself what could be causing the pain? Extension, side flexion, rotation and flexion of the neck should normally be pain free. Check for axillary nerve function by checking for sensation at the top of the deltoid muscle. Check radial, median and ulnar nerve sensation distally at the hands. Feel distal pulse at the brachial and radial arteries and compare both limbs. Assess distal perfusion, limb temperature and capillary refill.

Elbow

Before looking at the elbow, examine the shoulder for any abnormal pathology or restrictions in range of movement. Then assess for any deformity of the elbow joint and check for obvious swelling, bruising, inflammation, muscle wasting, or previous injury or surgery. Support the patient's forearm so that the elbow is flexed to approximately 70 degrees. Palpate bony landmarks and feel for inflammation, heat or swelling over the olecranon (bursitis). Passively flex the elbow to 90 degrees and apply downward force to the palmar surface of the patient's hand whilst supporting under the elbow. The elbow's normal range of movement includes flexion and extension of the elbow and pronation/ supination of the forearm.

Wrist and hand

Inspect the hand for swellings, deformities, muscle wasting, scars (particularly carpal tunnel release scars), skin changes, rashes, nail biting (onycholysis), nail fold vasculitis and palmar erythema. Note which joints are involved and whether any changes are symmetrical.

Now feel the hands. This part of the examination should be as smooth as possible, and you will need to develop your own technique. Based on our own experience, we would recommend the following approach, starting proximally and working distally towards the fingers:

- Begin by feeling the radial pulses and the wrist joints with the two thumbs on the extensor surface and the index fingers on the flexor surface. Then feel the muscle bulk in the thenar and hypothenar eminences.

- In the palms, feel for any tendon thickening and assess the sensation over the relevant areas supplied by the radial, ulnar and median nerves.

- As with all other joints, you should assess the temperature over the joint areas and compare these with the temperature of the forearm.

- Now squeeze over the row of metacarpophalangeal joints whilst watching the patient's face for any discomfort. You should then move onto any metacarpophalangeal joints that are noticeably swollen. Palpate these bimanually with your two thumbs on the dorsum and two index fingers on the palm.

- Move onto the interphalangeal joints and again palpate any that are swollen. This palpation is done with one of the thumbs on the top and the other on one of the sides. The index fingers go on the vacant sides of the joint.

- At this point, the underside of the elbows should be checked for any psoriatic plaques and rheumatoid nodules. Psoriatic plaques could suggest the presence of psoriatic arthritis.

- Test for extension and flexion of the wrists and fingers, adding abduction of fingers and thumbs and lastly thumb opposition.

One special test that you may like to employ is Phalen's manoeuvre, which is a diagnostic test for carpal tunnel syndrome (Rawles *et al.* 2010, Purcell 2010). Forced flexion of the wrist, either against the other hand or by the examiner for 60 seconds, will recreate the symptoms of carpal tunnel syndrome (Arthritis UK 2011).

Froment's sign is a test that may also be used to check ulnar nerve function. This test is performed by asking the patient to hold a piece of paper between their thumb and index finger in order to check the function of the adductor pollicis (Rawles *et al.* 2010, Purcell 2010). In a patient with ulnar nerve palsy, the interphalangeal joint of the thumb will flex to compensate.

Hip

Ask the patient to stand and observe them for any muscle wasting. Ask them to stand on one leg at a time (the Trendelenberg test). This assesses muscle strength of the hip and gluteal muscles. If there is weakness, the pelvis will drop on the opposing side. Following this, ask them to walk away and then towards you assessing for an abnormal gait.

Then position the patient lying flat and face up. Observe for any scars that may indicate previous surgery. Is there any discrepancy in the length of the legs? Is there any external rotation of one or both of the legs?

Palpate the area over the greater trochanter for tenderness (Arthritis UK 2011), and assess for full hip flexion (keep knee flexed at 90 degrees). Then, with the hip and knee flexed at 90 degrees, assess external and internal rotation.

Knee

Consider the alignment of the tibia with the femur (Q angle – less than 15 degrees). Look for bowlegged or knocked knees. Observe the patient's quadriceps for signs of wasting and asymmetry. Examine the pelvis and hip joint and report any abnormalities. Compare both knee joints and observe any signs of obvious inflammation. Palpate the bones of the knee, check for signs of fluid and note any difference in the joint temperature. Utilise passive, active and resisted movement to take the joint through its normal range of movements. Note any abnormal pathology.

Ankle and foot

Ask the patient to remove their shoes and observe shoes for uneven wear. With the patient standing, check foot and ankle alignment. Observe the foot and ankle for calluses, swelling, inflammation, deformity and the height of the arches of the foot (Rawles *et al.* 2010, Bachmann *et al.* 2003). Palpate the knee and calf. Check for signs of inflammation behind the knee and note any swelling or pain in the calf. Palpate the ankle joint, fibula, calcaneum, malleoli and fifth metatarsal, noting any swelling, pain, inflammation and/or nodules (over the Achilles tendons). Listen and note any audible noises whilst moving the joint. Positive findings may require an x-ray (Bachmann *et al.* 2003). In the absence of swelling, carry out passive, active and resisted movement tests.

Box 7.1: Case study – presenting condition

Ms A was a 52-year-old married woman with two teenage children who presented with pain, reduced range of movement and swelling of the left ankle following a fall whilst playing netball. The assessment of this patient was carried out at the scene of the incident.

Global overview

Immediate assessment of Ms A established that her airway, breathing, systemic circulation and conscious level were unaffected by the injury. She was able to confirm her name and appeared completely lucid. Exposure of the injury was completed later. Overall impression at this stage was that she was a normal healthy individual with no obvious abnormalities that could have contributed to this injury. Her behaviour was consistent with her presentation. She was unable to walk on the injured limb.

The mechanism of injury involved a collision with another player and subsequently landing on her ankle from a height of approximately 60cm. It was important to consider the biomechanical forces involved, namely the speed of the collision as well as the height of the fall. These considerations raised suspicion that this injury could have caused more damage to the underlying structures of the ankle and lower leg.

Ms A reported hearing a 'tearing' sound as she landed on the outside of her ankle. The pain was immediate and was accompanied by what she described as swelling and redness on the outer aspect of the ankle.

Ms A had pertinent past medical history. She had a history of repeated ankle injury (due to her participation in netball) and had often returned to her sport too soon after previous injuries. Other than occasional 'gastric' pain, she reported being fit and healthy. She commented that she had been having 'hot flushes and heart palpitations'. Following these symptoms, her GP prescribed hormone replacement therapy (HRT) with no further investigations.

She had taken no medications before the assessment. Her current medications were HRT and NSAIDs for recurrent musculoskeletal pain. She had no known allergies. She had been treated by physiotherapists on a number of occasions for previous sporting injuries to her ankles.

Ms A was adopted but had met her biological mother, who suffered from osteoporosis and osteoarthritis. She had no siblings and was unaware of the health of her biological father.

She had worked as a dentist for the last 20 years, establishing her own practice with five employees. She stated that she maintained a healthy diet and had only had one day off work in the last two years. She had been a competitive amateur netball player for over 30 years. She admitted that this had 'taken its toll' on her ankles and knees, with an ever-increasing injury rate, accompanied by protracted recovery times and soreness of the joints. She had never smoked and only consumed alcohol occasionally.

Impression: A 52-year-old woman with an ankle ligament sprain following a fall at a netball match.

Physical examination

The physical examination commenced with removal of Ms A's shoes and socks. The socks were cut with scissors to reduce movement and aid removal. The lower leg (from knee to toes) was exposed. The garments on the opposing side were also removed and the uninjured side compared. No gross deformity, suggesting a fracture or dislocation, was evident; nor were there any breaks in the skin from bone displacement.

Swelling was evident over the lateral malleolus with erythema. (Rapid onset swelling suggests a more serious injury; swelling will continue to develop for 6 to 24 hrs.)

The patient's pain was assessed, scoring 6 on a 0–10 scale and localised to the area of swelling. Distal pulses were present (dorsalis pedis and posterior tibial) and the skin well perfused. The injured foot felt marginally warmer.

If the pulse is absent, it is important to document the time of this pertinent negative.

Ms A was able to wiggle her toes as requested and could distinguish between a sharp and soft object, thereby confirming that she had no loss of neurological function.

The ankle was then palpated, proximal to distal, with constant comparison to the uninjured side. Palpation began just below the knee, assessing calf muscle, tibia and fibula (with thought to the kinematics involved as some ankle injuries have associated proximal tibia fractures). No further abnormalities were found during this part of the examination.

Whilst palpating the medial and lateral malleoli and all tarsal bones, we attempted to distinguish between bone and soft tissue pain; Ms A appeared to have pain associated with soft tissue only.

The navicular and cuboid were squeezed together, followed by the proximal ends of the first and fifth metatarsals. Ms A did not complain of pain during this part of the assessment. Pain during this palpation could represent a ligament tear from a bone associated with fracture.

The ankle was assessed for stability using the drawer test. Assessing talofibular ligaments, the leg is held proximal to both malleoli in one hand, and the foot grasped with the other. The foot is then pulled forward, while holding the leg still. The same procedure is completed on the opposite side, and the movement compared. Ms A appeared to have equal movement on both sides. From the same starting position, Ms A's ankle was inverted and everted, testing for instability within the tibial ligaments (see Figures 7.1, 7.2 and 7.3).

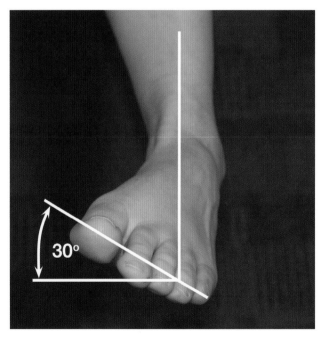

Figure 7.1: Ankle inversion, 30 degrees

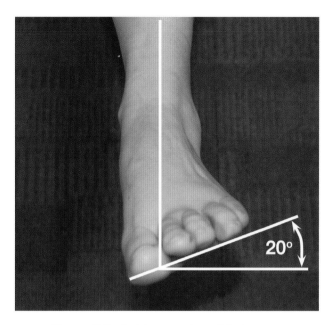

Figure 7.2: Ankle eversion, 20 degrees

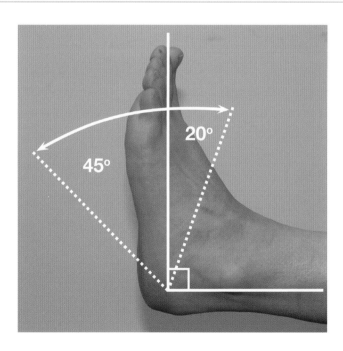

Figure 7.3: Testing for instability within the tibial ligaments, 45 and 20 degrees

Ms A's entire ankle appeared wider than the uninjured leg and she had significant pain, suggesting tibiofibular ligament damage.

Ms A was transported to hospital in order to rule out further significant injury. A sprain is simply a tearing of some of the ligament fibres holding the joint together, followed by an inflammatory response – hence the pain and swelling. The ankle joint has four sets of ligaments, anterior, posterior, medial and lateral, any of which can be damaged, depending on the kinematics involved at the time of the injury.

The most common of these presenting sprains, accounting for some 85% of presentations (Loveridge 2002), involves the inversion (adduction) that Ms A described as 'pushed over my ankle'. She was experiencing pain and swelling on the lateral aspect of the ankle. Ankle sprains are graded from 1 to 3 in increasing order of severity. A grade 3 injury involves disruption of the ligaments, instability, bruising and severe swelling; while a grade 1 injury is stable, with only microscopic tears in some ligament fibres and mild swelling (Loveridge 2002).

During the assessment, the practitioner's aim is to identify the most serious injuries and their secondary complications. The initial impression may be that of a sprain, but fractures are sometimes impossible to differentiate and should not be excluded from the differential diagnosis. Fractures may also have the added concern of circulatory compromise, which may result in reduced flow and haemodynamic instability. Dislocation may be present at the fracture site and may involve ligament injury.

When the practitioner looks at the site, they should consider the kinematics and the potential for associated damage. They may recognise a complicated fracture with systemic infections or, as with the case study, a simple strain or sprain. Remember that under-diagnosed fractures left untreated may have a significant impact on a patient's health, limiting the return of normal activities of daily living. Unfortunately, in a community setting, differentiating between skeletal and muscular injuries can be difficult or impossible.

The practitioner should always be prepared and willing to refer patients for further investigation if there is any doubt surrounding the findings of the musculoskeletal assessment.

In summary, this chapter has outlined the process and techniques involved in the assessment of the musculoskeletal system. Conditions involving this system can be surprisingly complex and therefore the importance of a systematic and thorough examination cannot be over-emphasised.

References

Arthritis Research UK (2011). Clinical Assessment of the Musculoskeletal System: a guide for medical students and healthcare professionals [online] Available at http://www.arthritisresearchuk.org/health-professionals-and-students/student-handbook.aspx Accessed 01/05/2012.

Bachmann, L.M., Kolb, E., Koller, M.T., Steurer, J. & ter Riet, G. (2003). Accuracy of Ottawa Ankle rules to exclude fracture of the ankle and mid-foot: systematic review. *British Medical Journal*. **326**, 417.

Doherty, M., Dacre, J. & Dieppe, P. (1992). The 'GALS' Locomotor screen. *Annals of the Rheumatic Diseases*. **51**, 1165–69.

Douglas, G., Nicol, F. & Robertson, C. (2009). *Macleod's Clinical Examination*. London: Churchill Livingstone.

Forsblad, D.H. & Jochems, C. (2008). Role of oestrogen deficiency in osteoporosis in post-menopausal rheumatoid arthritis. *European Musculoskeletal Review*. **3** (1), 76–79

Fujii, T., Luo, Z. P., Kitaaka, H.B. & An, K. N. (2000). The manual stress test may not be sufficient to differentiate ankle ligament injuries. *Clinical Biomechanics*. **15** (8), 619–23.

Judge, N.L. (2007). Assessing and managing patients with musculoskeletal conditions. *Nursing Standard*. **22** (1), 51–57.

Lillicrap, M.S., Byrne, E. & Speed, C.A. (2003). Musculoskeletal assessment of general medical inpatients; joint still crying out for attention. *Rheumatology*. **42**, 951–54.

Loveridge, N. (2002). Lateral ankle sprains. *Emergency Nurse*. **10** (2), 29–33.

Meadows, J.T.S. (1999). *Orthopaedic Differential Diagnosis in Physical Therapy*. New York, USA: McCraw Hill.

Moncrieff, J. & Pomerleau, J. (2000). Trends in sickness benefits in Great Britain and the contribution of mental disorders. *Journal of Public Health Medicine*. **22**, 59–67.

Monk, C. (2006). Measurement of the functional improvement in patients receiving physiotherapy for musculoskeletal conditions. *New Zealand Journal of Physiotherapy*. **34** (2), 50–55.

Purcell, D. (2010). *Minor Injuries: A Clinical Guide For Nurses*. London: Churchill Livingstone.

Rawles, Z., Griffiths, B. & Alexander, T. (2010). *Physical Examination Procedures for Advanced Nurses and Independent Prescribers. Evidence and Rationale*. London: Hodder Arnold.

Roche, A., Hunter, L., Pocock, N. & Brown, D. (2009). Physical examination of the foot and ankle by orthopaedic and accident and emergency clinicians. *Injury. International Journal of the Care of the Injured*. **40**, 136–38.

Schmidt, M., Christiansen, C.F., Mehnert, F., Rothman, K.J. & Sorensen, H.T. (2011). Non-steroidal anti-inflammatory drug use and risk of atrial fibrillation or flutter: population based case-control study. *British Medical Journal*. **4**, 343.

Seidel, H.M., Ball, J.W., Dains, J.E. & Benedict, G.W. (2006). *Mosby's Guide to Physical Examination*. St Louis, USA: Mosby, Elsevier.

Walsh, M. (2006). *Nurse Practitioners: Clinical Skills and Professional Issues*. London: Butterworth Heineman.

Wardrope, J. & English, B. (2003). *Musculoskeletal Problems in Emergency Medicine*. Oxford: Oxford University Press.

Chapter 8

Obstetric assessment

Heather Passmore

This chapter will enable healthcare practitioners to undertake a clinical examination of a pregnant woman and determine the appropriate care and referral if they detect raised blood pressure. The responsibility for care of pregnant women rests primarily with registered midwives, obstetricians and GPs. However, there may be occasions when other practitioners are required to participate in their care and provide preconceptual advice to women with existing hypertension

It is common practice in the UK for all pregnant women to carry their own maternity notes. This is advantageous to healthcare practitioners, who can utilise these notes to compare current blood pressure recording with previous measurements, to facilitate evaluation of any change and to plan required intervention. The aim of management is to enable pregnancy to continue to a minimum of 37 weeks' gestation without compromising either maternal or fetal well-being. Hypertensive disorders remain a cause of maternal death, both in the UK (Knight *et al.* 2015) and worldwide (Patton *et al.* 2009), so clinical examination to enable early recognition is imperative. Walker (2000) indicates that approximately 12% of pregnancies are affected by hypertensive disorders that are unique to pregnancy. However, this figure varies due to the wide spectrum of presenting factors, ranging from mild to severe.

This chapter will briefly cover the causes of raised blood pressure in pregnancy, focusing on the most common presentation, pre-eclampsia. The clinical, haematological, biochemical and fetal indicators of raised blood pressure will be examined and applied to a case study to demonstrate the fundamentals of clinical examination in this condition.

Anatomy and physiology of blood pressure and changes in pregnancy

Blood pressure is defined as the pressure exerted on the interior walls of blood vessels and is measured in millimetres of mercury (Hg). In a healthy young adult at rest, the systolic pressure in the aorta as the ventricles contract is approximately 120mmHg, falling to a diastolic pressure of 80mmHg when the heart is at rest. Blood pressure is dependent upon two factors – cardiac output and peripheral resistance.

Cardiac output is the heart rate multiplied by the stroke volume. The cardiac output may increase in response to exercise, an increase in blood volume or if blood vessels are damaged by atherosclerosis. Peripheral resistance is the extent to which the diameter of a blood vessel resists the flow of blood, and this can be affected by blood volume, the viscosity of the blood, blood vessel lining, length and diameter (Rankin *et al.* 2005). The peripheral resistance is significantly influenced by the vessels of the arterioles, capillaries and venules. The vessel walls contain smooth muscle that responds to certain hormones or temperature, and the resultant vasodilation or constriction can affect peripheral resistance.

The pulse pressure is the difference between the systolic and diastolic pressure, and is influenced most by stroke volume and the rigidity of the arteries. An average value for arterial pressure, the mean arterial pressure (MAP), represents the 'pressure pushing blood through the arteries and is therefore indicative of tissue perfusion' (Rankin 2005, page 231). Control of blood pressure is complex; it requires a mechanism to adjust to the body's different activities and the needs of different organ systems. The medulla oblongata in the brain provides central regulation, with baroreceptors in the walls of arteries, veins and the right atrium creating physiological adjustments to maintain blood pressure. Chemoreceptors in the carotid artery and aorta detect changes in oxygen, carbon dioxide levels and pH, which are interpreted by the medulla to alter cardiac rate or rhythm. Blood pressure is also controlled by several hormones:

- Adrenaline and noradrenaline, from the adrenal cortex, increase cardiac output and affect the diameter of blood vessels.
- Antidiuretic hormone, from the hypothalamus, causes vasoconstriction.

- Renin-angiotensin pathway increases blood pressure by vasoconstriction and release of aldosterone, which increase sodium and water reabsorption in the kidneys.
- Atrial natriuretic peptide is released from cells in the atria of the heart when blood pressure is high, resulting in vasodilation and the loss of salt and water.

During pregnancy, the increase in circulating levels of progesterone secreted by the placenta causes relaxation of smooth muscle. The walls of the veins relax and this causes a reduction in maternal blood pressure, which is most marked in the second trimester. After this time, the physiological increase in plasma volume (most marked in the third trimester and up 40–50% on non-pregnant volume) returns the blood pressure to its non-pregnant level.

Pathological changes in blood pressure

There are various theories regarding the pathology of pre-eclampsia. However, a two-stage model has been proposed for the pathophysiology, involving a placental trigger preventing abnormal invasion of the spiral arteries in the uterus and a maternal systemic response, which is likely to be responsible for variation in presentation and progression of the condition. The abnormal implantation of the placenta can cause ischaemic disease of the placenta and subsequent impaired placental perfusion, resulting in widespread vascular endothelial cell dysfunction throughout the body (Yerby 2010, Nicoll 2009). This is part of a more extensive maternal intravascular inflammatory reaction, which provides an explanation for the clinical features of pre-eclampsia (Redman et al. 1999). These include raised blood pressure, proteinuria, oedema, coagulopathy, impaired renal function and liver dysfunction (Stevenson & Billington 2007). Foetal growth is affected by the diminished placental blood flow.

Peripheral resistance is increased in pre-eclampsia, as opposed to the normal decrease in pregnancy. In addition, the increase in sensitivity to angiotensin II raises blood pressure further (Sarris et al. 2009, page 215). The mean arterial pressure (MAP) is thought to reflect the degree of hypovolaemia associated with the condition (Stevenson & Billington 2007, page 103); and in their systematic review Cnossen et al. (2008) found that MAP was a better predictor for pre-eclampsia than either systolic, diastolic blood pressure or an increase in blood pressure. Systolic pressure and MAP are known to be higher before the onset of clinical disease, and at 18 and 28 weeks (Shennan & Halligan 1999, cited in Leslie et al. 2011).

Raised blood pressure occurring in pregnancy (gestational hypertension) is classified as mild, moderate or severe – according to a range of systolic and diastolic measurements. The former diagnosis of a rise in diastolic pressure >15mmHg above booking blood pressure is no longer regarded as appropriate in these definitions. The classification assists practitioners in determining the required clinical examination, investigation and care (see Tables 8.4 and 8.5 below). The NICE antenatal care guideline recommends that hypertension in which there is a single diastolic blood pressure of 110mmHg, or two consecutive readings of 90mmHg at least 4 hours apart and/or significant proteinuria (1+), should prompt increased surveillance. If the systolic blood pressure is above 160mmHg on two consecutive readings at least 4 hours apart, treatment should be considered (NICE 2008).

Raised blood pressure in pregnancy (gestational hypertension) is classified as follows:

- Mild: 140/90–149/99mmHg
- Moderate: 150/100–159/109mmHg
- Severe: > 160/110 mmHg

(Adapted from the National Collaborating Centre for Women's and Children's Health [NCCWCH] 2010)

The differential diagnosis of raised blood pressure in pregnancy is shown in Table 8.1 below, which indicates the significance of urinalysis to detect proteinuria, and haematological and biochemical investigation as an essential part of the diagnostic process.

Table 8.1: Definitions of raised blood pressure in pregnancy

(Adapted from NCCWH 2010)

Definition	Differential diagnosis
Chronic hypertension	Hypertension present at booking visit or before 20 weeks, or women already treated with antihypertensive medication
Gestational hypertension	New hypertension presenting after 20 weeks, without significant proteinuria
Pre-eclampsia	New hypertension presenting after 20 weeks, with significant proteinuria
Severe pre-eclampsia	Pre-eclampsia with severe hypertension and/or symptoms, and/or biochemical and/or haematological impairment
HELLP syndrome	Haemolysis, elevated liver enzymes and low platelet count

Eclampsia	A convulsive condition associated with pre-eclampsia
Significant proteinuria	Diagnosed when the urinary protein:creatinine ratio is greater than 30mg/mmol or a validated 24-hour urine collection result shows greater than 300mg protein

Hypertension in pregnancy has been the focus of much research. While the precise cause remains elusive, risk factors for developing pre-eclampsia have been established and differentiated into moderate and high (see below). The presence of significant hypertension and/or proteinuria should alert the healthcare professional to the need for increased surveillance of both maternal and foetal well-being. More frequent blood pressure measurements should be considered for pregnant women who have any of the risk factors listed below. These factors should lead healthcare practitioners to be vigilant in history-taking and clinical examination and determine appropriate care pathways for women found to be at risk of developing raised blood pressure in pregnancy.

Risk factors for pre-eclampsia are as follows:

Moderate

- First pregnancy
- Age > 40 years
- Pregnancy interval > 10 years
- BMI >5 kg/m² at first visit
- Family history of pre-eclampsia
- Multiple pregnancy

High

- Hypertensive disease during previous pregnancy
- Chronic kidney disease
- Autoimmune disease such as systemic lupus erythematosis or antiphospholipid syndrome
- Type 1 or type 2 diabetes
- Chronic hypertension

Women who are at moderate and high risk of developing pre-eclampsia are advised to take 75mg of aspirin daily from 12 weeks until the birth of the baby (NCCWCH 2010).

Pre-pregnancy advice for women with chronic hypertension

Women should be encouraged to obtain a BMI of 20–25 and conceive, if possible, before the age of 40. They should also keep their dietary sodium intake low to help reduce blood pressure. The use of antihypertensive medicine should be reviewed with particular reference to the increased risk of congenital abnormalities in women who take angiotensin-converting enzyme (ACE) inhibitors, angiotensin II receptor blockers (ARBs) and chlorothiazide. The use of ACE inhibitors and ARBs should be stopped within 2 days of pregnancy confirmation. Women with chronic hypertension should be referred for consultant obstetric care (NCCWCH 2010).

Recording blood pressure

Accurate blood pressure recording is essential during pregnancy. Manual measurement can be made with an anaeroid or oscillatory machine. There is increased use of automated electronic blood pressure recording, though underestimation of blood pressure with these devices has been reported (NCCWCH 2010). This underestimation needs to be remembered when caring for women with any form of hypertension in pregnancy. All equipment should be regularly serviced and services clearly marked on the sphygmomanometer.

Irrespective of the machine used to measure blood pressure, the following guidelines should be observed:

- The patient should be seated for at least 5 minutes, relaxed and not moving or speaking.
- The arm must be supported at the level of the heart. Ensure that no tight clothing constricts the arm.
- Place the cuff on neatly, with the centre of the bladder over the brachial artery. The bladder of the cuff should encircle at least 80% of the arm (but not more than 100%).

Measurement of blood pressure using manual recording equipment:

- Estimate the systolic beforehand:
  Palpate the brachial artery
  Inflate cuff until pulsation disappears
  Deflate cuff
  Estimate systolic pressure
- Then inflate to 30mmHg above the estimated systolic level needed to occlude the pulse.

- Place the stethoscope diaphragm over the brachial artery and deflate at a rate of 2–3mm/sec until you hear regular tapping sounds.
- If a mercury sphygmomanometer is used, the column of mercury must be vertical, and at the observer's eye level (Beevers et al. 2001).

Measurement of blood pressure using electronic recording equipment:

- Most monitors allow manual blood pressure setting selection, where you choose the appropriate setting. Other monitors will automatically inflate and re-inflate to the next setting if required.
- Repeat three times and record measurement as displayed. Initially test blood pressure in both arms and use arm with highest reading for subsequent measurement.

Selection and use of the appropriate cuff for blood pressure measurement is imperative (see Table 8.2 below). Use of a bladder that is too small (undercuffing) can lead to overestimation of BP by as much as 30mmHg in obese women. Less frequently, overcuffing can result in an underestimation of BP ranging from 10 to 30mmHg.

Table 8.2: Blood pressure cuff sizes *(Adapted from O'Brien et al. 2003)*

Indication	Width (cm)* =	Length (cm)* =	BHS guidelines Bladder width and length (cm)*	Arm circumference (cm)*
Small adult/child	10–12	18–24	12 x 18	< 23
Standard adult	12–13	23–35	12 x 26	< 33
Large adult	12–16	35–40	12 x 40	< 50
Adult thigh cuff **	20	42		< 53

* The ranges for columns 2 and 3 are derived from recommendations from the British Hypertension Society (BHS), European Hypertension Society (ESH) and the American Heart Association.
Columns 4 and 5 are derived from only the BHS guidelines.

** Large bladders for arm circumferences over 42cm may be required.

= Bladders of varying sizes are available so a range is provided for each indication (applies to columns 2 and 3)

Determination of systolic pressure is clearly established as the first auditory sounds in the brachial artery as the cuff is released. Korotkoff sounds guide the measurement of blood pressure and are shown in Table 8.3 below. The clinical significance, if any, of phases II and III has not been established. Measurement of the diastolic endpoint has been equivocal. However, there is now a general consensus that disappearance of sounds (Korotkoff V) should be used. When the Korotkoff sounds persist down to zero (not uncommon in pregnancy), muffling of sounds (phase IV) should be recorded for diastolic pressure, and a note made to this effect (O'Brien & Fitzgerald 1994).

Table 8.3: Korotkoff auscultatory sounds to measure blood pressure
(Adapted from O'Brien & Fitzgerald 1994)

Phase I	The first appearance of faint, repetitive, clear tapping sounds that gradually increase in intensity for at least two consecutive beats is the systolic blood pressure.
Phase II	A brief period may follow, during which the sounds soften and acquire a swishing quality.
Auscultatory gap	In some patients, sounds may disappear altogether for a short time.
Phase III	The return of sharper sounds, which become crisper, to regain or even exceed the intensity of phase I sounds.
Phase IV	The distinct, abrupt muffling of sounds, which become soft and blowing in quality.
Phase V	The point at which all sounds finally disappear completely is the diastolic pressure.

Women with gestational hypertension should be offered an integrated package of care, covering admission to hospital, treatment, measurement of blood pressure, testing for proteinuria and blood tests as indicated in Table 8.4 below.

Table 8.4: Management of pregnancy with gestational hypertension

(Adapted from NCCWCH 2010)

	Mild hypertension (140/90 to 149/99mmHg)	Moderate hypertension (150/100 to 159/109mmHg)	Severe hypertension (160/110mmHg or higher)
Admit to hospital	No	No	Yes (until blood pressure is 159/109mmHg or lower)
Treat	No	With oral labetalol as first-line treatment to keep: • diastolic blood pressure between 80 and 100mmHg • systolic blood pressure less than 150mmHg	With oral labetalol as first-line treatment to keep: • diastolic blood pressure between 80 and 100mmHg • systolic blood pressure less than 150mmHg
Measure blood pressure	Not more than once a week	At least twice a week	At least four times a day
Test for proteinuria	At each visit, using automated reagent-strip reading device or urinary protein:creatinine ratio	At each visit, using automated reagent-strip reading device or urinary protein:creatinine ratio	Daily, using automated reagent-strip reading device or urinary protein:creatinine ratio
Blood tests	Only those for routine antenatal care	Test kidney function, electrolytes, full blood count, transaminases, bilirubin. Do not carry out further blood tests if no proteinuria at subsequent visits.	Test at presentation and then monitor weekly: kidney function, electrolytes, full blood count, transaminases, bilirubin.

In women with mild hypertension presenting before 32 weeks or at high risk of pre-eclampsia, measure blood pressure and test urine twice weekly. In women receiving outpatient care for severe gestational hypertension, after it has been effectively controlled in hospital, measure blood pressure and test urine twice weekly and carry out weekly blood tests. Hospitalisation and bed rest is not a treatment for gestational hypertension.

Table 8.5: Management of pregnancy with pre-eclampsia

(Adapted from NCCWCH 2010)

	Mild hypertension (140/90 to 149/99mmHg)	Moderate hypertension (150/100 to 159/109mmHg)	Severe hypertension (160/110mmHg or higher)
Admit to hospital	Yes	Yes	Yes
Treat	No	With oral labetalol as first-line treatment to keep: • diastolic blood pressure between 80 and 100mmHg • systolic blood pressure less than 150mmHg	With oral labetalol as first-line treatment to keep: • diastolic blood pressure between 80 and 100mmHg • systolic blood pressure less than 150mmHg
Measure blood pressure	At least four times a day	At least four times a day	More than four times a day, depending on clinical circumstances
Test for proteinuria	Do not repeat quantification of proteinuria	Do not repeat quantification of proteinuria	Do not repeat quantification of proteinuria
Blood tests	Monitor using the following tests twice a week: kidney function, electrolytes, full blood count, transaminases, bilirubin	Monitor using the following tests three times a week: kidney function, electrolytes, full blood count, transaminases, bilirubin	Monitor using the following tests three times a week: kidney function, electrolytes, full blood count, transaminases, bilirubin

Consultant obstetric staff should document in the woman's notes the maternal (biochemical, haematological and clinical) and foetal thresholds for elective birth before 34 weeks in women with pre-eclampsia.

Clinical examination

Clinical history

Previous medical, obstetric and social history should be assessed and recorded at the first booking interview. If necessary, interpreting services should be used to ensure effective communication.

A comprehensive history should be taken at each antenatal examination to:

- **Ascertain experience of any severe headaches and their nature (related to tension, frontal, unilateral/bilateral, duration)**
- **History of visual disturbances, such as blurring or flashing before the eyes**
- **Severe pain just below the ribs (epigastric pain), which is a common symptom of significant pre-eclampsia**
- **Nausea or vomiting**
- **Sudden swelling of the face, hands or feet**

Over 20 weeks' gestation, foetal movement should be checked, although foetal movement charts are not recommended (NICE 2008). If foetal activity is abnormal, cardiotocography should be performed, preferably in a consultant unit, where the holistic well-being of mother and foetus can be assessed. The use of personalised GROW charts assists in the assessment of foetal growth (NICE 2008).

All pregnant women should be made aware of the need to seek immediate advice from a healthcare professional if they experience any of the above symptoms suggesting pre-eclampsia.

As good practice in information sharing, CMACE & Lewis (2011, page 165) recommend that a GP should, whenever possible, give a named community midwife confidential access to the woman's full written and electronic records, with the woman's consent. If this is not possible, the GP should supply a named community midwife with a summary of the woman's past medical history, with the woman's consent.

The first port of call for a pregnant woman with epigastric pain (an important symptom of severe pre-eclampsia) may well be her GP. This problem needs to be urgently addressed. The significance of epigastric pain in pregnancy also needs to be better understood in Emergency Departments as described in the report *Saving Mothers' Lives:*

A woman presented to an Emergency Department in early third trimester with epigastric pain. Her blood pressure was >150/90 mmHg and she had proteinuria +++. She was diagnosed as having 'gastritis' and discharged home, where she collapsed and died shortly afterwards. Autopsy showed a cerebral haemorrhage and the typical histological features of pre-eclampsia.
(CMACE & Lewis 2011)

Physical examination

At each visit to a healthcare professional, the physical examination should include accurate measurement of blood pressure, especially if the woman is feeling unwell.

Urinalysis for proteinuria should also be carried out, utilising dipstick measurement at each visit, especially if the woman is feeling unwell. Quantitative measurement is necessary:

>1+ protein on urine dipstick is significant

(approximate equivalents 1+ = 0.3g/l, 2+ = 1g/l, 3+ = 3g/l).

The healthcare professional should check for worsening peripheral and periorbital oedema. Jaundice in a pregnant woman requires immediate investigation and admission. Foetal growth should be assessed by measuring fundal height and foetal activity.

After 28 weeks, perform ultrasound fetal growth and amniotic fluid volume assessment and umbilical artery Doppler velocimetry (indicates abnormal adaptation of spiral arteries during placentation).

Investigations and related symptoms

- Haemoconcentration – low haemoglobin with haemolysis, low platelets
- Urea and electrolytes – raised creatinine (mean levels: first trimester 60μmol/l, second trimester 54μmol/l, third trimester 64μmol/l) and urea
- Liver function – full blood count: raised haemoglobin and haematocrit with liver function test (LFT): raised transaminases (alanine aminotransferase [ALT] and aspartate aminotransferase [AST] and alkaline phosphatase); normal pregnancy levels are 20% lower than non-pregnant levels.
- Urate – levels equate to gestation (i.e. <320μmol/l at 32 weeks, <360μmol/l at 36 weeks) but raised in pre-eclampsia
- Clotting – abnormal LFT or low platelets could indicate disseminated intravascular coagulation
- Mid-stream urine – to exclude infection as a cause of proteinuria
- 24-hour urine – the most accurate measurement for proteinuria

- Protein:creatinine ratio – this can be a one-off measurement accurate in predicting significant proteinuria (Sarris et al. 2009, page 214)

Recording findings

All healthcare professionals should record their actions and findings in the woman's medical records, which will include the mother's own hand-held maternity notes. Depending upon the practitioner and situation, this may also be recorded in the mother's obstetric records or on a computer system.

Reporting findings and referral

Any deviation from normal must be referred onwards and concerns escalated to a medical colleague of appropriate seniority. Due to the potential consequences for pregnancy, referral to the local obstetric unit and consultant-led care, if not already in place, will become appropriate.

Any discussion between clinical staff about a woman with pre-eclampsia should include explicit mention of the systolic pressure. Severe, life-threatening, hypertension must be treated effectively. Management protocols should recognise the need to avoid very high systolic blood pressures (over 160mmHg). The latest report on confidential enquiries into maternal deaths says that the single most serious failing in the clinical care provided for mothers with pre-eclampsia was the inadequate treatment of their systolic hypertension. In several cases, this resulted in a fatal intracranial haemorrhage. Systolic hypertension was also a key factor in most of the deaths from aortic dissection (CMACE & Lewis 2011).

Maternal and fetal well-being will be improved by appropriate referral when abnormalities are detected. However, referral does not equate to treatment. Where an urgent response is required, a senior clinician should be telephoned, and the call should be backed up by a written letter, email or fax. The referral letter should include:

- Current problem and reason for referral
- Details of any past medical history, including mental health history, even if this is not directly relevant to the presenting problem
- All medications she is currently on or has recently stopped
- Investigations carried out so far.

GPs should always refer a woman with pre-eclampsia for specialist care and should only start anti-hypertensives in primary care if a woman is severely unwell, before her emergency admission. In this situation, the treatment of choice is oral labetalol (CMACE & Lewis 2011).

An interprofessional approach to pregnant women whose blood pressure becomes elevated will improve maternal and foetal outcomes. Collaborative action and good communication between midwives, general practitioners, obstetricians, ultra- sonographers, haematologists, biochemists, anaesthetists and paediatricians and early engagement of intensive care specialists (where appropriate) will enable planning for the optimal delivery time in relation to maternal and foetal condition. GPs should be conversant with the Action on Pre-Eclampsia guidance for detection and referral for pre-eclampsia and eclampsia (APEC 2004).

Case study

Clinical history

Lily was a lady from Sub-Saharan Africa (name changed to ensure anonymity and protect confidentiality [Nursing and Midwifery Council [NMC] 2015]). She was a multiparous lady, having had two previous pregnancies by the same partner, both complicated by raised blood pressure.

Her first pregnancy was complicated by pre-eclampsia with labour induced at 36 weeks, resulting in a normal delivery of a live infant weighing 2.3kg (25th centile).

Her second pregnancy was again complicated by pre-eclampsia and was treated with labetalol (200mg three times a day) from 28 weeks' gestation. As her blood pressure continued to rise (despite the antihypertensive treatment) and intrauterine growth retardation was suspected, associated with a diminished volume of amniotic fluid, an emergency lower segment Caesarean section was performed at 36 weeks' gestation. The baby weighed 2.53kg (50th centile).

Lily reported no continuation of raised blood pressure following her two previous pregnancies but there was a family history of raised blood pressure in the family, and her mother experienced raised blood pressure and pre-eclampsia in her pregnancies.

Aged 31 with a BMI of 28, Lily was booked for antenatal care at 9 weeks' gestation, in accordance with antenatal care guidance (NICE 2008). Due to her previous obstetric history, Lily was booked for consultant-led care to be delivered at the District General Hospital, with neonatal intensive-care facilities. Her plan of care allowed for more frequent antenatal visits than the seven usually recommended for multiparous women, due to her history of raised blood pressure in pregnancy.

Clinical examination

Table 8.6 (below) charts the frequency of antenatal care visits with the examinations performed and resultant intended care. This should be compared with Table 8.5 (see page 134) to determine appropriate clinical investigations and care for a woman with pre-eclampsia. At 24 weeks' gestation Lily's systolic blood pressure showed a range from 140 to 162mmHg with no proteinuria or other symptoms, and she was not admitted to hospital. Clinical examination of full blood count, coagulation screen, urea and electrolyte measurement and liver function tests may have provided information regarding the apparently rising blood pressure.

Table 8.6:
Lily's antenatal care record, from booking to 28 weeks' gestation

Gestation (weeks)	Blood pressure (mmHg)	Urinalysis	Other observations/ investigations (pertinent to raised blood pressure)	Care plan
9 + 3	140/80	Nothing abnormal detected (NAD)	FBC	Consultant-led care; regular antenatal checks
18 + 4	140/80	NAD	Fundus = dates Foetal movement felt	
19+	140/90	Trace protein → MSU – NAD	Fundus = dates Foetal movement felt	Congenital anomaly scan MW/GP weekly blood pressure measurement Review 24/40 Scan + Doppler + consultant review at 28/40 and 32/40
24 + 2	Systolic pressure 140–162	+ve – nitrite Trace blood Trace protein → MSU – NAD	Abdomen soft, non-tender Fundus = dates	Headache yesterday No epigastric pain

cont.	Diastolic pressure 83–90 MAP = 107–120 With Dynamap recording on three occasions		Foetal movement felt Foetal heart rate 150 beats per minute	No visual disturbance No oedema Not admitted to hospital Consultant review if BP>160/100 Mother made aware of symptoms requiring her to contact unit 2-weekly monitoring of BP by midwife
28 + 4	165/102 62/98	Protein +	Abdomen soft, non-tender Fundus = dates Foetal movement felt Foetal heart rate 144 beats per minute Haematological test – FBC and coagulation screen Uric acid, glomerular filtration rate, magnesium, bicarbonate	Headache No epigastric pain No visual disturbance Slight oedema of left foot Admitted to hospital Commenced treatment with oral Labetalol 200mg tds (3 hours after 1st dose BP 143/84, pulse 80) Ultrasound scan to assess growth and umbilical artery Doppler

(Blood tests and ultrasound scans performed as part of the antenatal screening programme are not shown here. Information and a schedule of screening tests can be accessed at htttp://www.screening.nhs.uk/england.)

Table 8.7: Clinical investigations – haematology

Test	Results	Units	Reference range	Hi/Lo flag
Coagulation screen				
Prothrombin time	10.2	s	(10.0–15.0)	
INR	0.9			
APTT	27	s	(26–37)	
APTT Ratio	0.8			
Fibrinogen	5.01	g/L	(2–4.5)	Abnormal
Full blood count				
Hb	11.1	g/L	(11.5–16.0)	Caution
WBC	7.8	x 10^9/L	(4.0–11.0)	
Platelets	191	x 10^9/L	(135–450)	
RBC	3.82	x 10^12/L	(3.80–4.8)	
MCV	84	fl	(80–100)	
Haematocrit	0.32	L/L	(0.35–0.45)	Abnormal
MCH	29.1	pg	(27–34)	
RDW	13.4		(10–15)	
Neutrophils	5.3	x 10^9/L	(2.0–7.5)	
Lymphocytes	1.5	x 10^9/L	(1.0–4.0)	
Monocytes	0.7	x 10^9/L	(0.1–1.0)	
Eosinophils	0.2	x 10^9/L	(0.0–0.5)	
Basophils	0.0	x 10^9/L	(0–0.2)	

These haematological tests indicate some impact from raised blood pressure. While the low haemoglobin may be caused by physiological haemodilution in pregnancy and mild anaemia, the raised fibrinogen level and low haematocrit are likely to be the results of hypertension caused by abnormal placentation.

Table 8.8: Biochemical tests

Test	Results	Units	Reference range	Hi/Lo Flag
Urea & electrolytes				
Urea	1.6	mmol/L	(2.5–8.5)	Abnormal
Na (Sodium)	139	mmol/L	(132–144)	
K (Potassium)	2.8	mmol/L	(3.2–5.0)	Abnormal
Creatinine	50	umol/L	(55–108)	Abnormal
Liver function tests				
ALP	262	u/L	(80–260)	Abnormal
Total protein	61	g/L	(65–80)	Abnormal
Albumin	31	g/L	(33–50)	Abnormal
Globulin	30	g/L	(22–38)	
ALT	15	u/L	(0–37)	
Total Bilirubin	7	umol/L	(0–20)	
Uric acid				
Uric acid	0.23	mmol/L	(0.11–0.35)	
EGFR				
eGFR	>150	ml/min		
Magnesium				
Mg	0.65	mmol/L	(0.70–1.03)	Abnormal
Bicarbonate				
Bicarbonate	23	mmol/L	(24–33)	Abnormal

These results demonstrate that a moderate level of hypertension in pregnancy can have a wide-ranging impact on a variety of biochemical clinical markers. The systolic pressure reading at 28 weeks (of above 160mmHg) is concerning, and would indicate a worsening condition. This was the rationale for commencement of labetalol (200mg three times a day) as antihypertensive treatment.

Treatment

There was no indication from the antenatal care record that Lily had received prophylactic aspirin 75mg. This was contrary to the recommendation that if at least two moderate risk factors are present, or at least one high risk factor for pre-eclampsia, women should be advised to take 75mg aspirin per day from 12 weeks' gestation until birth (Askie *et al.* 2007, NCCWCH 2010). The rationale for this is the alterations in the balance of thromboxane and prostacyclin, along with platelet activation and endothelial dysfunction in pre-eclampsia (Redman *et al.* 1999). The benefit this may have offered would have been a reduction in blood viscosity, with some possible lowering of blood pressure. Other treatment instigated for continuing antenatal care was in accordance with Table 8.5 (see page 134), with plans for discharge home if labetalol had the desired effect of lowering blood pressure – in the absence of any other signs of worsening disease.

Required care in labour

The timing of delivery will be an interprofessional decision to maximise maternal and foetal well-being. As a multigravida, Lily may be able to have a planned vaginal delivery though her previous Caesarean section will be taken into consideration.

If epidural analgesia is used, the woman should not be preloaded with fluids prior to commencement, and fluid replacement should be at 80ml/hour unless compensation for other fluid loss is required.

Intramuscular oxytocin (Syntocinon), not syntometrine, should be the routine drug for active management of the third stage of labour in hypertensive women (MacDonald *et al.* 2004).

Postnatal care

While associated with altered placentation, pre-eclampsia and eclampsia can still present in the postnatal period. Women who have experienced raised blood pressure in pregnancy should have their blood pressure measured regularly until 10 days following delivery and follow-up at 6–8 weeks (NCCWCH 2010).

Risk of recurrence of hypertensive disorders of pregnancy

For women who have had gestational hypertension:

- Risk of gestational hypertension in a future pregnancy ranges from about 1 in 6 (16%) pregnancies to about 1 in 2 (47%) pregnancies
- Risk of pre-eclampsia in a future pregnancy ranges from 1 in 50 (2%) to about 1 in 14 (7%) pregnancies

143

For women who have had pre-eclampsia:

- Risk of gestational hypertension in a future pregnancy ranges from about 1 in 8 (13%) pregnancies to about 1 in 2 (53%) pregnancies
- Risk of pre-eclampsia in a future pregnancy is up to about 1 in 6 (16%) pregnancies
- Risk of pre-eclampsia in a future pregnancy is about 1 in 4 (25%) pregnancies if their pre-eclampsia was complicated by severe pre-eclampsia, HELLP syndrome or eclampsia and led to birth before 34 weeks, and about 1 in 2 (55%) pregnancies if it led to birth before 28 weeks (NCCWCH 2010)

Pre-conception care to reduce the risk of raised blood pressure in pregnancy

Women who are at increased risk of raised blood pressure should be advised to seek pre-pregnancy care from their GP. Women with chronic hypertension who take angiotensin-converting enzyme (ACE) inhibitors or angiotensin II receptor blockers (ARBs) should receive pre-pregnancy counselling on the increased risk of congenital abnormalities if these drugs are taken during pregnancy. The health professional responsible for managing their hypertension should switch them to other antihypertensive treatment (NCCWCH 2010).

The task of prevention and reducing the risk of raised blood pressure in pregnancy is complicated by the lack of precise aetiology. Pre-pregnancy advice may be beneficial for all women and in particular those with existing hypertension. In women with a body mass index over $35kg/m^2$, weight reduction and regular exercise may help to reduce the fourfold increase in risk of pre-eclampsia (Duckitt & Harrington 2005). The role of maternal diet has received increased attention recently in a quest to understand the aetiology of pre- eclampsia. Studies on nutrients such as antioxidants, fatty acids and calcium and magnesium remain limited, which means that dietary advice to reduce raised blood pressure lacks an evidence base (Xu et al. 2009).

Predicting and improving outcomes for women who develop pre-eclampsia (with its associated maternal and perinatal morbidity) continues to be problematic. Screening methods utilising placental biomarkers (placental growth factor) are likely to improve diagnosis but currently lack satisfactory sensitivity and specificity for widespread use (Lewis 2011). Early recognition and instigation of increased surveillance and treatment of raised blood pressure in pregnancy remain vital, and continued vigilance in clinical examination by healthcare practitioners remains the primary means of achieving these ends.

References

Action on Pre-Eclampsia [APEC] (2004). *Pre-Eclampsia Community Guideline (PRECOG guideline).* London: APEC. Available at: http://action-on-pre-eclampsia.org.uk/wp-content/uploads/2012/07/PRECOG-Community-Guideline.pdf (Accessed 27/2/2017).

Askie, L.M., Duley, L. & Henderson-Smart, D.J. (2007). Antiplatelet agents for prevention of pre-eclampsia: a meta-analysis of individual patient data. *Lancet.* **369** (9575), 1791–98.

Beevers, G., Lip, G.Y.H. & O'Brien, E. (2001). ABC of hypertension blood pressure measurement, Part I – Sphygmomanometry: factors common to all techniques. *British Medical Journal.* **322**, 981–85.

Centre for Maternal and Child Enquiries [CMACE] & Lewis, G. (2011). Saving mothers' lives: Reviewing maternal deaths to make motherhood safer 2006–2008 The eighth report of the Confidential Enquiries into Maternal Deaths in the United Kingdom. *BJOG: An International Journal of Obstetrics & Gynaecology.* **118** (1), 1–203.

Cnossen, J.S. & Vollebregt, K.C. (2008). Accuracy of mean arterial pressure and blood pressure measurements in predicting pre-eclampsia: systematic review and meta-analysis. *British Medical Journal.* **336** (1117), 8–120.

Duckitt, G. & Harrington, D. (2005). Risk factors for pre-eclampsia at antenatal booking: Systematic review of controlled studies. *British Medical Journal.* **330** (7491), 565–71.

Knight, M., Tuffnell, D., Kenyon, S., Shakespeare, J., Gray, R. & Kurinczuk, J.J. (eds) on behalf of MBRRACE-UK (2015). *Saving Lives, Improving Mothers' Care – Surveillance of maternal deaths in the UK 2011–13 and lessons learned to inform maternity care from the UK and Ireland Confidential Enquiries into Maternal Deaths and Morbidity 2009–13.* Oxford: National Perinatal Epidemiology Unit, University of Oxford.

Leslie, K., Thilaganathan, B. & Papageorghiou, A. (2011). Early prediction and prevention of pre-eclampsia. *Best Practice in Clinical Obstetrics and Gynaecology.* **25**, 343–54.

Lewis, J. (2011). Placental biomarkers can help the clinical management of pre-eclampsia. *British Journal of Midwifery.* **19** (11), 738–41.

McDonald, S.J., Abbott, J.N. & Higgins, S.P. (2004). Prophylactic ergometrine-oxytocin versus oxytocin for the third stage of labour. Cochrane Database Syst Rev 2004; Issue 1: CD000201.

National Collaborating Centre for Women's and Children's Health [NCCWCH] (2010). *Hypertension in Pregnancy: The Management of Hypertensive Disorders During Pregnancy.* National Institute for Health and Clinical Excellence Guideline 107. London: RCOG, August 2010. Available at: http://guidance.nice.org.uk/CG107/ (Accessed 23/6/2016).

National Institute for Health and Clinical Excellence [NICE] (2008). *Antenatal Care Guideline.* London: National Institute for Health and Clinical Excellence.

Available at: https://www.nice.org.uk/guidance/cg62 (Accessed 27/2/2017).

Nicoll, A. (2009). Pregnancy-induced hypertension, pre-eclampsia and eclampsia. In Magowan, B., Owen, P. & Drife, J. (eds) *Clinical Obstetrics and Gynaecology.* Edinburgh: Elsevier.

Nursing and Midwifery Council [NMC] (2015). *The Code: Professional Standards of Practice and Behaviour for Nurses and Midwives.* London: NMC.

O'Brien, E. & Fitzgerald, D. (1994). The history of blood pressure measurement. *Journal of Human Hypertension.* **8**, 73–84.

O'Brien, E., Asmar, R., Beilin, L., Imai, Y., Mallion, J-M., Mancia, G., Mengden, T., Myers, M., Padfield, P., Palatini, P., Parat, G., Pickering, T., Redon, J., Staessen, J., Stergiou, G. & Verdecchia, P. (2003). European Society of Hypertension recommendations for conventional, ambulatory and home blood pressure measurement. *Journal of Hypertension.* **21** (5), 821–48.

Patton, G.C., Coffey, C., Sawyer, S.M., Viner, R.M., Haller, D.M., Bose, K., Vos, T., Ferguson, J. & Mathers, C.D. (2009). Global patterns of mortality in young people: a systematic analysis of population health data. *Lancet.* **374**, 881–92.

Rankin, S.H., Stallings, K.D. & London, F. (2005). *Patient Education in Health and Illness.* London: Lippincott, Williams and Wilkins.

Redman, C., Sacks, G. & Sargent, I. (1999). Pre-eclampsia: an excessive inflammatory response. *American Journal of Obstetrics and Gynaecology.* **180** (2), 499–506.

Sarris, I., Bewley, S. & Agnihotri, S. (eds) (2009). *Training in Obstetrics and Gynaecology: The Essential Curriculum.* Oxford: Oxford University Press.

Stevenson, M. & Billington, M. (2007). 'Hypertensive disorders and the critically ill woman' in M. Billington & M. Stevenson (eds) *Critical Care in Childbearing for Midwives.* Oxford: Blackwell.

Walker, J. (2000). Pre-eclampsia. *Lancet.* **356** (9237), 1260–65.

Wylie, L. (2005). *Essential Anatomy and Physiology in Maternity Care.* Edinburgh: Elsevier.

Xu, H., Shatenstein, B., Lou, Z-C, Wei, S. & Fraser, W. (2009). Role of nutrition in the risk of pre-eclampsia. *Nutrition Reviews.* **67** (11), 639–57.

Yerby, C. (2010). 'Cardiac and hypertensive disorders' in D. Stables & J. Rankin (eds) *Physiology in Childbearing.* Edinburgh: Elsevier.

Chapter 9

Mental health assessment

Helen Rees and Dr Gareth Rees

Introduction

Mental illness costs the economy approximately £105 billion per year and reduces life expectancy by an average of 20 years (an impact similar to that of smoking) (Department of Health 2011). Mental illness is the greatest cause of disability in the United Kingdom; and mental health symptoms are also common and affect people of all ages, ethnicities and cultures. In the 2007 Adult Psychiatric Morbidity Survey, 23% of adults admitted to experiencing symptoms of mental illness within the last week, providing the often quoted statistic that 1 in 4 adults experience a mental disorder (National Centre for Social Research 2007). As healthcare workers, you will therefore inevitably meet people who have experienced, or are currently experiencing, symptoms of psychiatric illness.

The distinction between physical and mental health assessment is ultimately an arbitrary one; not only are people with mental health problems at increased risk of poor physical health but people with physical health problems are also more likely to develop a psychiatric illness. This is reflected in the title of the government's mental health strategy document 'No Health without Mental Health', which calls for so-called parity of esteem between mental and physical health and an end to the stigmatisation and healthcare inequalities that have long dogged those experiencing psychiatric illness (Department of Health 2011). It is therefore essential that healthcare professionals from all disciplines can competently assess people with mental health problems; indeed there is a growing body of evidence that the prognosis for people with mental health problems can be improved dramatically by offering them timely assessments and guiding them towards appropriate evidence-based interventions (Department of Health 2011). This chapter will outline a structured approach to the assessment of people with mental disorders, using case studies where necessary to highlight key learning points.

Setting the scene

Mental health assessment is a two-way process that can be influenced by a variety of internal and external factors. The following issues should therefore be borne in mind when conducting an assessment of an individual's mental wellbeing.

Safety

The most important consideration in any assessment of mental or physical health is your personal safety. Whilst most people with mental health problems pose no risk to others, it must be remembered that anyone experiencing severe emotional distress (such as confusion, fear or anxiety) may present in an agitated and unpredictable manner. It is therefore essential to collect information about risk before initiating contact with the person. It may be possible to ameliorate some of these risks by assessing somebody with a colleague and/or the police; however, if you are unable to guarantee your own safety then nobody will criticise you for not completing the assessment. In such a situation, you should document the reasons for this and escalate your concerns to a more senior member of staff.

When deciding whether it is safe to conduct an assessment, make sure that you also spend some time scanning the environment for anything that could be used to cause harm. You are also strongly advised to position yourself nearest to the door so that you can leave the assessment quickly if the risk of you being harmed escalates.

Environment

The assessment environment is important because if the person being assessed doesn't feel safe, cared about, and listened to, they are unlikely to divulge important or private information (which may be essential to understanding the nature of their difficulties). If possible, try to conduct mental health assessments in a quiet, well-lit room that is free of any obvious distractions. Tell your colleagues where you will be and put any mobile phones/pagers on silent in order to avoid any unnecessary interruptions. Avoid unnaturally prolonged eye contact (which some individuals may find confrontational or aggressive) by arranging the seating in the room so that the individual and assessor sit at a 90-degree angle to each other (Egan 2013).

On commencing the assessment, you should introduce yourself, your role and the purpose of the assessment; it is also important to carry some form of identification and make sure it is clearly visible. Try to be calm, empathetic and understanding so that the person you are assessing feels relaxed and comfortable; evidence suggests that undergoing a mental health assessment is a stressful experience for many (National Collaboration Centre for Mental Health 2012). If someone is experiencing acute distress, their ability to engage in a mental health assessment may be greatly reduced; in these instances, it is advisable to reduce the length of assessment (if possible) or rearrange the assessment for a more appropriate time.

Supporters

People with mental health concerns are often accompanied by supporters, such as friends, family members or advocates who wish to be present during the assessment itself. In such cases, it is important to gain consent from the individual being assessed to confirm that they are happy for the supporter to be present. If the person is unable to give this consent (for instance, because they are acutely unwell and lack the mental capacity to make this decision), the assessor should decide whether the supporter being present is in the person's best interests. Even if a supporter is permitted to stay, you should routinely ask to talk to the person being assessed privately for a short period afterwards; this gives the individual an opportunity to discuss matters which they feel unable to discuss with anyone else present. It is also good practice to document who is present during any mental health assessment (including supporters and other professionals).

Communication

Therapeutic communication is founded upon empathy, the use of open and non-threatening body language, appropriate eye contact, using a range of open and closed questions, and active listening (Egan 2013). Normalising statements (such as stating that mental health problems are common and affect people indiscriminately) may help to reassure somebody who is anxious or apprehensive about being assessed. You should also emphasise that your intention is to explore their mental health concerns so that you can help them and that, although some of your questions may be quite personal, there is no requirement for them to answer anything that they feel uncomfortable discussing. Remember that, as with other forms of healthcare assessment, you must keep the person's information confidential – unless you believe that maintaining confidentiality will be putting somebody at risk of significant harm; it is important that everyone in the assessment is aware of this.

Cultural considerations

Culture is multifactorial and includes the language, values, customs and beliefs associated with specific ethnic, religious or social groups. Differences in culture are therefore likely to affect how somebody understands their mental wellbeing and/or attributes their symptoms. For instance, some religions may believe that those who experience auditory hallucinations are hearing the word of God. Dismissing or ignoring someone's cultural beliefs, particularly their illness attributions, is likely to negatively affect the therapeutic alliance and will make people less likely to see your assessment as appropriate or useful to them. Assessors should therefore be respectful of other people's cultures and, where possible, help them to understand their difficulties in a cultural context; talking to a person's family or friends is often a useful way of determining whether certain beliefs or behaviours expressed during an assessment are in keeping with that person's culture.

Assessors should also ensure that their own culture and beliefs do not adversely affect the assessment process. In particular, beware of making assumptions about people based on stereotypes. For example, one of the factors suggested by investigations into the over-representation of Afro-Caribbean males within British psychiatric intensive care inpatient units is the covert misperception that, when acutely unwell, such men are particularly dangerous and cannot be safely managed within less restrictive settings (Prins *et al.* 1993).

Box 9.1: Case study 1

Isaac is an 11-year-old schoolboy who attends your clinic (with his father), complaining of red, painful and cracked skin on both his hands. Isaac states that this has got a lot worse since he started secondary school earlier this year. Isaac's father reports that his son has stopped playing football with his friends and seems to be washing his hands up to thirty times a day. During the interview, Isaac stares at the floor and says very little; his father quickly responds to any questions on his behalf.

- Think about the how the environment may affect the mental health assessment.

- How might you try to gain more information about Isaac's symptoms?

- What could you do to encourage Isaac to be more involved in the assessment? How would you give him the opportunity to speak to you alone?

The mental health history

History taking is a core component of every medical assessment; when done well, it not only provides practitioners with sufficient information to make accurate diagnoses, but can also be the foundation of a therapeutic alliance. In mental health, good history taking involves a systematic clinical enquiry into a person's emotional, psychological and social wellbeing. The mental health history (see Box 9.2) is very similar in format to the general medical history outlined in Chapter 1 of this book. There are, however, some subtle but important differences and these are discussed below.

Box 9.2: The mental health history

- Presenting complaint(s)
- History of presenting complaint(s)
- Past psychiatric history
- Past medical/surgical history
- Drug history
- Family history
- Personal history
- Social history
- Drug and alcohol history
- Forensic history
- Pre-morbid personality

History of presenting complaint(s)

In addition to describing the features of a person's mental health symptoms, it is important to document how these symptoms affect the person's quality of life and/or level of functioning. This is not only an important way of determining the severity of somebody's symptoms but also gives an indication of the kind of holistic interventions that might be required to support them in their recovery. To do this, it may be useful to ask the individual to describe their 'normal day' and how this has been affected by their symptoms. For instance, is the person still able to get out of bed, dress themselves, prepare food and so on? Make sure you also take a holistic view of the different areas of life that may be affected by mental health problems, such as employment, relationships, leisure activities and sex life.

Past psychiatric history

When people present with mental health symptoms, it is important to have an understanding of their past psychiatric history. This should include asking about any previous contact with mental health services, diagnoses and past/current treatments (both pharmacological and psychological). It is also useful to know whether those who have been admitted for psychiatric care accepted treatment voluntarily or were detained under the provisions of the Mental Health Act 1983 (amended 2007).

Drug history

It is important to make a list of all the medications a person is taking (including both prescribed medications and over-the-counter remedies), their concordance with these treatments, and whether or not they are experiencing any unpleasant side effects. Even though you are conducting a mental health assessment, make sure that you also document any physical health medications they may be taking. Drug-induced psychosis, for example, is a well-recognised phenomenon associated with many routinely prescribed treatments (see Box 9.3).

Box 9.3: Prescribed medications associated with drug-induced psychosis

- Corticosteroids (e.g. Prednisolone)
- Antihistamines (e.g. Promethazine)
- Anticonvulsants (e.g. Phenytoin)
- Anticholinergics (e.g. Atropine)
- Dopaminergics (e.g. L-dopa)
- Fluoroquinolone antibiotics (e.g. Ciprofloxacin)
- Stimulants (e.g. Dexamphetamine)
- Anaesthetics (e.g. Ketamine)
- Benzodiazepines (e.g. Diazepam)

Family history

There appears to be a genetic component to many mental disorders. For example, when both parents of a child have a diagnosis of schizophrenia, the child's risk of developing the condition later is increased by approximately 40% (Cardno *et al.* 1999). It is therefore important to ask people with mental health concerns whether they have a family history of psychiatric illness. This may also be an appropriate time in the mental health history to ask people about the composition of their family, the quality of their relationships and any other forms of social support.

Personal history

The stress vulnerability model proposed by Zubin and Spring (1977) suggests that mental illness is the product of both biological vulnerabilities and stressful life events. It is therefore important that any assessment of mental health takes into account the stressful experiences a person has experienced during their life so far, such as childhood abuse, bullying, relationship breakdowns and bereavement (Turvey *et al.* 1999). This can be achieved by discussing a person's life chronologically, identifying and enquiring about salient life events along the way.

Forensic history

Although individuals with mental health problems are more likely to be victims of crime than perpetrators of crime (Hughes *et al.* 2012), it is important to ask people about their forensic history in order to formulate an assessment of the safety risk they present to others.

Pre-morbid personality

Only by having an appreciation of somebody's pre-morbid personality can healthcare professionals understand the impact and extent of their mental health symptoms. It is therefore essential to ask people what they were like before their symptoms started; this could include asking about their relationships, character, leisure interests, aspirations, fears, belief systems, etc. When people are acutely unwell, they may struggle to answer questions about their pre-morbid state; in these situations, collateral history (from friends, family and colleagues) becomes extremely valuable.

Collateral history

Although the clinical interview provides a significant amount of information about the person you are assessing, you should also take into account any other sources of information available to you. This so-called 'collateral history' is a useful way of corroborating the person's mental health history and highlighting new information that may not have already been disclosed. Possible sources of collateral history include GP/hospital records, family and friends, the emergency services and secondary mental health services.

Asking difficult questions

In order to fully understand the context of somebody's mental health problems it may be important to explore some very private aspects of their lives. People are more likely to volunteer sensitive information about themselves if they feel safe, comfortable and satisfied that their information will be kept confidential. However, asking personal questions is difficult and feelings of uneasiness, embarrassment and a desire not to offend can prevent assessors from being able to ask people about sensitive topics. The following advice applies to asking difficult questions in general, with specific examples listed afterwards.

General advice

- Asking about difficult topics routinely, rather than selectively, avoids the risk of missing information because of stereotypes and/or not wishing to offend people from specific cultures and religions. For instance, if you routinely ask everybody whether they drink alcohol then you are less likely to miss out on identifying people who you might assume were abstinent (such as those of the Muslim faith). Incorporating difficult questions into the routine assessment also allows assessors to introduce sensitive topics of conversation more easily and reduces the likelihood of causing offence – for example, when asking an elderly person whether they use illicit drugs.

- Try to ask open questions as much as you can, rather than questions that invite a yes/no answer. These give the person being assessed the opportunity to provide information on their own terms and in a way that makes sense to them.

- Beware of asking leading questions, which invite a particular answer or response. Leading questions may in fact expose your own negative feelings of unease regarding a subject and will make the person less likely to respond in a truthful or helpful manner – for instance, 'You don't want to kill yourself though, do you?'

- Normalising statements are useful because they let the person you are assessing know that they are not alone in having certain experiences. This makes it easier and more acceptable for that person to make a disclosure. Making a normalising statement doesn't mean that you are colluding with the person; it simply indicates that you are open to discussing difficult topics further. For instance, you might say 'When people feel very depressed they quite commonly experience feelings of not wanting to be alive; is this something you can relate to?'

Asking about childhood abuse

Sadly, a significant proportion of people who experience severe and enduring mental illnesses as adults have also been victims of abuse in childhood. Abuse can take many forms but is usually categorised as either physical, sexual, emotional or neglect (NICE 2009). Do not collude with abuse by ignoring, dismissing or minimising anything that is disclosed; instead acknowledge that by disclosing abuse the person has undertaken something extremely difficult. It may be helpful to ask how old they were when the abuse took place, the identity of the perpetrator and whether that person was ever brought to justice. If you are worried that the perpetrator of child abuse may still have contact with children, this is a safeguarding issue and you must act accordingly (see 'Safeguarding', page 163).

Suggested questions may include:

- **What were the best and worst bits of your childhood?**
- **Did you have a good relationship with your parents when you were growing up?**
- **When you were a child, did anyone ever do something sexual that made you feel uncomfortable?**

Relationship abuse

Relationship abuse is associated with several mental health problems including depression, post-traumatic stress disorder and suicide attempts (Golding 1999). The National Institute for Health and Clinical Excellence therefore recommends that assessors routinely ask people about this form of abuse (NICE 2014). In order to maintain the person's safety, it is important that this discussion takes place in private. This is because individuals may be at risk of further harm if perpetrators think that they have disclosed something to a healthcare professional, and the individual may also be prevented from accessing health services in the future. It is not advisable to encourage individuals to leave abusive relationships without the support of wider agencies, as this is often when they are most at risk.

Suggested questions may include:

- **Do you feel safe in your relationship at the moment?**
- **You mentioned that you and your partner are arguing a lot – have you ever threatened or hurt each other?**

Suicidal ideation and self-harm

Suicidal ideation is generally linked to depression but is also associated with adverse life events, such as bereavement, divorce, bullying, alcohol or substance misuse and several other mental health conditions. It is important to remember that most people who experience suicidal thoughts do not act on them; there is also good evidence that asking somebody whether they have thought about ending their life does not make completed suicide any more likely (Gelder 2000). If you are worried that somebody is at significant risk of suicide, it is important to escalate your concerns and document your assessment carefully.

Suggested questions may include:

- **Have you ever felt that life is no longer worth living?**

Self-harm is an umbrella term for a wide range of practices, including cutting, burning, hair pulling, scratching, punching and swallowing poisonous substances, and it affects as many as 1 in 12 young people in the United Kingdom (Moran et al. 2012). Many people who self-harm do so because they feel it helps them to cope with mental health problems and provides them with temporary relief from emotional distress; it is less commonly associated with the intention of ending life. Assessors should also ask about the pattern of self-harming behaviours; consider seeking additional support if somebody presents with increased frequency, increased secrecy, increased desperation, using life-threatening methods, cutting arteries or muscles, etc.

Box 9.4: Case study 2

Benjamin is a 60-year-old retired teacher who lives by himself. You are asked to see him, to dress a wound on his leg which he sustained after falling down the stairs last week. Whilst you are there, you notice that his house is untidy and that he is wearing the same clothes he was wearing last week. When you ask him about this, he reports feeling miserable and unmotivated to clean the house. On his coffee table, you notice a half-drunk bottle of vodka and three unopened boxes of Citalopram.

- How would you ask Benjamin about suicidal ideation in a way that conveys empathy and a non-judgemental attitude?
- What impact is Benjamin's mental state having on his activities of daily living?
- How can you find out about Benjamin's pre-morbid personality?

Mental state examination

Like the physical examinations conducted in other healthcare specialties, the mental state examination is a structured framework for collecting objective observations about an individual's presenting complaints (see Box 9.5). The mental state examination can be performed by any practitioner and can be done anytime, anywhere and without any special equipment. Also, unlike the physical examinations described elsewhere in this book, the mental state examination is not performed separately from history taking but, rather, as an ongoing process which starts the moment the assessment begins. Assessors can therefore still conduct a mental state examination on somebody who is unwilling to engage in any other form of mental health assessment – for instance, a person who believes the assessor is involved in a conspiracy against them and refuses to answer any questions.

Box 9.5: The mental state examination

- Appearance
- Behaviour
- Speech
- Mood
- Thoughts
- Perception
- Cognition
- Insight

Appearance and behaviour

From the moment you meet somebody presenting with a mental health problem you can start making observations about their appearance and behaviour. What is this person's physical appearance? Are they under- or over-weight? Do they look their stated age? Are they dressed appropriately for the time of day/year? Do they have distinguishing features, such as piercings, tattoos or deformities? Are they clean, or does it look as if they are neglecting their personal hygiene? Do you see any evidence of possible self-harm, such as lacerations, burns or scarring? When making observations about somebody's appearance, it is also essential to consider what is considered 'normal' for somebody of the same age, culture and educational background and to keep comments objective and evidence based.

In terms of behaviour, try to describe what you see the person doing. Are they co-operating with the assessment process? Are they able to sit calmly or are they anxious, agitated, distracted or tearful? Are they hyperactive, slow or fidgety? Are they able to hold normal eye contact or are they staring or looking at the floor or looking around the room? Do they seem to be responding to hallucinations, e.g. talking to themselves or reacting to unseen objects?

Speech

When assessing speech, you should take into account both the content and form of what the person is saying. In terms of content, is the person able to engage in coherent conversation? Are they preoccupied by any particular subjects or themes? Do they answer the questions you have asked or change the subject to something completely different? Are they using any unusual or made-up words? (These are called neologisms and are sometimes used by people experiencing psychosis.) In terms of the form of their speech, pay attention to the rate, rhythm, tone and volume of their conversation. For instance, somebody experiencing a manic episode may present with 'pressured speech' – this is a tendency to speak in a rapid, loud and unrelenting manner, which the assessor may find difficult to follow or interrupt.

Mood

Every mental state examination should include both a subjective and objective assessment of mood. Subjective mood refers to the person's evaluation of their own emotional state, which can be assessed using a simple rating scale, e.g. asking them to give their mood a score from 0 (the lowest their mood has ever been) to 10 (the best their mood has ever been). It may also be useful to ask people if they are feeling hopeful about the future – somebody with a very low mood may struggle to think about the future, whereas somebody experiencing a manic episode may suggest lots of plans that seem unlikely to come to fruition.

When assessing mood objectively, it is essential to pay attention to the person's facial expression, posture and activity levels. You may also wish to comment on their appetite, sleeping, motivation, concentration and libido, which can all be affected by mood disturbance. You should also pay attention to any other emotions expressed, which may include anxiety, guilt, fear and suspiciousness, for example. People experiencing psychosis may even present with an absence of emotion (described as 'blunted affect') or incongruous mood (e.g. laughing and smiling when talking about something most people would feel sad about, such as a recent bereavement).

When assessing somebody's mood, you should always ask about suicidal ideation and thoughts of self-harm. If an individual *does* disclose thoughts about harming themselves, you should document this clearly and, where necessary, escalate your concerns to a more senior member of staff.

Thoughts and perceptions

Gaining information about somebody else's thoughts can be difficult but it's an important part of the mental state examination. Firstly, consider the form of the person's thought processes. For instance, are they making sense or changing from one subject to another? Do they report having too many or too few thoughts? Do they feel in control of their own thinking (sometimes people with psychosis may believe that their thoughts are being broadcast to others or being added/taken away from their minds by an external force)?

Next, consider the content of somebody's thoughts and whether their thinking is congruent with the rest of their presentation. Somebody with depression, for example, is more likely to express negative or pessimistic thought content, such as 'I am no good at anything' or 'I would be better off dead'. If somebody reports experiencing repetitive or intrusive thoughts, this may suggest obsessive compulsive disorder (OCD), post-traumatic stress disorder (PTSD) or an autistic spectrum disorder (ASD). You may find that people experiencing psychosis express delusions; these are false, fixed beliefs (outside the person's cultural or educational background), held despite superior evidence to the contrary (e.g. 'I know the pregnancy test was negative but I am sure that I am going to give birth to a fox').

Perceptual disturbances may involve any of the body's senses, such as sight, hearing, taste, touch or smell. The most common type of perceptual abnormality you are likely to see are hallucinations; this is where somebody has a sensory experience without there being any obvious external stimulus, such as hearing somebody's voice when nobody else is around. These experiences can be very distressing for individuals and may influence other areas of the mental state examination. (For instance, somebody who is seeing ghosts passing through the walls of the assessment room may struggle to concentrate on your questions about mood.) Remember that perceptual abnormalities are not always necessarily pathological – hypnogogic hallucinations (i.e. transient sensory events) experienced during the transition between waking and sleep (such as hearing a voice calling your name) are in fact commonly experienced by people who have no underlying mental health problems.

Cognition

Cognition can be defined as the process of knowing; it is a broad term that encompasses various functions of the brain. Firstly, consider the conscious level of the person you are assessing: are they alert, or are they struggling to remain awake long enough to answer your questions? Are they orientated in time, place and person, i.e. do they know what time of day it is, where they are and who they are? Cognition also involves intellectual level and memory – is the person you are assessing able to understand your questions? Are they able to recollect recent events with clarity? Impaired cognition may indicate that somebody is experiencing dementia and/or an acute confusional state (delirium). If you have concerns about somebody's cognition you may wish to assess this further, using one of the many standardised screening tools available: the Cognitive Impairment Test (6-CIT) consists of only six questions and takes approximately 5 minutes to complete (Brooke & Bullock 1999).

Insight

In terms of the mental state examination, insight refers to somebody's ability to recognise that they are mentally unwell. This may become apparent very quickly, early in the assessment, or may take a more subtle form. When people with mental health problems lose insight, it can be very difficult to manage them in community settings because they are unlikely to see the need to attend planned outpatient appointments or take prescribed medications consistently. This will ultimately affect their prognosis.

Box 9.6: Case study 3

Maria is 30 years old and unemployed. She was brought to hospital at 2am after being found in the middle of the road by a local taxi driver; she told the taxi driver that she felt unsafe and was being monitored by the government. When you ask to talk to Maria, she becomes visibly agitated and starts shouting loudly that the government will not break her. She will not engage with you any further and states that there is nothing wrong with her and she wants to go home.

Maria is wearing a hoodie, which she frequently pulls over her face so that she is unable to see you. She sits with her arms folded and repeatedly taps her right foot on the floor during the assessment. You can hear Maria mumbling but cannot understand what she is saying because her speech is so fast; at times you observe her laughing for no apparent reason. One of the nurses in the hospital tells you that Maria has a history of self-harm and was detained under the Mental Health Act 1983 (amended 2007) last year.

- **Write a mental state examination for Maria, based on the information available in the case study.**
- **Think about what questions you might want to ask the taxi driver who brought Maria to hospital.**
- **What additional information would you want to know about Maria's past psychiatric history?**

Risk assessment and safeguarding

People experiencing mental health problems are often exposed to a variety of different risks, such as suicide, self-harm, violence, exploitation and neglect. Evaluating these risks involves balancing various risk and protective factors to estimate the likelihood of an event taking place. Like mental state examination, risk assessment is an information-gathering exercise which should take place throughout the mental health assessment. Whilst risk is not fixed and cannot be completely eliminated, adopting an objective approach to risk assessment is an important way of safeguarding people with mental health problems. If you are worried that the person you are assessing is at immediate risk of harm, you have a responsibility to escalate these concerns immediately.

Risk of completed suicide

Evidence suggests that over 25% of people who end their lives access mental health services in the year preceding their death (Centre for Mental Health and Safety 2015); asking about suicidal ideation should therefore be a routine part of every mental health assessment. However, just because somebody discloses suicidal thoughts does not automatically mean they are at high risk of completed suicide. As previously mentioned, most people experiencing suicidal ideation do not attempt to end their own lives.

Individuals at higher risk of suicide tend to have attempted to end their lives previously (Gelder *et al.* 2000). You should also be more concerned about people who are unable to distract themselves from these thoughts or who have expressed a definite intent to act on them by planning their suicide or engaging in final acts, such as writing a suicide note, making a will or stockpiling medication. Try to determine whether the person you are assessing has access to the means of ending their life: this is why doctors, dentists and farmers have a higher incidence of suicide (Roberts *et al.* 2013).

Also, be aware of individuals who express generalised guilt, feeling hopeless about the future, or newfound motivation following a period of pervasive low mood. Most mental illnesses are associated with an increased risk of suicide; people with schizophrenia, for example, are at least ten times more likely to end their own lives compared to the general population (Dutta *et al.* 2010). There are also certain demographic factors that might make somebody more likely to act on suicidal ideation, including male gender, older age, unemployment, homelessness, harmful use of alcohol/illicit drugs, low socioeconomic group and lack of emotional support (Mental Health Foundation 2015).

When determining somebody's suicide risk, it is also important to take into account their protective factors. Protective factors include anything that reduces risk or gives the individual strength, such as engaging with health services, keeping regular appointments, the presence of good coping strategies and supportive relationships. Supporting individuals to strengthen their protective factors can be a useful way of keeping them safe.

Self-harm

As already stated in this chapter, self-harm is common – particularly amongst adolescents and young adults. It is therefore important that you ask about self-harming routinely as part of your assessment. Don't be judgemental about somebody who tells you that they self-harm; this may be their only way of coping with significant psychological distress. Some forms of self-harming put people at greater risk of long-term damage; you should therefore attempt to explore this during your assessment. For people who cut themselves, for example (one of the commonest forms of self-harm), ask how deep they are cutting, whether they are using clean implements, and whether they are avoiding muscle, veins and arteries. There are many reasons why people self-harm; only in a small proportion of cases do people who self-harm wish to bring about their own death.

Aggression and violence

Although individuals with mental health problems are more likely to be victims of violence than perpetrators (Monahan *et al.* 2001), it is important to ask people whether they have a history of aggression in order to determine whether they pose a risk to others. You should also ask people about their forensic history, as convictions for certain offences may give clues to their propensity towards violence, e.g. assault or rape. Other factors that increase a person's risk of harming others include alcohol or illicit drug misuse, paranoia and 'command hallucinations' (for instance, somebody who hears voices telling them to harm others).

Vulnerability and neglect

Certain mental health problems expose individuals to a higher risk of self-neglect. These include depression, young age, physical or intellectual disability. Homelessness and use of alcohol or illicit drugs also make people with mental health problems vulnerable to being abused by others. During your assessment, it is therefore important to look for signs of neglect or abuse: this could include unexpected weight loss, social withdrawal, dishevelled appearance and/or unexplained injuries.

Safeguarding

Safeguarding is the framework for promoting the welfare of children and vulnerable adults and protecting them from unnecessary harm; this is everybody's responsibility, no matter which area of healthcare you work in. Many people with mental health problems are vulnerable due to their symptoms or wider circumstances. If you think somebody may be the victim of abuse, you must document your concerns carefully and refer appropriately to your local safeguarding team.

People with mental health problems can also be perpetrators of abuse. Indeed, psychiatric illness, domestic violence and parental substance misuse form the 'toxic trio' of risk factors identified by a report that looked into the deaths of children due to abuse (Brandon et al. 2010). It is therefore important to routinely ask people whether they have children and/or caring responsibilities (making a note of names and dates of birth) and seek safeguarding advice if they also present with the toxic trio features. If you fear that a child or vulnerable person is at significant risk of harm, you have a statutory duty to report this immediately; infants and children with disabilities are at particularly high risk. Nobody will ever criticise you for raising concerns about the safety of a child or vulnerable person; however, the potential consequences of ignoring such concerns do not bear thinking about.

Physical health and investigations

The beginning of this chapter alluded to the fact that the distinction between mental and physical health is an arbitrary one and has led to people with mental health problems being stigmatised and subjected to a host of healthcare inequalities. There are therefore several valid reasons why the evaluation of somebody's physical wellbeing should be an integral part of every mental health assessment (and vice versa).

Mimickers

Several mental health problems share symptoms with physical health conditions. The conditions listed in Box 9.7, for example, are commonly misdiagnosed as depression because these individuals can present with symptoms of low mood, disturbed sleep, avolition, etc. Acute changes in mental state and/or impaired consciousness may also suggest an underlying physical cause. Individuals presenting with mental health symptoms should therefore undergo some basic investigations as a routine part of the assessment process.

Box 9.7: Physical health mimickers of depression

- Obstructive sleep apnoea
- Hypothyroidism
- Cushing's syndrome
- Addison's disease
- Multiple sclerosis (MS)
- Hyperparathyroidism
- Premenstrual syndrome
- Systemic lupus erythematosus (SLE)
- Cerebrovascular accidents (CVAs)

Somatisation

Somatisation can be defined as the subconscious tendency to experience emotional distress in the form of physical health symptoms. For instance, an individual with a depressive illness may present with headaches, chest pains and limb weakness. People with somatoform disorders are usually convinced that their symptoms have a physical cause and sometimes undergo a series of unnecessary physical investigations before the underlying psychological stress is identified. Somatisation is particularly prevalent among children and young adults and should always be considered when somebody presents with medically unexplained symptoms.

Challenging healthcare inequalities and health promotion

As stated in the introduction to this chapter, people with mental health problems have a significantly lower life expectancy than the general population, with evidence suggesting that most of this excess mortality is associated with physical illness (Vreeland 2007). The reasons for this are likely to be three-fold. Firstly, some psychiatric conditions have been shown to have a direct link to physical illness; for instance, being diagnosed with severe mental illness is an independent risk factor for cardiovascular disease (De Hert et al. 2009). Secondly, many of the medications used to treat mental health problems are also associated with physical ill-health; for example, some antipsychotic drugs are linked to type 2 diabetes mellitus and metabolic syndrome (Hasnain et al. 2010). Thirdly, people with mental health problems have been shown to be more likely to engage in unhealthy lifestyle behaviours, such as smoking, excessive alcohol consumption and poor diet. (Parks et al. 2006).

Health promotion

Every time you conduct a mental health assessment, you should include an evaluation of physical health and a health behaviours discussion. By doing this you will also be in a position to provide health promotion and individualised advice about smoking cessation, exercise, healthy eating, health screening and access to other services, such as dentists and opticians. At the very least, you should record the person's basic physical observations, such as blood pressure and pulse, body mass index (BMI), and alcohol consumption.

Specific mental health assessments

Alcohol and substance misuse

People who present to healthcare professionals with substance misuse problems represent only a small proportion of the people who use alcohol and/or drugs. Alcohol and substance use can therefore be seen as existing on a continuum, from abstinence and recreational use at one end to harmful use and dependence at the other. Since substance misuse remains extremely stigmatised in most cultures, it is important to adopt a non-judgemental attitude towards people who admit to misusing alcohol and/or illicit drugs.

When assessing somebody with a substance or alcohol misuse problem, it is important to determine what they are using (remember that people can become dependent on prescribed and over-the-counter medications as well as illicit drugs), how much they are using, and how often they are using them. Features of dependence include cravings, tolerance (needing to use more of the substance to achieve the same effect), withdrawal symptoms and unsuccessful attempts to reduce.

Several screening tests exist for the assessment of alcohol and substance misuse. The CAGE questionnaire, for example, is a four-point questionnaire designed to identify individuals who may be alcohol dependent (and therefore require further assessment) (Ewing 1984). Physical examination and routine drug testing are also useful ways of determining the extent of a person's alcohol or substance misuse.

It is important to remember that intoxication, and withdrawal from alcohol and/ or illicit drugs, can have an acute impact on somebody's mental state. For instance, cocaine use is associated with euphoria, over-talkativeness, reduced appetite, confusion, paranoia, anxiety and hallucinations. This may make it difficult to complete an accurate assessment of somebody's underlying mental wellbeing.

In the long term, substance misuse also places individuals at increased risk of several psychiatric conditions. For instance, individuals who are alcohol dependent are more likely than the general population to develop major depression (Davidson 1995). Where possible, it is therefore advisable to assess people when they are drug-free.

Eating disorders

It is important to recognise and treat eating disorders early on because they are associated with impaired growth in children and high mortality rates. The two eating disorders most commonly diagnosed in the United Kingdom are anorexia nervosa and bulimia nervosa; both these conditions are driven by an intense preoccupation with food and share many of the same signs and symptoms. To assess somebody who presents with disordered eating, you should therefore enquire about their body image, eating patterns (e.g. restricting calorie intake and/or bingeing), and purging (e.g. induced vomiting and laxative and/or diuretic abuse). Asking somebody what they eat in a typical day/week can also be very enlightening.

Since eating disorders are associated with a large range of physical health complications, it is important to take a detailed medical history. For instance, endocrine problems associated with anorexia nervosa can cause menstrual problems (in women) and erectile dysfunction (in men). Body mass index (BMI) is also used when diagnosing and monitoring adults with anorexia nervosa but is less helpful with other types of eating disorder.

Since early detection and treatment of eating disorders improves prognosis, various assessment tools and screening tests are available for assessors to use. Perhaps the most commonly used screening test is the SCOFF questionnaire, which consists of five questions and re quires no specific training or equipment to complete (Morgan et al. 1999). This questionnaire does not diagnose eating disorders but identifies people who are likely to need a more in-depth assessment.

Dementia

Dementia is an umbrella term for several conditions associated with a global decline in brain functioning. Although the risk of dementia increases with age (affecting 3% of people over the age of 65), it is important to remember that dementia can affect people at any point during their lives (Alzheimer's Society 2014). The form of dementia that is most commonly diagnosed in both the over- and under-65s is Alzheimer's disease (approximately 70% of cases); other forms of dementia include vascular dementia, Lewy body dementia and frontotemporal dementia (Alzheimer's Society 2014).

Assessing people with dementia can be difficult because the condition can present with a varied range of symptoms, depending on which areas of the brain have been affected. Commonly reported symptoms include memory loss, impaired judgement and difficulties using and understanding language. Asking about the chronology of these symptoms can also give an indication of the type of dementia somebody may be suffering from. For example, Alzheimer's disease usually presents as a slow progressive decline in cognitive function, whereas in vascular dementia this deterioration is described as 'step-wise'. It is also important to remember that delirium (an acute confusional state) can present in a similar way to dementia and should be ruled out before a diagnosis of dementia is made.

If you suspect that somebody has dementia, the most commonly used screening tool is the Mini Mental State Examination (MMSE) (Folstein et al. 1975). This 30-point questionnaire takes approximately ten minutes to complete and examines various different areas of cognitive function. You do not need any specific equipment or training to be able to conduct this test and if somebody scores less than 24 marks out of 30 you should consider referring them for a specialist cognitive assessment. Using the MMSE does not replace the need to take a detailed clinical history. As with any mental health problem, you should gain as much collateral history as possible, assess what impact the person's symptoms are having on their ability to function, and ensure safety.

Children and young people

Although many psychiatric disorders start in early life, assessing the mental health of children and young people can be difficult due to the different ways in which young people communicate mental and emotional distress. Assessors should therefore try to utilise varied and creative ways of collecting information about the person's symptoms, such as playing, drawing and observing behaviour.

When conducting a mental health assessment, it is also important to take into account the developmental stage of the child or young person you are assessing. This is particularly significant when diagnosing specific neurodevelopmental disorders such as autism or hyperkinetic disorder. Failure to meet key developmental milestones is a good indication that a child requires a more detailed investigation of their mental and physical health. Taking a detailed developmental history and close liaison with other professionals (such as school nurses and health visitors) are therefore essential aspects of the assessment process.

Uncharacteristic school refusal can be one of the first indicators of mental distress in young people. Asking a child about school can therefore give a useful insight into their level of functioning. You could also try to obtain collateral history about the child's performance at school, peer relationships, and how they do with creative and imaginative tasks. In order to uphold your responsibility to keep children safe, it is also important to ask children and young people about abuse and bullying (including cyber-bullying). As highlighted earlier in this chapter, self-harming is becoming increasingly common among young people and so asking about this should also be a routine part of your assessment.

Intellectual disability

Intellectual disabilities (previously known as learning disabilities or mental retardation) affect approximately 20 per 1000 people in the United Kingdom. These are neurodevelopmental disorders characterised by an impairment of intellect (defined as an IQ less than 70) and adaptive functioning (Learning Disabilities Observatory 2013). They can be sub-classified as mild (IQ 50–69), moderate (IQ 35–49), severe (IQ 20–34) and profound (IQ <20) (World Health Organisation 1992).

Although 30 to 50% of people with intellectual disabilities will experience co-morbid mental health problems (a higher proportion than the general population) (Smiley 2005), assessing the mental health of people with intellectual disabilities can be challenging. Firstly, it is important to be mindful of the language you use to ask questions: use short sentences where possible and avoid asking leading questions or using metaphors and/or jargon. Also, remember that some people will need longer to respond to your questions or additional support to share their symptoms. For those people who are unable to communicate verbally, you should pay attention to the non-verbal ways in which people express their distress (i.e. through their behaviour). Where possible, make sure that you assess somebody with an intellectual disability in a calm and non-threatening environment; healthcare settings can be busy and loud, which may make some people with intellectual disabilities feel anxious, agitated or vulnerable.

Conclusion

Regardless of which area of healthcare you work in, you will see people with mental health problems. This chapter is therefore not meant to be prescriptive. Instead, it provides you with a basic framework for assessing somebody experiencing emotional distress. Only by treating these people with dignity and respect can the healthcare profession begin to address the longstanding stigma and health inequalities faced by those with mental health problems.

References

Alzheimer's Society (2014). *Dementia UK Update.* London: Alzheimer's Society.

Brandon, M., Bailey, S. & Belderson, P. (2010). *Building on the learning from serious case reviews: a two-year analysis of child protection database notifications 2007–2009.* University of East Anglia: Department for Education.

Brooke, P. & Bullock, R. (1999). Validation of a 6 item cognitive impairment test with a view to primary care usage. *International Journal of Geriatric Psychiatry.* **14** (11), 936–40.

Cardno, A.G., Marshall, E.J., Coid, B., Macdonald, A.M., Ribchester, T.R., Davies, N.J., Venturi, P., Jones, L.A., Lewis, S.W., Sham, P.C., Gottesman, I.I., Farmer, A.E., McGuffin, P., Reveley, A.M. & Murray, R.M. (1999). Heritability estimates for psychotic disorders: the Maudsley twin psychosis series. *Archives of General Psychiatry.* **56** (2), 162–65.

Centre for Mental Health and Safety (2015). *National confidential enquiry into suicide and homicide by people with mental illness.* Manchester: Centre for Mental Health and Safety.

Davidson, K.M. (1995). Diagnosis of depression in alcohol dependence: changes in prevalence with drinking status. *British Journal of Psychiatry.* **166**, 199–204.

De Hert, M., Dekker, J.M., Wood, D., Kahl, K.G., Holt, R.I. & Moller, H.J. (2009). Cardiovascular disease and diabetes in people with severe mental illness. Position statement from the European Psychiatric Association (EPA), supported by the European Association for the Study of Diabetes (EASD) and the European Society of Cardiology (ESC). *European Psychiatry.* **24**, 412–24.

Department for Health (2011). *No Health without Mental Health: A Cross Government Mental Health Strategy for People of All Ages.* London: The Stationery Office.

Dutta, R., Murray, R.M., Hotopf, M., Allardyce, J., Jones, P.B. & Boydell, J. (2010). Reassessing the long-term risk of suicide after a first episode of psychosis. *Archives of General Psychiatry.* **67** (12), 1230–37.

Egan, G. (2013). *The Skilled Helper. A problem-management and opportunity development approach to helping.* 10th edn. California: Brooks Cole.

Ewing, J.A. (1984). Detecting Alcoholism. The CAGE Questionnaire. *Journal of the American Medical Association.* **252** (14), 1905–907.

Folstein, M.F., Folstein, S.E. & McHugh, P.R. (1975). Mini-mental state: a practical method for grading the cognitive state of patients for the clinician. *Journal of Psychiatric Research.* **12** (3), 189–98.

Gelder, M., López-Ibor, J. & Andreasen, N. (2000). *New Oxford Textbook of Psychiatry.* Oxford: Oxford University Press.

Golding, J.M. (1999). Intimate partner violence as a risk factor for mental disorders: a meta-analysis. *Journal of Family Violence.* **14**, 99–132.

Hasnain, M., Fredrickson, S.K. & Vieweg, W.V.R. (2010). Metabolic syndrome associated with schizophrenia and atypical antipsychotics. *Current Diabetes Reports.* **10**, 209–216.

Hughes, K., Bellis, M.A., Jones, L., Wood, S., Bates, G., Eckley, L., McCoy, E., Mikton, C., Shakespeare, T. & Officer, A. (2012). Prevalence and risk of violence against adults with disabilities: a systematic review and meta-analysis of observation studies. *The Lancet.* **379** (9826), 1621–29.

Learning Disabilities Observatory: Royal College of General Practitioners: Royal College of Psychiatrists (2013). *Improving the Health and Wellbeing of People with Learning Disabilities: An Evidence-Based Commissioning Guide for Clinical Commissioning Groups (CCGs).* London: Learning Disability Observatories.

Mental Health Foundation (2015). *Fundamental Facts About Mental Health.* London: Mental Health Foundation.

Monahan, J., Steadman, H.J., Silver, E., Appelbaum, P.S., Robbins, P.C., Mulvey, E.P., Roth, L.H., Grisso, T. & Banks, S. (2001). *Rethinking risk assessment: the MacArthur study of mental disorder and violence.* New York: Oxford University Press.

Moran, P., Coffey, C., Romaniuk, H., Olsson, C., Borschmann, R., Carlin, J.B. & Patton, G.C. (2012). The natural history of self-harm from adolescence to young adulthood: a population-based cohort study. *The Lancet.* **379** (9812), 236–43.

Morgan, J.F., Reid, F. & Lacey, J.H. (1999). The SCOFF questionnaire: assessment of a new screening tool for eating disorders. *The British Medical Journal.* **319**, 1467.

National Centre for Social Research and the Department of Health Sciences, University of Leicester (2007). *Adult psychiatric morbidity in England, 2007. Results of a household survey.* London: The Health & Social Care Information Centre.

National Collaboration Centre for Mental Health (2012). *Service User experience in Adult Mental Health. NICE guidelines on improving experience of care for people using adult mental health.* London: Royal College of Psychiatrists and the British Psychological Society.

National Institute for Health and Care Excellence (2007). *Public health toolkit 6: behaviour change at population, community and individual level.* London: NICE.

National Institute for Health and Care Excellence (2009). *Child maltreatment: when to suspect maltreatment in under-18s.* London: NICE.

National Institute for Health and Care Excellence (2011). *Service user experience in adult mental health: improving the experience of care for people using adult NHS mental health services.* London: NICE.

National Institute for Health and Care Excellence (2014). *Domestic violence and abuse: how services can respond effectively.* https://www.nice.org.uk/advice/lgb20/chapter/introduction (Accessed 28/2/2016).

Parks, J., Svendsen, D. & Singer, P. (eds) (2006). *Morbidity and mortality in people with serious mental illness.* Alexandria: National Association of State Mental Health Program Directors (NASMHPD).

Prins, H., Blacker-Holst, T., Francis, E. & Keitch, I. (1993). *Report of the committee of inquiry into the death in Broadmoor Hospital of Orville Blackwood and a review of the deaths of two other Afro-Caribbean patients. Big, Black and Dangerous?* London: Special Hospitals Service Authority.

Read, J., Hammersley, P. & Rudegeair, T. (2007). Why, when and how to ask about childhood abuse. *Advances in Psychiatric Treatment.* **13** (2), 101–10.

Roberts, S.E., Jaremin, B. & Lloyd, K. (2013). High-risk occupations for suicide. *Psychological Medicine.* **43** (6), 1231–40.

Roper, N., Logan, W.W. & Tierney, A.J. (2000). *The Roper-Logan-Tierney model of nursing: based on activities of living.* London: Churchill Livingstone.

Royal College of Psychiatrists (2010). *No health without public mental health: the case for action.* London: The Royal College of Psychiatrists.

Smiley, E. (2005). Epidemiology of mental health problems in adults with learning disabilities: an update. *Advances in Psychiatric Treatment.* **11**, 214–22.

Turvey, C.L., Carney, C., Arndt, S., Wallace, R.B. & Herzog, R. (1999). Conjugal loss and syndromal depression in a sample of elders aged 70 years or older. *American Journal of Psychiatry.* **156** (10), 1596–1601.

Vreeland, B. (2007). Treatment decisions in major mental illness: weighing the outcomes. *Journal of Clinical Psychiatry.* **68** (12), 5–11.

World Health Organisation (1992). *ICD-10 Classifications of Mental and Behavioural Disorder: Clinical Descriptions and Diagnostic Guidelines.* Geneva: World Health Organisation.

World Health Organisation (2000). *Preventing suicide: a resource for general physicians.* Geneva: WHO.

Zubin, J. & Spring, B. (1977). Vulnerability: a new view on schizophrenia. *Journal of Abnormal Psychology.* **86**, 103–26.

Chapter 10

Perioperative assessment

Hannah Abbott

Perioperative care is a complex speciality that involves a number of different professional groups delivering care in different clinical settings throughout the perioperative journey. The complexity of the procedures undertaken, and the variety of patient factors, results in a number of potential risks to the patient. Nevertheless, the risk of death or major complications is low and this can be attributed to advances in surgical and patient care (NCEPOD 2011). Patient assessment prior to surgery and anaesthesia is a vital component in identifying potential risks as a precursor to devising appropriate management plans. However, to optimise patient outcomes, it is also essential that patients are assessed throughout their perioperative journey. This chapter will explore perioperative assessment for patients undergoing elective surgery under general anaesthesia.

Pre-operative preparation

Prior to admission

The pre-operative preparation process is designed to assess the patient before surgery and anaesthesia, whilst also providing an opportunity for pre-optimisation and health promotion as appropriate. This process was previously termed 'pre-assessment'. However, the new title more accurately reflects the scope of the process and acknowledges the holistic nature of patient preparation. Pre-operative preparation may be conducted in a designated assessment unit or in the day surgery unit for day cases. Wherever it takes place, it is important that the patient is comfortable and is afforded privacy so that they feel able to discuss any concerns they may have.

Pre-operative preparation processes are usually informed by local policy and specific screening tools that enable healthcare professionals to assess the patient and identify any specific pre-operative investigations or preparations that may be needed. The screening tools also aid in the identification of more complex cases, which require a detailed anaesthetic assessment prior to admission, or when collaboration with other specialist services in the hospital is required. These screening tools will enable the practitioner to carry out a detailed pre-operative assessment, which will include past medical history, previous surgery and anaesthesia, baseline observations and current medications. The assessment will also indicate when pre-operative testing is required.

The pre-operative preparation process is also an opportunity for health promotion as part of the Making Every Contact Count initiative, which aims to use every opportunity to improve health and wellbeing. This is designed to focus on proactive prevention and the wider determinants of health. Practitioners should therefore use pre-operative preparation appointments as an opportunity to provide brief advice that will help improve the patient's overall health and wellbeing (NHS 2014).

Part of the pre-operative preparation process is consideration of the risk of venous thromboembolism (VTE). VTE is a blood clot that forms in a vein; this is typically in the deep veins of the legs, known as a deep vein thrombosis (DVT). Three general factors are considered to contribute to the risk of VTE:

- **Venous stasis**
- **Damage to the vessel wall**
- **Hypercoagulability**

Perioperative patients are immobile for the duration of their procedure and in the early stages of their recovery so the venous stasis factor applies to all patients. The other two factors are considered in further detail upon admission. Pre-operative preparation presents an opportunity to educate the patient regarding VTE and to initiate any pre-operative measures that may reduce their risk, such as cessation of oestrogen-containing oral contraceptives or hormone replacement therapy four weeks before elective surgery. Educating the patient regarding the importance of mobilisation (where possible), the rationale for graduated compression stockings and the importance of hydration, for example, may enable them to reduce their risk post-operatively (NICE 2010), especially if they are going to be discharged soon after the procedure and will complete their recovery at home.

The importance of temperature maintenance is also explained to the patient as part of pre-operative preparation, and they should be advised to bring appropriate clothing to hospital with them, such as a dressing gown and slippers (NICE 2008).

Box 10.1: Case study 1

Karl was a 45-year-old patient presenting for an elective circumcision. Circumcision had been identified as being a suitable day case procedure so a suitably trained member of the multi-disciplinary team assessed his suitability as a day case. Assessment for day cases considers three key elements: the surgical procedure, medical factors and social considerations.

The procedure had already been deemed suitable for day surgery and so the clinical assessment proceeded.

Medical factors: Karl's overall general health was good. He undertook gentle exercise on a regular basis and did not have any co-morbidities. Karl had a BMI of 36.7. However, obesity is no longer considered a sole contra-indication for day surgery, as the pre-operative assessment should consider the patient's overall health (Verma *et al.* 2011).

Social considerations: It is usual for a patient's social circumstances to be assessed using a local hospital tool, which will generally include the suitability of the patient's home in the immediate post-operative period and the provision of support for the patient. The practitioner undertaking the pre-assessment had to confirm that Karl had an adult who was willing to accompany him home and, as he was having a general anaesthetic, he also required an adult to spend the first 24 hours with him (Verma *et al.* 2011). Karl lives in a modern house approximately 4 miles from the hospital and his partner was going to be with him after the procedure and therefore there were no specific social contra-indications to a day surgery procedure.

Upon admission

Upon admission, all perioperative patients will have baseline observations completed and recorded. Some patients may also have detailed manual handling or pressure area care assessments completed as required and in accordance with any local policy.

All perioperative patients should be assessed for their risk of VTE upon admission. This assessment comprises:

- **The risk factors attributed to the surgical procedure**
- **The patient-specific risk factors**

These risk factors are shown in Table 10.1 below.

Table 10.1: Risk factors for VTE *(Adapted from NICE 2010)*

Procedure risk factors	Patient-specific risk factors
• Total anaesthetic and surgical time >90 minutes. • For procedures involving the pelvis or lower limb, a total anaesthetic time of >60 minutes. • Anticipated significant reduction in mobility. • Acute surgical admission with inflammatory/intra-abdominal condition.	• Over 60 years of age • Obesity (BMI >30) • Taking oestrogen-containing contraceptives. • Taking hormone replacement therapy. • Known thrombophilias. • Dehydration. • Patient history/family history (first degree relative) of VTE. • Varicose veins with phlebitis. • Cancer or undergoing treatment for cancer. • Significant medical co-morbidities. • Admission to critical care unit.

Perioperative patients are considered at risk of VTE if they fulfil any one of the procedure risk factors or one or more of the patient-specific risk factors (NICE 2010). Once the patient's risk has been assessed, suitable methods of VTE prophylaxis will be selected. Perioperative patients are typically fitted with anti-embolism stockings upon admission. It is essential that these are sized correctly for the patient and used according to the manufacturer's instructions, with particular regard to any contra-indications. Intermittent pneumatic compression devices are also used frequently for perioperative patients; however, these are generally applied in theatre. Pharmacological VTE prophylaxis may also be considered, but the patient must be assessed for risk of bleeding. This assessment should be repeated if the clinical situation changes, or within 24 hours after admission, to ensure that methods of VTE prophylaxis remain appropriate.

Patients should also be assessed for the risk of inadvertent perioperative hypothermia. They are considered at increased risk if any two of the criteria in Box 10.2 (below) apply. In the hour before transfer to theatre, it is important that the patient's temperature is taken and recorded. If this is below 36.0°C, active warming should commence via a forced air warmer and the patient should not be transferred to theatre until their temperature is a minimum of 36.0°C, unless clinical urgency dictates otherwise (NICE 2008).

Box 10.2: Risk factors for inadvertent perioperative hypothermia

- ASA grade 2–5.
- Pre-operative temperature <36.0°C where pre-operative warming is not possible.
- Combined general and regional anaesthesia.
- Intermediate or major surgery.
- Risk of cardiovascular complications

(Adapted from NICE 2008)

Anaesthetic assessment

Anaesthetic assessment is an essential component of the perioperative assessment process and patients should be admitted with sufficient time to allow the anaesthetist to conduct a full pre-operative assessment. This must include all the elements identified in Box 10.3 (below).

Box 10.3: Essential components of anaesthetic pre-operative assessment

- Confirm patient's identity.
- Review case notes and interview patient regarding past medical and anaesthetic history.
- Carry out physical examination including airway assessment.
- Review results of pre-operative investigations and consider any additional tests required.

- Consider risk factors and how to manage them.
- Discuss anaesthetic technique.
- Explain pre-operative fasting, intended pain relief and any risks.
- Confirm the patient's understanding of the procedure and gain consent.
- Record discussions in anaesthetic record.
- Prescribe any pre-medication required.

(Adapted from RCoA 2016)

The anaesthetic assessment will include a detailed review of the presenting condition, the surgical urgency and the patient's medical history. The patient will be asked about their medical history with particular emphasis on the respiratory and cardiovascular system. The gastrointestinal system is also pertinent with regard to anaesthesia, as it is important to determine whether the patient experiences reflux or has a hiatus hernia. The patient's anaesthetic history and previous anaesthetic records are assessed with a particular focus on any complications experienced. The healthcare professional needs to determine the exact nature of the complications reported by the patient, as some minor complications may concern the patient but not necessarily affect the delivery of the anaesthetic.

The patient's family history will also be assessed, with regard to any hereditary conditions. This is particularly important if the patient has not had a previous anaesthetic, as malignant hyperthermia is a life-threatening hereditary condition that is triggered by volatile anaesthetic agents or suxamethonium. An assessment of the patient's medication history must consider all concurrent medication and any potential interactions with anaesthetic agents. The impact of withdrawing existing medications must also be assessed. It is important to determine whether the patient has any drug allergies and the exact nature of any reported reactions; any allergies to foods, adhesives or latex also need to be assessed. In addition to assessing the patient's current prescribed medication, any other drug use (including alcohol consumption and smoking) must also be assessed.

Following an assessment of the patient's medical condition, pre-operative investigations may be required. The investigations needed will depend on the clinical assessment and the surgical procedure. The NICE (2016) guidelines make recommendations for preoperative testing prior to elective surgery. However, any tests carried out should be based on assessment of the patient, rather than simply employing routine pre-operative testing (Verma *et al.* 2011).

Following clinical assessment, it is possible to assign an ASA grade (see Table 10.2, below) to the patient. This is a description of their physical state, and is used as a prospective assessment tool that has been shown to correlate with the risks of anaesthesia. However, this tool only considers physical health with regard to systemic disease and therefore does not take into account additional factors that may affect anaesthetic risk – for example, the potential for difficult airway, or the complexity of the surgical procedure.

Table 10.2: ASA Grading *(Adapted from American Society of Anesthesiologists 2013)*

ASA Grade	Definition
1	Healthy patient
2	A patient who has a mild systemic disease
3	A patient who has a severe systemic disease
4	A patient who has a severe systemic disease which is a constant threat to life
5	A patient who is near death and is not expected to survive without the surgery
6	A patient who has been pronounced brain-dead and who is undergoing organ retrieval

Physical assessment

A physical assessment is undertaken routinely as part of the anaesthetic assessment. This will generally concentrate on airway assessment, although anatomy for regional anaesthesia will also be examined as appropriate.

Assessment of the airway is crucial in order to anticipate and prepare for difficult airways. All patients should therefore undergo a comprehensive airway assessment, which is documented as part of the anaesthetic record. However, this assessment cannot anticipate *all* potential complications so it is crucial that the team discuss any potential difficulties and how they will be managed, including ensuring that emergency equipment is located and checked (Frerk et al. 2015). An initial visual assessment of the patient can yield important information, which may suggest a more difficult airway – for example, obesity, short neck or receding jaw. In addition, numerous bedside assessments should be undertaken with the intention of predicting a difficult airway.

The Mallampati assessment is a simple grading system that is routinely employed in pre-operative airway assessment, as it grades the amount of space available in the mouth for laryngoscopy and intubation. The assessment is performed with the patient sitting with their head in the neutral position. The patient is asked to open their mouth as widely as possible and protrude their tongue. The Mallampati score is then determined, based on the observed structures (see Table 10.3, below).

Although the Mallampati assessment should be undertaken with the patient sitting, this is not always possible due to the patient's clinical presentation and it may therefore be necessary to undertake this assessment with the patient lying supine. It has been shown that this change in posture results in a significant difference in Mallampati grade, with higher Mallampati grades when the patient is in supine position. A slight decrease in mouth opening has also been observed in the supine position, although this was not of sufficient magnitude to be considered clinically relevant (Singhal *et al.* 2009).

Table 10.3: Mallampati classification *(Adapted from AnaesthesiaUK 2010)*

Mallampati classification	Structures visible
Class 1	Soft palate, fauces, uvula and pillars
Class 2	Soft palate, fauces and some of the uvula
Class 3	Soft palate and bottom of the uvula
Class 4	Hard palate

The inter-incisor gap assessment may be undertaken at the same time as the Mallampati. The patient is asked to open their mouth to its maximum extent. The distance between the upper and lower incisors is then measured, using a ruler or fingerbreadths. As adequate mouth opening is important for the establishment of the airway, a measurement of less than 3cm (or two fingerbreadths) is considered indicative of a difficult airway (Ong & Pearce 2011). When undertaking an inter-incisor gap and Mallampati assessment for a patient with trauma to the face or jaw (such as a fractured mandible), it should be remembered that the patient's mouth opening may be limited by pain and the opening may therefore increase following induction of anaesthesia. Nevertheless, to ensure patient safety, preparation for the establishment of the airway should be based upon the actual assessment.

Head and neck extension is essential in the safe establishment of the airway and this assessment is therefore important in assessing the patient's range of neck movement. The patient is asked to fully extend their head and neck (this is the start position); they are then asked to flex their neck fully (the finish position). The assessor then estimates the angle through which they have moved. This is graded as: above, below or equal to 90°. Less than 90° is considered indicative of difficult intubation (Ong & Pearce 2011).

An assessment of thyromental distance (TMD) is conducted to predict the measurement of the TMD prior to laryngoscopy and intubation. During laryngoscopy, the tongue is displaced into the thyromental space and so a short TMD indicates that there is reduced space for compression of the tongue, thus impairing visualisation of the glottis and vocal cords. The assessment is performed by asking the patient to fully extend their head and neck and measuring the horizontal distance between the mandible and the thyroid prominence. (The mouth is closed throughout this assessment.) The TMD is measured in centimetres, using a ruler or fingerbreadths. There have been numerous studies suggesting various measurements as predictors of difficult intubation. These predictive measurements generally vary between 6 and 7cm (or three fingerbreadths). A TMD less than this is considered to be an indicator of difficult intubation (Kiser et al. 2011).

In the mandibular protrusion assessment, the patient is asked to protrude the lower jaw. In a normal mandibular protrusion, the lower incisors can be protruded anterior to the upper incisors; difficult intubation is anticipated when the protrusion of the lower incisors either meets the upper or cannot meet the upper incisors. The upper lip bite test (ULBT) also indicates the range of motion of the lower teeth and has been shown to be a 'reasonable predictor' of difficult intubation. The assessment is performed with the patient in the sitting position and they are asked to bite their upper lip with their lower teeth. Class I and II can bite the upper lip, with class I above the vermilion line and class II below. In class III, the lower incisors cannot bite the lip, thus suggesting difficult intubation (Hester et al. 2007).

Assessment of submental space or submental sign (SMS) has been proposed as a qualitative indicator of difficult intubation. This assessment is conducted with the patient in the supine position, with a neutral head position, and the examination is performed during expiration. The normal anatomical submental space is a thin layer of adipose tissue and a deep curve that can be easily compressed to allow palpation of the hyoid bone and laryngeal cartilage. When the submental sign is positive, however, the submental space consists of a tissue mass that is non-compliant, and the hyoid bone cannot be palpated. This positive submental sign is considered indicative of difficult intubation (Javid 2011).

Box 10.4: Case study 2

Gabrielle was a 32-year-old female patient presenting for a laparoscopic cholecystectomy. Gabrielle had a BMI of 23 and was generally fit and well. However, in the assessment of her past medical history she disclosed that she had had extensive surgery following a traffic accident. Upon review of the anaesthetic notes, Gabrielle had a number of orthopaedic procedures immediately following the accident and then faciomaxillary reconstructive surgery a few days later. The anaesthetic for both procedures was uneventful.

As with all patients, the anaesthetist conducted a full airway assessment. While Gabrielle had full neck extension, she had a Mallampati of 3, an inter-incisor gap of 2cm and was unable to protrude her lower incisors to meet the upper.

Gabrielle explained that the limited mandibular mobility was following her reconstructive surgery. However, all these clinical assessments indicated a difficult airway. The anaesthetist was therefore able to develop an anaesthetic plan to safely manage Gabrielle's airway; this was discussed with the designated anaesthetic assistant, a role usually undertaken by an Operating Department Practitioner (ODP). Nurses may also undertake this role following successful completion of post-registration training where they have achieved the competencies stipulated in the College of Operating Department Practitioners (CODP) curriculum or those in NHS Education for Scotland (AAGBI 2012).

Induction

When the patient is received in the operating department, a number of checks will be carried out to confirm their identity, consent for the procedure, any allergies, time of last oral intake of both fluids and solids, and any other procedure-specific details. It is important to confirm that the patient is able to respond to these questions. For example, a patient may have removed their hearing aid prior to theatre or may have left their glasses on the ward and will therefore be unable to read the consent form.

Throughout the anaesthetic preparation, the team should explain all interventions to the patient and seek consent prior to carrying out any intervention. Baseline observations are recorded prior to induction. These will consist of non-invasive blood pressure (NIBP), electrocardiograph (ECG) and oxygen saturation via pulse oximeter. In some cases, such as paediatrics, it may not be possible to apply all these monitoring devices prior to induction. However, pulse oximetry must be applied, as this is considered a key component of safe anaesthetic care. The World Health Organisation (WHO 2009) advises the verbal confirmation of the placement and functionality of the pulse oximeter prior to induction. Prior to induction monitoring of airway gases and airway pressure must be prepared, and these should be monitored throughout.

In accordance with NICE (2008) guidelines, the patient's temperature should be taken, and documented, prior to induction of anaesthesia. In the anaesthetic room, a temporal scanner will typically be used to measure the patient's temperature, as this is generally considered more accurate than a tympanic thermometer, due to consistency of use. It may also be more acceptable to the patient than a tympanic device, as the temporal scanner is non-invasive and works by measuring the heat emitted from the skin over the temporal artery when scanned over the forehead. To ensure that accurate measurements are obtained, the device must be used in accordance with the manufacturer's instructions.

In addition to the physical assessments undertaken prior to induction, it is important to assess the patient's emotional state and to respond accordingly. Surgery (and anaesthesia) is a stressful experience and each patient may respond to this stress in a different way. It is therefore important that the patient is offered support throughout in a manner that is acceptable to them. For example, some patients may find hand holding comforting during induction, while others may find this uncomfortable.

Intra-operative assessment

Throughout surgery and anaesthesia, the patient requires continuous physiological assessment, which is achieved by clinical observation supported by monitoring devices. However, it is important that the patient is actually assessed, rather than simply relying on the monitoring devices available. Clinical assessments include palpation of the pulse, auscultation of breath sounds, pupil size and chest and/or reservoir bag movement. It is essential that the patient is monitored throughout anaesthesia by pulse oximetry, ECG, NIBP, airway pressure and airway gases; a nerve stimulator must also be available when muscle relaxants are used (AAGBI 2015). These monitoring devices support a number of clinical assessments throughout the procedure, including adequacy of ventilation and anaesthetic depth. Some patients may also require continuous assessment via invasive monitoring – for example, arterial blood pressure and/or central venous pressure (CVP). The decision to use invasive monitoring devices will be made based upon the magnitude of the procedure and the assessment of the patient and their physiological status.

When the procedure takes longer than 30 minutes, the patient's temperature must also be monitored (AAGBI 2015) and recorded every 30 minutes throughout (NICE 2008). Depending on the duration and type of procedure, the most appropriate method of temperature monitoring will be selected. Where temperature monitoring is required only every 30 minutes, the temporal scanner should prove a suitable method. For longer cases or more extensive surgery, however, it may be considered necessary to employ continuous assessment of the patient's temperature via an invasive temperature probe. These may be inserted either orally into the lower oesophagus or rectally. Oesophageal temperature monitoring is preferred, as this provides an accurate reflection of core temperature. Rectal temperature is less accurate in surgical patients, where the temperature changes may be relatively fast and therefore due to the time 'lag', rectal temperature does not accurately represent core temperature.

Assessment of consciousness during general anaesthesia is essential to minimise the risk of awareness. This risk is greatest during relaxant anaesthesia when the patient is paralysed, as they are unable to move, and movement is a clear indicator of light anaesthesia. Numerous methods are used to assess depth of anaesthesia, including clinical observations, isolated forearm technique, end-tidal agent monitoring and bispectral index. There are also a number of clinical observations that are used for the same purpose. Autonomic reflex activity (for example, tachycardia and hypertension) are indicators of light anaesthesia and can be assessed as part of the normal anaesthetic monitoring. The PRST score can be used to assess autonomic activity and is the sum of the score from each of the four parameters, which are scored from 0 to 2 (AnaesthesiaUK 2005):

P (systolic blood pressure)
R (heart rate)
S (sweating)
T (tears)

While this is a relatively simple assessment, there is potential for significant variation between different practitioners, which suggests that it is not a reliable system. It is also essential to consider these parameters in the context of the clinical situation (AnaesthesiaUK 2005).

While variations in clinical observations may be associated with depth of anaesthesia, they are not considered to be completely reliable. End-tidal agent monitoring is commonly used in clinical practice to assess anaesthetic depth. This is related to the concept of minimum alveolar concentration (MAC). Anaesthetic monitors calculate MAC from the end-tidal agent (AnaesthesiaUK 2007). However, this is only possible when volatile anaesthetic agents are used and is therefore not suitable in total intravenous anaesthesia (TIVA); hence bispectral index (BIS) monitoring has been recommended for patients receiving TIVA (NICE 2012). It has been suggested that BIS offers a more effective method of assessing depth of anaesthesia and can thus be used to guide anaesthetic drug administration (Punjasawadwong *et al.* 2007). BIS is derived from the electroencephalogram (EEG) and offers a measurement of anaesthetic depth, which is independent of most drugs (Luginbühl *et al.* 2003). While BIS has been suggested as a beneficial addition to perioperative assessment, it has not yet been routinely employed. However, it is recommended where there is a specific risk of awareness or very deep anaesthesia (NICE 2012).

When the patient is paralysed using muscle relaxants, it is also necessary to assess the neuromuscular blockade. This can be assessed by observing for the return of muscle tone, which is typically seen as movement of the face. In addition, return of muscle tone around the wound may be reported by the operating surgeon. Return of muscle tone can also present as an increase in airway pressure or attempts at respiratory effort. Again, these are observed using the routine anaesthetic monitoring. A peripheral nerve stimulator can be used as a quantitative measurement of muscle relaxation; this uses a train-of-four stimulus, and the number of responses is used to assess the degree of neuromuscular blockade.

Good fluid management has been identified as key in improved post-operative patient outcomes so it is essential that fluid balance is monitored throughout. In procedures where suction is used to clear the operative site, the volume of blood in the suction bottle is recorded and added to the intra-operative fluid balance record. The volume of blood in the suction needs to be as accurate as possible, and the volume of irrigation fluid to the surgical site is therefore also recorded and subtracted from the total suction volume. A significant amount of blood may also be lost on the surgical swabs. This is also measured by weighing the wet swabs and subtracting the dry swab weight. Again, any irrigation must be accounted for, to ensure that the measurement is as accurate as possible.

Assessment within the post-anaesthetic care unit (PACU)

Upon arrival in the post-anaesthetic care unit (PACU), the qualified recovery practitioner will receive a patient handover from the anaesthetist and another member of the theatre team as per local policy. This handover will provide information regarding the patient's care in theatre and specific requirements in the immediate post-operative period. It is essential that the patient is monitored by pulse oximetry, ECG and NIBP as a minimum throughout the period of care in PACU; where a patient is intubated or has a supraglottic airway in situ, continuous capnography is also required (AAGBI 2013). A nerve stimulator (for assessment of neuromuscular blockade), difficult airway equipment, and a thermometer and patient warming device must also be available (AAGBI 2013). The patient's temperature should be measured upon arrival, and subsequent measures taken every 15 minutes until the patient is discharged to the ward (NICE 2008).

Patients may be transferred to the recovery room in varied states of consciousness, ranging from alert and orientated to unconscious with an airway in situ. The recovery practitioner will greet the conscious patient upon admission, and this can provide a useful initial assessment of the patient's consciousness and airway patency.

In the PACU, all patients must be monitored on a one-to-one basis until they have regained airway control, cardiovascular stability and the ability to communicate. All patients must also be monitored throughout the post-anaesthetic recovery period and these observations recorded (AAGBI 2013). The recovery practitioner will undertake a comprehensive systematic assessment of the patient using the Airway, Breathing, Circulation, Disability, Exposure (ABCDE) algorithm, communicating interventions throughout:

Airway

Assessment of the post-operative airway is crucial to identify obstruction, which may be attributed to a number of causes, including secretions/blood/gastric aspirate, swelling or oedema. A physical observation of the patient and the airway will alert the practitioner to any deviations from normal that could indicate obstruction – for example, use of accessory muscles when breathing or cyanosis. Airway obstruction may also be characterised by airway sounds such as gurgling when there is fluid in the upper airways, crowing in laryngeal spasm, or inspiratory stridor when obstruction is above the larynx. However, it should be remembered that there is *no sound* in the event of complete airway obstruction.

Patients will frequently be transferred to the PACU with a supraglottic airway in situ and these patients must be cared for by a practitioner who has been trained in the management and removal of these airways (AAGBI 2013). Where a patient is transferred to PACU with an endotracheal tube in situ, it is the anaesthetist's responsibility to remove this. However, this task may be delegated to an appropriately trained practitioner who is willing to accept this responsibility (AAGBI 2013).

Breathing

The recovery practitioner should assess respiratory rate by counting the patient's respirations for a full minute, and any deviations from the normal range must be reported to the anaesthetist. It should be remembered that respiratory rate in post-operative patients may be at the lower end of the normal range due to the intra/post-operative administration of opioid drugs. At the same time as counting the respiration rate, the practitioner should observe the patient for bilateral chest movement, any signs of abdominal breathing or use of accessory muscles; the patient's colour should also be observed for cyanosis.

Circulation

Assessment of circulation and fluid management is an essential component of post-anaesthetic care and has been associated with overall post-operative outcomes. The recovery practitioner should assess and record heart rate and rhythm (AAGBI 2013), and this should include palpation of peripheral pulse for a full minute. A capillary refill time greater than 2 seconds is a sign of poor cardiac output and therefore this assessment should be undertaken; a peripheral measurement of less than 2 seconds may be followed by a central measurement. Measuring peripheral capillary refill time also allows the practitioner to feel the patient's hand, as cool pale extremities are another sign of poor cardiac output.

The recovery practitioner will monitor the patient's fluid balance and maintain an accurate record of this. This will include monitoring the patient's urine output and any losses from wound drains, in addition to any intravenous fluid infusions or blood transfusions.

Disability

Checking the patient's consciousness level is an important element in post-operative assessment. This should be checked and recorded using the AVPU tool, which assesses whether the patient is Alert, responds to Voice, responds to Pain or is Unresponsive. The AVPU tool is simple to use and is not subject to interpretation. However, there may be occasions when a more in-depth neurological assessment is required in the PACU.

Blood sugar level assessment may be required in the PACU, based on individual patient requirements and any local policy. For example, patients with diabetes will always have their blood sugar level assessed.

Pain and emesis are important assessments within the PACU, and no patient should return to the ward until these are controlled (AAGBI 2013). There are numerous tools to support these assessments, which are discussed later in this chapter.

Exposure

The recovery practitioner should conduct a full body exposure assessment of the patient, whilst taking care to maintain the patient's dignity throughout. This is an important post-operative procedure, as it allows assessment of the wound site and dressings, and any drain sites. The wound should be observed for any strikethrough on the dressing or excessive bleeding. Any unexpected bleeding should be reported to the surgeon as a matter of urgency. In some ear, nose and throat (ENT) procedures, there may be no visible dressings so the patient should be observed for signs of bleeding; for example, excessive swallowing following tonsillectomy may indicate bleeding.

This assessment also provides an opportunity to remove any theatre/transfer sheets from underneath the patient. When rolling the patient to remove these sheets, posterior assessment should also allow identification of any pressure areas.

Pain assessment

Assessment of post-operative pain is a key component of patient care within the PACU, as uncontrolled post-operative pain can have adverse physiological and psychological effects. Although perception of pain is subjective, it is important that the level of pain experienced by the individual is assessed and managed appropriately. There are numerous pain assessment tools that can be employed to measure the level of pain experienced, and it is important that the recovery practitioner selects a tool that is suitable for the patient's age and ability.

It is often suggested that asking the patient about their pain may raise their awareness of pain. However, it is essential that the patient has an opportunity to verbalise pain so that the prescribed analgesic regime may be initiated. In addition to assessment scales, physiological measurements can also be used to gauge pain – for example, by taking basic observations. However, where possible, pain needs to be distinguished from other causes of distress, as some of the signs and symptoms may be the same. These pain scales enable practitioners to measure pain as a sole factor.

The verbal pain rating scale uses simple words to describe pain:

- 'No pain'
- 'Mild pain'
- 'Moderate pain'
- 'Severe pain'

This pain rating scale is simple to use and may therefore be well suited for patients in the early phases of recovery from anaesthesia. However, the simplicity of this assessment makes it more difficult to differentiate between small changes in level of pain. These verbal descriptors may be assigned numerical values (0 for no pain and 4 for severe pain) for ease of recording, but it is important that a suitable key is used and that these are not confused with values from the numerical rating scale.

The visual analogue scale (VAS) pain assessment tool consists of a 10cm line, with 'no pain' at one end and 'worst pain ever' at the other end. The patient is asked to point to or mark the line to represent their pain. This can then be measured from the 'no pain' point to give the patient's pain score a numerical value. It is useful to employ this method of translating the point on the scale to a numerical descriptor, as small changes in pain score can then be identified and recorded.

The numerical rating scale is commonly used for patients in the post-operative period, as it is simple to use, whilst also allowing differentiation between changing levels of pain. This assessment is performed verbally by asking the patient to rate their pain between 0 and 10, with 0 being 'no pain' and 10 being 'the worst pain ever'. This scale is easily understood by patients, is quick to use and pain scores can easily be recorded. However, it should be remembered that it may not be suited to all patients.

The Wong-Baker FACES® scale is commonly used for paediatric patients in the PACU, as it provides a visual descriptor of pain. The patient is shown six faces, ranging from a happy face depicting 'no pain' to a sad, crying face depicting 'worst pain'. The patient then points to the face that most closely represents their pain/how they are feeling. To aid recording, these faces are assigned numerical values, with 0 for 'no pain' and 5 for 'worst pain'. This is generally used for paediatric patients, and may also be employed for adults for whom the other scales are not suitable or practical – for example, this scale transcends language barriers.

Assessment of post-operative nausea and vomiting (PONV)

Post-operative nausea and vomiting (PONV) is undesirable, as it is distressing for the patient, presents a risk of aspiration, and delays discharge from the PACU or day surgery unit. Consequently, the risk of PONV should have been assessed pre-operatively, and appropriate anti-emetic therapy administered intra-operatively.

PONV should be assessed by the recovery practitioner as part of routine patient care in the PACU. While vomiting can be easily assessed, it is also important to determine the level of nausea experienced by the patient. This could be simply asking the patient whether they feel nauseous, but this lacks any scale and therefore, as with pain assessment, different scoring systems may be employed. The most commonly used scale is the verbal descriptive scale (VDS), which uses word categories to describe the level of nausea experienced – for example, 'none', 'mild', 'moderate', 'severe'. These categories can then be assigned numerical values for recording. A visual analogue scale has been shown to be a suitable tool for assessment of nausea, with 'no nausea' at one end of the scale and 'unbearable nausea' at the other (Boogaerts *et al.* 2000). Similarly, other scales may be adapted for the assessment of nausea. It is important that it is clear what scale has been used when recording the findings and that the practitioner adheres to any local policy.

Discharge from the PACU

Discharge from the recovery room is the responsibility of the anaesthetist, but this is usually delegated to the qualified recovery practitioner who adheres to strict discharge criteria (AAGBI 2013). The recovery practitioner will assess the patient to determine whether they adequately meet the set discharge criteria. These criteria are set locally. However they will include the following, as defined by AAGBI (2013):

1. The patient is conscious, able to maintain a patent airway and exhibits protective airway reflexes.
2. Acceptable respiration and oxygenation.
3. Cardiovascular stability with pulse and blood pressure approximate to normal values, adequate perfusion and no persistent bleeding.
4. Controlled pain and emesis with appropriate analgesia and anti-emetics prescribed.
5. Temperature within an acceptable range as the hypothermic patient should not be returned to the ward.
6. Appropriate intravenous and oxygen therapy prescribed.
7. All invasive devices, including intravenous cannulae, drains and catheters, should have been checked.
8. All patient documentation should be complete.

Assessment and the perioperative team

The perioperative environment is unique in the sense that a number of different professionals work within this environment to assess, plan and deliver care to the patient. While this chapter has explored the range of perioperative assessments that are routinely undertaken, it is usual for different professionals to undertake different assessments. Consequently, to deliver effective care within the perioperative environment, it is essential that the findings of these assessments are communicated effectively.

The World Health Organisation (WHO) surgical safety checklist was launched in June 2008 as a result of the 'Safer Surgery Saves Lives' initiative, which aimed to address key safety issues, including poor communication within the perioperative team, avoidable surgical site infection and anaesthetic safety. The checklist consists of three phases:

- **Sign in (before induction of anaesthesia)**
- **Time out (before surgical incision)**
- **Sign out (after closure of the wound, before transfer to the PACU)**

These three phases allow the perioperative team to share the outcomes of their clinical assessments and their implications for the patient's care. A subsequent edition of the checklist was produced in 2009 and a sample of this can be found on the WHO website. However, this checklist is frequently adapted to meet local needs and may be incorporated into local hospital documentation (WHO 2009).

'Patient Safety First' then incorporated the WHO Surgical Safety Checklist in their Perioperative Care Intervention, which advocated a five-step approach to patient safety and promoted a team culture (NPSA 2010). The first step is a pre-operative briefing, which is conducted before the commencement of the list and includes all team members. This allows the team to assess the list and identify any potential challenges. It also allows sharing of information resulting from patient assessment, thus ensuring the provision of individualised care. Steps two to four correlate with those identified in the WHO Surgical Safety Checklist; and step five is a post-operative debrief that enables the team to assess the conduct of the list and identify any areas for improvements. However, it is important to recognise that this process will only be effective if the entire perioperative team engages with this and remains in the same theatre for the complete operating list (Abbott & Wordsworth 2016). The team must therefore be aware of changes during the list and ensure that they perform a full handover in the event of changes to the team, or pause to review when there are changes to the list.

The composition of the team itself must also be assessed to ensure that there are sufficient staff with an appropriate skill set to safely deliver care to the perioperative patient. It is a requirement of the National Safety Standards for Invasive Procedures (NatSSIPs) that there is 'an appropriate ratio holding a specific primary or postgraduate practice qualification applicable to the procedural area' (NHS England 2015, page 26) which, in the case of perioperative practice, means staff who hold the pre-registration Operating Department Practice award and/or nurses who have completed a post-graduate perioperative programme. It is recommended that at least one member of the non-medical surgical team must hold a specific qualification in perioperative care (CODP 2015) and this should therefore be considered when allocating staff to a theatre team.

The team must also be able to assess and monitor the non-technical factors that may impact upon their performance and the care of the patient, such as fatigue, stressful situations and poor team working (Abbott & Wordsworth 2016). It is important that individual practitioners can recognise these factors in themselves and also that they are able to recognise them in others and offer support or take action, as appropriate, to ensure the safe delivery of care.

Perioperative documentation

The findings of all assessments and interventions during the perioperative phase should be documented fully and accurately, as this is both a professional responsibility (HCPC 2016, CODP 2009, NMC 2015) and essential for the continuity of care. This is particularly pertinent for the perioperative patient who will be cared for by a range of professionals in different clinical areas and therefore clear, comprehensive documentation will be essential.

Conclusion

This chapter has explored the assessments required for the safe delivery of care for the perioperative patient. A wide range of assessments has been explored, and it should be noted that these will be undertaken by different professionals within the multidisciplinary team. Hence, effective communication between these professionals is essential for safe, effective patient care. While this chapter has focused on the routinely performed anatomical and physiological assessments, it is also vital to carry out on-going assessment of a patient's psychological and emotional needs. The perioperative experience can be extremely stressful so it is essential that each patient receives holistic care that meets their individual needs.

References

Association of Anaesthetists of Great Britain and Ireland (2013) Immediate Post-anaesthesia Recovery 2013. *Anaesthesia.* **68**, 288–97.

Association of Anaesthetists of Great Britain and Ireland (2015). Recommendations for standards of monitoring during anaesthesia and recovery. *Anaesthesia.* **71**, 85–93.

AAGBI (2012). *Statement on assistance for the anaesthetist* (25th September 2012) [online] available from: http://www.aagbi.org/news/latest-news (Accessed 17/02/2013).

Abbott, H. & Wordsworth, S. (2016). 'Introduction to perioperative care' in H. Abbott & S. Wordsworth (eds) *Perioperative Practice Case Book.* London: Open University Press.

AnaesthesiaUK (2005). *Clinical Signs* [online] available from: http://www.frca.co.uk/article.aspx?articleid=100494 (Accessed 8/12/2016).

AnaesthesiaUK (2007). *End-tidal agent monitoring* [online] available from: http://www.frca.co.uk/article.aspx?articleid=100759 (Accessed 8/12/2016).

AnaesthesiaUK (2010). *Assessment of the airway* [online] available from: http://www.frca.co.uk/article.aspx?articleid=257 (Accessed 8/12/2016).

American Society of Anesthesiologists (2013). *ASA Physical Status Classification System* [online] American Society of Anesthesiologists, available from: http://www.asahq.org/For-Members/Clinical-Information/ASA-Physical-Status-Classification-System.aspx (accessed 17/2/2013).

Boogaerts, J.G., Vanacker, E., Seidel, L., Albert, A. & Bardiau, F.M. (2000). Assessment of postoperative nausea using a visual analogue scale. *Acta Anaesthesiologica Scandinavica.* **44**, 420–74.

CODP (2009). *Record Keeping Guidance for Operating Department Practitioners.* London: College of Operating Department Practitioners.

CODP (2015). *Guidance on local implementation of the NHS England National Safety Standards for Invasive Procedures (NatSSIPs) – Workforce Issues* [online] Available from: https://www.unison.org.uk/content/uploads/2014/07/CODP_NatSSIPS_Position_Statement.pdf (Accessed 27/10/2015).

Cox, F. (ed.) (2009). *Perioperative Pain Management.* Oxford: Wiley-Blackwell.

Frerk, C., Mitchell, V.S., McNarry, A.F., Mendonca, C., Bhagrath, R., Patel, A., O'Sullivan, E.P., Woodall, N.M. & Ahmad, I. (2015), Difficult Airway Society 2015 guidelines for management of unanticipated difficult intubation in adults. *British Journal of Anaesthesia.* **115** (6), 827–48.

Hester, C.E., Dietrich, S.A., White, S.W., Secrest, J.A., Lindgren, K.R. & Smith, T. (2007). A comparison of the preoperative airway assessment techniques: the modified Mallampati and the upper lip bite test. *AANA Journal.* **75** (30), 177–82.

HCPC (2016). *Standards of Conduct, Performance and Ethics.* London: Health and Care Professions Council.

Javid, M.J. (2011). Examination of submental space as an alternative method of airway assessment (submental sign). *BMC Research Notes.* **4**, 221.

Kiser, M., Wakim, J.A. & Hill, L. (2011). Accuracy of fingerbreadth measurements for thyromental distance estimates: A brief report. *AANA Journal.* **79** (1), 15–18.

Luginbühl, M., Wüthrich, S., Petersen-Felix, S., Zbinden, A.M. & Schnider, T.W. (2003). Different benefit of bispectral index (BIS™) in desflurane and propofol anesthesia. *Acta Anaesthesiologica Scandinavica.* **47**, 165–73.

McArthur-Rouse, F. & Prosser, S. (eds) (2007). *Assessing and Managing the Acutely Ill Adult Surgical Patient.* Oxford: Blackwell Publishing.

NCEPOD (2011). *Knowing the Risk: A Review of the Peri-operative Care of Surgical Patients.* London: National Confidential Enquiry into Patient Outcome and Death.

NHS (2014). *An Implementation Guide and Toolkit for Making Every Contact Count* [online] Available from: http://www.england.nhs.uk (Accessed 08/12/2016).

NHS England (2015). *National Safety Standards for Invasive Procedures (NatSSIPs)* [online] Available from: https://www.england.nhs.uk/patientsafety/never-events/natssips/ (Accessed 27/10/2015).

NICE (2008). *The Management of Inadvertent Perioperative Hypothermia in Adults.* London: National Institute for Health and Clinical Excellence.

NICE (2010). *Venous Thromboembolism: Reducing the Risk.* London: National Institute for Health and Clinical Excellence.

NICE (2012). *Depth of Anaesthesia Monitors – Bispectral Index (BIS), E-Entropy and Narcotrend-Compact M.* London: National Institute for Health and Clinical Excellence.

NICE (2016). *Routine preoperative tests for elective surgery* [online] Available at: http://www.nice.org.uk/guidance/ng45 (Accessed 8/12/2016).

NMC (2015). *The Code.* London: Nursing and Midwifery Council.

NPSA (2010). *Five Steps to Safer Surgery.* London: National Patient Safety Agency.

Ong, C. & Pearce, A. (2011). Assessment of the airway. In Radford, M., Williamson, A. & Evans, C. (eds.) (2011). *Preoperative Assessment and Perioperative Management.* Keswick: M&K Publishing.

Punjasawadwong, Y., Phongchiewboon, A. & Bunchungmongkol, N. (2007). Bispectral index for improving anaesthetic delivery and postoperative recovery (Review). *Cochrane Database of Systematic Reviews.* Issue 4.

Radford, M., Williamson, A. & Evans, C. (eds.) (2011). *Preoperative Assessment and Perioperative Management.* Keswick: M&K Publishing.

RCoA (2016). Chapter 2, *Guidelines for the Provision of Anaesthesia Services: Guidance on the Provision of Anaesthesia Services for Pre-operative Assessment and Preparation 2016.* London: Royal College of Anaesthetists. [online] Available from: http://www.rcoa.ac.uk (Accessed 8/12/2016).

Singhal, V., Sharma, M., Prabhakar, H., Ali, Z. & Singh, G.P. (2009). Effect of posture on mouth opening and modified Mallampati classification for airway assessment. *Journal of Anaesthesia.* **23**, 463–65.

Verma, R., Alladi, R., Jackson, I., Johnston, I., Kumar, C., Page, R., Smith, I., Stocker, M., Tickner, C., Williams, S. & Young, R. (2011). Day case and short stay surgery: 2. *Anaesthesia.* **66**, 417–34.

WHO (2009). *Implementation Manual Surgical Safety Checklist.* (2nd edition). Geneva, Switzerland: World Health Organisation.

Chapter 11

Eye, ear, nose and throat assessment

Rachael Hosznyak, Esther Hosznyak, Alex Westaway and James Graveson

Introduction

The cranial cavity contains many vital structures, such as the major blood vessels, main sensory organs and cranial nerves, which lead to a variety of minor and major illness presentations. Eye, ear, nose and throat (EENT) conditions are the leading complaint for nearly 300,000 Emergency Department (ED) attendances in the UK annually (Baker 2015) and many more in primary care. This makes it vital for the primary healthcare practitioner to have an applied knowledge of the anatomy and physiology of the cranial cavity and throat, as well as a knowledge of common ENT ailments, presentations and assessment.

This chapter uses a case study (see Box 11.1) to facilitate an exploration of different EENT assessments. The assessment of the ears, eyes, nose and throat is important in its own right. However, as the patient's complaint involves unsteadiness and increased frequency of falling, practitioners need to rule out any potential red flags before continuing with the assessment, as these symptoms could be produced by cardiac or neurological pathologies.

Box 11.1: Case study

Ivy, an 82-year-old woman, has presented at her local healthcare practice complaining of having common cold-like symptoms for the past 10 days. After further questioning, she also states that she has been feeling 'unsteady' lately and has experienced an increased frequency of falling over but is otherwise healthy.

Initial observations

Walked in to the consultation alone and unaided. Appears in good health and has good nutritional status for age. Alert, orientated, appropriately dressed and in good spirits despite feeling unwell. Appears flushed but no obvious jaundice, anaemia, clubbing, cyanosis, oedema or lymphadenopathy.

- Respiratory rate: 18 per minute
- SpO_2: 97% on room air
- Heart rate: 80 beats per minute
- Blood pressure: 130/90 mmHg
- Capillary refill time: <2 seconds
- Tympanic temperature: 37.20C
- Blood sugar: 6.0

Cardiovascular system

Peripheral pulses regular, normal in volume and equal. Heart sounds S1 + S2 = 0, nil murmurs heard. Apex beat 5th intercostal space mid-clavicular line. Nil obvious clinical cardiac signs. Nil pertinent complaints.

Respiratory system

Effective breathing, bilateral rise and fall. Trachea central. Resonant percussion and tactile fremitus equal. Chest sounds normal, clear and nil adventitious sounds noted. Complains of nasal congestion and rhinorrhoea observed but otherwise nil pertinent complaints.

Central nervous system

Alert and orientated. –ve face, arms and speech test. Mini-mental score normal. Cranial nerves 1–12 intact. Complained of dizziness just prior to leaving the house.

Gastrointestinal system

Soft and non-tender abdomen. Unremarkable and nil complaints.

Genitourinary system

Unremarkable and nil complaints.

Musculoskeletal system

BMI 18. Slight kyphosis. Gait normal. Tone and reflexes normal.

After ruling out any potential life-threatening illnesses, it is apparent that the patient (illness aside) is in reasonably good health and the assessment can proceed. When considering the above patient case, there are several cues which indicate that an Eyes, Ears, Nose and Throat (EENT) assessment is now warranted. The patient is complaining of symptoms of a 'common cold', which indicates the assessment of the nose and throat. In addition, the patient has been feeling 'unsteady'. As equilibrium of balance is maintained through a combined input of proprioception, visual and vestibular information, an eyes and ears assessment is also necessary for patients with balance disturbances or those who have fallen, and this is the case for this particular patient.

From the initial presenting complaints, it seems that the patient has two main concerns. One is the generalised, non-descript complaint of 'cold-like' symptoms, and the other is a feeling of unsteadiness and increased frequency of falling. Whilst it is plausible that these may be two separate complaints, the possibility that they are linked should remain in the clinician's mind and each patient should be assessed on an individual basis. On many occasions, clinicians will treat and refer patients for incidental findings rather than the patient's initial presenting complaint.

An EENT history follows a similar structure to the medical model. However, it does not replace the medical model and a general history should be completed for all patients during consultations. With this in mind, a thorough history should be taken during the consultation in order to ensure that the patient's complaint(s) and presentation are fully understood; this will help the practitioner establish the likely cause of the patient's symptoms.

EENT history taking

History taking is a fundamental part of the diagnostic process, underpins the clinician–patient relationship, and is responsible for approximately 70% of all diagnoses. Information obtained during this initial dialogue with the patient will guide which investigations the clinician decides to perform, and will allow the development of potential differential diagnoses. These diagnoses may be included or excluded as the consultation progresses, and this process will directly influence the likelihood of patient compliance with the resulting treatment plan or pathway.

Any structured EENT assessment must include:

- **The history of the presenting complaint**
- **The patient's previous medical and surgical history**
- **The drug history**
- **The social history**
- **The family history.**

This format may be adapted as appropriate to suit the situation, and the experienced clinician may find that this structure flows naturally in conversation with the patient.

The history of the presenting complaint

In some circumstances, it can be difficult to accurately identify the patient's presenting complaint. In such situations, clinicians should be certain that they understand the full picture, revisiting and clarifying if necessary, before moving on to examining the patient. The clinician should try to establish whether the patient's symptoms have occurred simultaneously or not. This can help to decide whether they are linked together or as sequelae from the initial symptom.

Furthermore, additional details about the condition itself should be elicited, including: the main symptoms, their exact nature and duration; simultaneous occurrence or precedence; and order of occurrence. This information may enable the clinician to detect a developing pathology or disease progression or confirm separate pathologies. For instance, common EENT infections may follow the respiratory tract downwards; an initial complaint of earache and headache might progress to a sore throat, productive cough and palpable supraclavicular lymphadenopathy. As a general rule, unilateral symptoms should raise suspicion of a sinister pathology, such as malignancies or tumours, which initially have a unilateral presentation and will require appropriate referral for investigation.

Patients may use a variety of terms to describe a symptom. These terms might be interchangeable to the patient; yet to clinicians a particular term may have a specific medical inference. The clinician may therefore need to question the patient to confirm their intended meaning to build up a more accurate picture. Terms used to describe common cold-like symptoms may include but not be limited to: 'runny nose', 'blocked nose', 'flu' and 'sore' or 'swollen throat'. The clinician will need to differentiate between the term 'flu' (a condition severe enough to require bed rest) and symptoms of the common cold and a feeling of being generally unwell, though still able to carry out activities of daily living (ADLs). As with all consultations, the psychosocial and economic status of the patient will also need to be considered, in the context of potential exacerbating factors and compliance.

Common terms to describe a change in balance (or perception of such) may include but not be limited to: 'unsteadiness', 'vertigo', 'dizziness' and 'feeling faint or light-headed'. These terms may have been specifically chosen by the patient to try to describe their symptoms and differentiate their condition from other similar experiences. Alternatively, they may use terminology that does not specifically determine a differential symptom or cause. For this reason, it is important to start by understanding the true symptom the patient is experiencing – as terms such as 'feeling faint' may be synonymous or used interchangeably with symptoms such as 'general weakness' or 'wooziness', which may have a respiratory, cardiac, neurological or psychophysiological cause (see Table 11.1).

In addition, terminology used by the patient may often be inconsistent with accepted medical terminology. Healthcare practitioners must therefore bear all this in mind during history taking and, where possible, elicit the exact meaning of the descriptor used by the patient to prevent confusion and avoid missing a possible diagnosis or referral.

Table 11.1: Common dizziness descriptors and potential causes

Descriptor	Potential cause/s
'**Vertigo**' (a visualised spinning, tilting or dropping of the environment)	A unilateral or central lesion causing an imbalance in vestibular signals
'**Light-headed**' or '**woozy**'	Blood pressure, metabolic, pharmacological, vestibular, psychophysiological
Near-faint or **presyncope**	Diffuse decreased cerebral blood flow
'**Out of body**' **sensation, floating or spinning internally** (e.g. environment remains static and individual experiences these phenomena)	Psychophysiological

Motion sickness, intolerance or mal debarquement	Sensory conflict, visual-vestibular-proprioceptive mismatch
Gait unsteadiness	Proprioceptive, vestibular, cerebellar or motor function loss

(Adapted from Kerber & Baloh 2011)

Having discussed the history of the presenting complaint with Ivy, it can be determined that she has a sensation of 'light-headedness', which preceded the onset of her pharyngitis, sinusitis and rhinorrhoea by approximately two weeks. This suggests (though does not provide conclusive evidence of) two separate pathologies which require investigation on two fronts: both vestibular and EENT. Blood pressure and CVA may be considered and will probably be excluded, based on history and presentation. Referral for blood tests to exclude further metabolic disorders could also be considered.

The past medical or surgical history

Following general history taking, EENT-specific medical conditions and surgical interventions should be considered, especially those that are relevant to the presenting complaints and any which may affect treatment, compliance, physical fitness or ability to tolerate anaesthesia should the patient require surgical interventions. These may include but not be limited to: previous head injuries, broken nose, recurrent tonsillitis, tonsillectomies, peritonsular abscess, childhood illnesses (such as measles, encephalitis, chicken pox, meningitis and mumps) and congenital abnormalities (such as intrauterine infections, anoxia and gestational diabetes, which may all impact on physical development, sensory cognition or function). Environmental factors, such as compliance with ear protection in noisy environments, toxic exposures and combinations, should also be considered (see heavy metal exposure below).

When dealing with a patient complaining of symptoms affecting their senses, it is important to establish their norm. In other words, what are their vision and hearing and balance normally like? If this examination includes a neurological assessment, which is likely, then what is their sense of smell and taste normally like?

As clinicians, we are aware of many possible causes of deficit in these areas but most of us would agree on what we expect to be the 'norm' when it comes to a fully functioning sensory ability in these areas. However, one individual's 'norm' may not necessarily be the same as someone else's. For instance, 3% of the population has some form of synaesthesia, a rare condition in which their sensory perceptions are blended and they may experience 'tasting words', 'hearing motion' or 'feeling colour'.

The drug history

Pertinent questioning, with direct relevance to the EENT complaint and examination, should include asking about prescribed anticoagulants, as these will affect any surgical management or simple management of epistaxis. You should also ask about other medications that cause otoxicity (damage to the cochlear and auditory nerves and the vestibular system) and any new medications or recent dose changes.

Medications causing ototoxicity

Some common medications are known to cause ototoxicity, with consequences that may be reversible or irreversible. Common antibiotic aminoglycosides (such as gentamicin or tobramycin) may cause irreversible damage and may therefore be counter-medicated with N-acetylcysteine to counter these effects. For instance, Meniere's disease has been treated with gentamicin in some individuals. However, gentamicin stops their episodes of vertigo but causes permanent destruction of the inner ear, resulting in permanent deafness.

Macrolides, such as erythromycin, are associated with reversible ototoxicity. Loop-diuretics (such as furosemide in high doses) may result in hearing loss. Chemotherapy agents containing platinum, such as cisplatin and carboplatin, have been known to cause tinnitus and cochleotoxicity.

Other agents that may cause ototoxicity include non-steroidal anti-inflammatories (NSAIDs) such as high-dose aspirin and other salicylates, medications for erectile dysfunction (such as sildenafil), quinine, and heavy metals such as lead and mercury. A synergistic effect can occur between exposure to loud noise and chemicals such as xylene, styrene or toluene, causing damage to the cochlear hair cells.

New medications or recent dose changes

New or recent changes in medications, such as analgesics, antihypertensives, diabetic medications, diuretics, selective serotonin re-uptake inhibitors (SSRIs), anti-psychotics, anti-epileptics and sedatives, may cause dizziness or increase the risk of falling. These effects may occur through different mechanisms, such as reduced blood pressure, reduced glucose availability, reduced dopamine levels, increased serotonin levels or neuronal impedance, and these possibilities should all be considered when differentiating the likely cause of new onset dizziness.

As with all drug histories, any conversation regarding the presence of allergic or anaphylactic symptoms should be documented, as well as asking about drug compliance. Drug compliance is a vital aspect of any history or diagnosis because healthcare professionals normally assume that the patient is appropriately medicated and their condition is therefore suitably managed. Non-compliance makes this assumption erroneous. Herbal dietary supplements should also be considered, as they are increasingly popular amongst patients. These supplements can either enhance or blockade existing medications.

The social history

The social history gives clues to inherited, pre-existing or contemporaneous exacerbating factors such as:

- Employment
- Home environment
- Alcohol intake and smoking history.

Employment

As noted previously, certain types of employment (such as the manufacture of paints, thinners, solvents, lacquers or products containing petroleum) may expose the patient to risk factors for EENT conditions.

Home environment

The patient's home environment should be discussed or visualised to check for exacerbating and precipitating factors such as oil burners (for sources of carbon monoxide), mould or damp conditions.

Alcohol intake and smoking history

Alcohol intake and smoking history (including previous but now ceased) should be discussed and correctly ascertained, as it provides an insight into the potential deleterious effect on the patient's immune status and upper respiratory tract functionality. Alcohol withdrawal or overuse may result in unsteadiness and declining motor function, and Wernicke's encephalopathy should always be considered in patients who may be misusing alcohol.

The family history

This should again be revisited in relation to EENT-specific conditions, as many (such as glaucoma, migraine and retinitis pigmentosa) can be inherited.

Asking about symptoms

Unsteadiness or falls

Questions you may consider asking regarding unsteadiness or falls include (but are not limited to):

- Are there any associated symptoms?
- Do you feel a sense of motion?
- What is the pattern of onset? Do symptoms occur after head movement?
- How long do the symptoms last?

- Do you have any auditory symptoms (loss of hearing, abnormal or persistent sound)?
- Have you experienced recent head or neck trauma?
- Do you have associated neurological symptoms (such as weakness or loss of muscle tone, or difficulty speaking)?

'Unsteadiness' is a very generalised symptom and can be caused by a variety of factors. We maintain our balance through proprioceptive, visual and vestibular input. Detailed history taking, coupled with a thorough examination, can help us establish which of these factors is causing the patient's symptoms.

Cold-like symptoms

Questions you may consider asking regarding cold-like symptoms include (but are not limited to):

- Can you describe all your symptoms?
- Do you have any pain in your throat or nose?
- Have your symptoms got progressively worse or better?
- Are you producing any sputum? If so, what colour is it?
- Do you feel as though you have a high temperature or a fever?
- How long have these symptoms persisted? (Try to help the patient define quantifiable timeframes for their symptoms, such as 'days/weeks/months' (Bickley 2013).)

Dizziness, unsteadiness or vertigo

In the presence of more ominous symptoms, such as dizziness and increased frequency of falls, it may be possible to overlook a patient reporting that they have a cold or cold-like symptoms. As a common cause of dizziness (and not necessarily true vertigo) is viral illness, further consideration needs to be given to this during an EENT assessment.

Note: Examination of a patient who is experiencing unsteadiness or vertigo-like symptoms should not be limited to the EENT assessment, as there may be a serious underlying cardiac, psychiatric or neurological condition.

Eyes

A loss or change in a person's vision can make them feel unbalanced. Without correct visual input, it is hard for an individual to centre themselves in their physical environment and any visual-vestibular mismatches will worsen this effect.

In this situation, questions should be open-ended to allow the patient to express themselves in their own words and describe their own experience. However, closed questions may then be required to narrow down pertinent timeframes and other aspects. For instance, 'How is your vision?' or 'Have you had any trouble with your eyes?' are useful opening gambits. Confirm with the patient whether they require adjuncts (such as glasses, reading glasses or contact lenses) to correct an already diagnosed defect. All tests should be performed with the appropriate adjunct whenever available.

Further questions may include:

- **Do you have any pain in or around your eyes? Are you experiencing more or less redness, excessive tearing or watering?** These symptoms may be indicative of common conditions such as infective or allergic conjunctivitis, subconjunctival haemorrhage and general corneal injury or infection. However, more sinister pathologies (such as acute iritis or acute angle closure glaucoma) should also be considered, excluded or immediately referred for assessment and management.

- **Is your vision worse during close work or distance?** This will help differentiate hyperopia, presbyopia and myopia.

- **Do you have blurred vision? Has the onset been gradual or acute? Is it acute and unilateral? Is it acute, unilateral, and with or without pain?** A painless acute unilateral visual loss may suggest a diabetic or traumatic vitreous haemorrhage, occlusion of a retinal vein or central retinal artery, macular degeneration or detachment of the retina. Stroke should also be considered as part of any visual loss differential.

Painful causes commonly occur in the anterior chamber and the cornea (for example, corneal ulcers, uveitis, traumatic hyphema, acute glaucoma or an optic neuritis from multiple sclerosis), though giant cell arteritis may also be considered. Independent of diagnosis or cause, an immediate referral is required.

Acute bilateral visual loss

Acute bilateral visual loss is a rare occurrence and may be attributed to medications that alter the eye's ability to process refraction, such as cholinergics, anticholinergics or steroids. However, chemical or radiation exposure should be considered in bilateral painful visual loss. Gradual bilateral visual loss is commonly caused by macular degeneration and cataracts, which may be diagnosed from dilated fundoscopy and referral for further testing such as fluorescein angiography.

Further questions may include:

- **Is the blurring complete or partial?** Consider macular degeneration or nuclear cataracts as a cause of slow central loss and advanced open-angled glaucoma in peripheral loss. Hemianopia and quadrantic effects should be considered in one-sided loss.

- **Are you experiencing any additions to vision or blind spots? Have you noticed 'flashing lights', with or without vitreous floaters?** 'Floaters' are moving specks or strands in the patient's vision, suggestive of vitreous floaters or detachment of vitreous from the retina, which may also be associated with the presence of a 'flashing light' symptom. In contrast, fixed blind spots (scotomas) suggest lesions in the retina itself or the associated visual pathways. Both these symptoms require an immediate eye consultation for investigation and treatment.

- **Any double vision? Does it persist with one eye closed? Which side is affected?** Diplopia may present as horizontal (side by side) or vertical (one on top of the other). Diplopia may be caused by brainstem or cerebellar lesions, weakness or paralysis of the extra-ocular muscles (horizontal diplopia of CN III/VI palsies or vertical diplopia of CN III/IV, consistent with their actions upon the eyeball). A unilateral diplopia which persists with one eye closed is suggestive of corneal or lens pathology. Benign physiologic horizontal diplopia may be discriminated by holding one finger upright, approximately 15cm in front of your face, and a second at arm's length. When focusing on one finger, the other image is doubled. This is a normal physiological presentation and the patient may be reassured.

- **Are there any particular environments, activities, fluorescent lights or patterns that change your vision by appearing to cause movement of objects, patterns or writing or a sense of unsteadiness?** This may lead you to consider Irlen Syndrome, also known as Meares-Irlen Syndrome. Patients with this syndrome experience scotopic sensitivity or visual stress. Although this is not an eye problem (but rather a problem with the way the brain is interpreting the visual data), it may become apparent during questioning in this part of the assessment. There may be similarities with dyslexia and indeed a dual diagnosis. However, unlike dyslexia, this syndrome will affect more than communication and language. Colourimetry or coloured overlays should be considered for dyslexia and an appropriate referral made for this assessment. This assessment may also be considered for migraine patients, as it is thought that pattern glare may cause certain migraines. A similar assessment and colour lens treatment is recommended for Irlen Syndrome patients. However, this differs from colourimetry and a specialist referral will need to be made.

Ears

In Ivy's case (see Box 11.1, page 196), it is possible that the underlying cause for her increased frequency of falls and feeling of unsteadiness is related to her ears. One of the three ways we maintain balance (vestibular input) relies on the semi-circular canals and vestibules of the inner ear, which contains the balance structures of the saccule and utricle. There are a variety of conditions which can affect these balance structures and lead to a sense of unsteadiness known as vertigo. As such, in the dizzy or unbalanced patient, an ear assessment should form part of your examination.

Not all dizziness is caused by vertigo, and you should consider all other possible causes of dizziness within your assessment to ensure that no conditions are overlooked. True vertigo can be defined as an 'illusion' or 'hallucination' of movement and is thought to account for at least 50% of patients complaining of some type of 'dizziness'. Additionally, vertigo may be of peripheral or central origin. Peripheral vertigo is caused by an inner ear problem; whereas central vertigo is caused by a neurological impairment, commonly related to the VIII cranial nerve, where the symptom is caused by a misinterpretation of information. To ensure that no neurological conditions are missed, the cause of the vertigo must first be identified as either central (neurological) or peripheral (vestibular).

To establish the origin of the vertigo, there are several tests that can be utilised. Novice clinicians should consider performing a structured examination, including all these tests, in order to build experience and familiarity with the method of examination and with normal, abnormal and pertinent findings which will allow them to exclude specific tests as experience is developed. The experienced clinician should consider returning to full structured examinations when they have not been exposed to certain tests for some time, have identified a gap in their own knowledge and simply to maintain current best practice. 'Skill fade' is a common issue throughout medical practice and should be addressed annually (or earlier if identified).

Head Impulse or 'head thrust' Test (HIT)

For this test, you will need to ask the patient to look directly at you and focus on an area of your face (usually the nose). You will then need to move the patient's head (not body) quickly to the side and look for correct eye movement. If a corrective saccade (jerky) movement of the eyes is made in order to refocus on the point of reference, then the patient's vertigo probably has an underlying vestibular cause.

Note: The importance of the general history taking, to exclude pertinent 'red flags' (such as recent neck trauma), cannot be over-emphasised here.

Romberg test

For this test, you should ask the patient to stand with their feet together and eyes closed whilst trying to maintain their balance. If the patient cannot maintain their balance with their eyes open, the cause is likely to be central in origin. In contrast, a patient who only loses their balance with their eyes closed is more likely to have a proprioceptive or vestibular underlying cause.

Fukuda-Unterberger test

For this test, you will need to ask the patient to march on the spot, with their eyes closed. Rotation may indicate damage to the labyrinth (inner ear) on the side of the recorded rotation.

Note: If the cause of vertigo is found to be central, complete a neurological assessment or refer as appropriate.

Peripheral vertigo

If the vertigo is found to be of peripheral origin, the next step is to identify the specific cause. Common types of peripheral vertigo include:

- **Viral – vestibular neuronitis and labyrinthitis**
- **Benign paroxysmal positional vertigo (BPPV)**
- **Vertebrobasilar ischaemia**
- **Eustachian tube dysfunction**
- **Meniere's disease.**

Other less common causes originating from the inner ear may include:

- **A build-up of wax**
- **Acoustic neuroma**
- **Otitis media**
- **Vestibular schwannoma.**

You may be able to rule in (or rule out) some of these conditions based on detailed history taking alone.

Mastoiditis

When assessing the patient's ear, you should include a brief examination of the mastoid area for swelling, tenderness and erythema. Patients with a history of mastoid surgery, and a subsequent mastoid cavity, will be prone to dizziness; mastoid assessment is therefore particularly pertinent to Ivy's case (see Box 11.1, page 196). Paediatric patients presenting with mastoiditis must be admitted as an emergency.

BPPV

Benign paroxysmal positional vertigo (BPPV) is the most common cause of vertigo and is caused by calcium carbonate crystals (octonia) within the semi-circular canal of the inner ear. It is particularly common in the older adult patient group. As its prevalence increases as age increases, there is often a significant delay in treating this condition. On average, patients will suffer without effective treatment of BPPV for over 70 months. Patients with untreated BPPV may experience increased falls, loss of confidence in their ability to move safely, muscle wasting and depression, which may lead to strains on the healthcare system.

Before treatment, clinicians will first need to identify that the patient is suffering from BPPV. BPPV elicits symptoms such as dizziness, nystagmus, nausea and vomiting. Patients with BPPV will often describe the onset of symptoms occurring after a change in head position; a typical example is turning over in bed or looking upwards. Studies have shown that a history of episodes of dizziness lasting <15 seconds is an indicator for diagnosing BPPV.

BPPV can also be diagnosed using the Dix-Hallpike manoeuvre. To perform this manoeuvre, you should:

1. Position the patient on a couch in a sitting position, with their legs up and in front of them, and the back of the couch laid flat, ready for the patient to lie flat.

2. The patient should then be guided to lie back flat whilst turning their head 45 degrees towards the suspected affected side. They should now be looking to either the left or right. If no affected side is suspected, the test can be repeated for each side.

3. The clinician should now look for signs of nystagmus. If present, the clinician should reassure the patient and wait for the symptoms to cease before moving the patient.

With a positive finding of nystagmus, a diagnosis of BPPV can be made. If trained to do so, the clinician can continue with treatment using the Epley manoeuvre (of which the Dix-Hallpike is already the first step). If not suitably trained, then a referral for this treatment should be made.

Hearing loss

When taking a history from a patient during an ear examination, your questioning should establish any possible hearing loss. It is important to bear in mind that there are many causes of hearing loss. However, these can all be categorised into two main types: conductive and sensorineural. Questions and examination should be targeted towards establishing the presence of any associated related symptoms if hearing loss is reported.

Sensorineural hearing loss may be caused by:

- Advancing age
- Acoustic trauma
- Infection
- Drugs
- Acoustic neuromas
- Meniere's disease
- A variety of neurological causes.

Conductive hearing loss may be caused by:

- Blockage of the Eustachian tube
- Fluid in the middle ear caused by a virus such as the 'common cold' as seen in Ivy's case (see Box 11.1, page 196)
- Impacted ear wax or a foreign body
- Ear infection
- Perforated tympanic membrane (PTM).

Rinne test

The Rinne test can be used to assess hearing loss. This test involves placing a vibrating tuning fork on the patient's mastoid bone and asking the patient to tell you when they can no longer hear the sound. At this point, you should move the tuning fork to about 1cm from the patient's external auditory meatus and ask them if they can hear the sound again. A normal response would be for the patient to hear the noise for twice as long with the tuning fork in this position, compared to the first position. This is due to the fact that air conduction of sound should be greater than bone conduction. The test should be repeated in both ears.

If the patient hears the sound for less than twice as long when the tuning fork is in front of the ear, they may have sensorineural hearing loss. This can be the case for one or both ears.

If the patient has an 'abnormal' response to the test and reports hearing the sound for longer when the tuning fork is placed on the mastoid bone than when placed near the external auditory meatus, the patient is considered to have conductive hearing loss.

Once the type of hearing loss has been established, you should investigate and manage the potential causes appropriately.

At a suitable point, either during or after a consultation with the patient, you should take the opportunity to discuss any relevant health promotion topics. In relation to a patient with ear-related symptoms these conversations may include:

- The possible requirement to have a hearing test
- Guidance on the use of a hearing aid
- Social support and adjustment in relation to hearing loss or tinnitus
- Occupational hazards that may lead to or be related to hearing loss
- The inappropriate use of cotton buds or other items to clean the inner ear and alternative advice on how the patient can approach ear hygiene.

If the patient is complaining of earache/pain (otalgia), the clinician should look for signs of:

- Mastoiditis
- Otitis externa
- Otitis media
- Other signs of associated with ENT or upper respiratory tract infection (URTI) infection such as pyrexia, sore throat, nasal discharge or blockage
- Otorrhoea – discharge due to otitis externa, trauma, otitis media with perforated tympanic membrane
- Tinnitus – perceived ringing/whistling/rushing sound. Popping sounds may also be reported and this may be due to temporo-mandibular joint (TMJ) issues.
- Vertigo – this may either be an inner ear problem or related to an underlying neurological condition
- CSF otorrhoea – which will display as a clear fluid discharge and is an indicator of a possible base of skull fracture.

It is important to ask the patient:

- If they have had any previous surgery involving their ears or any past problems

- If they have experienced any systemic illnesses that may cause hearing loss such as meningitis, mumps and measles
- If there is any familial link – i.e. any family members with hearing loss
- Any medications and/or allergies – e.g. erythromycin and vancomycin may cause deafness/tinnitus/balance problems; and streptomycin and gentamicin may cause ataxia (hearing loss through destruction of labyrinthine function)
- Any recent use of cotton buds or other items in the ear that may have resulted in trauma or infection.

Ivy presents with a mainly normal ear assessment, though a build-up of ear wax in the left ear, obscuring the tympanic membrane, is noted. This may be responsible for her sense of imbalance and can be easily treated with ear drops for a minimum 3–5 days to initially soften wax and facilitate irrigation if required. However, it should be noted there is currently a paucity of clinical evidence and this treatment regime is based on expert opinion (Burton & Doree 2009). Ivy should also be made aware that drops may worsen her symptoms, causing transient hearing loss as the wax softens and changes position, or skin irritation.

Nose

As the primary passage for air to flow in and out of the body during ventilation, the nasal passages can act as entry points for pathogens, resulting in many unwanted symptoms, such as rhinitis. In fact, the viruses and bacterial responsible for many meningococcal infections reside within the nasal passage but they are normally well suppressed by the innate immune system. In particular, infections that affect and inflame the sinuses can lead to symptoms of dizziness and can include blurred vision. In Ivy's case, this may be a contributing factor to the feeling of unsteadiness and a possible cause of falling.

Common cold

When patients comment on suffering from cold-like symptoms, clinicians should seek to define exactly what symptoms are being experienced. To clarify, a common cold is usually the result of a viral infection in the upper respiratory tract. On entry, a cold virus can attach to the lining of the nasal passages and/or sinuses. The surrounding cells then become infected and begin releasing histamine, causing local swelling/congestion and an increase in mucous production (rhinitis or coryza).

Generalised coryzal symptoms can include rhinorrhoea, congestion, epistaxis, anosmia or hyposmia, coughing, sneezing, nasal deformity and pain in the nose or throat.

Nasal inspection

Examination should always begin with inspection. In this case, the nose and nasal passages should be assessed in reference to normal anatomy, noting any congenital abnormality, deformity from swelling or trauma and deviation. The patient's nose should then be elevated at the tip to provide a view of the anterior nares and, once again, any abnormality noted.

Transillumination

After initial inspection of the nasal passages, assessment of the nasal sinuses should take place to examine if any congestion is present. To carry out this assessment, the room must firstly be dark and the patient sitting comfortably. Hold the light from a pen torch over the sinuses for examination. As the sinuses are hollow, a normal presentation would show the light passing through as a red glow. In the presence of any congestion, the light would no longer be able to shine through and would appear as opaque.

Testing for anosmia and the olfactory nerve

For this test, you should ask the patient to close their eyes and, using a familiar, potent and non-irritable substance such as coffee, vanilla or lemon, cover or occlude one nostril at a time and ask the patient to identify the smell. In the clinical environment, these substances may not be available. Alcohol may be appropriate and readily available from wipes or hand gel, though this substance can be offensive. As the patient inhales, olfactory receptors are triggered. If the odour is detected, anosmia is not present. Previous facial injuries (with damage to the cribiform plate) may cause transient or permanent anosmia – hence the importance of taking a complete history prior to testing.

Complaints of phantosmia (an olfactory hallucination or 'phantom smell') should also be considered. Potential causes can range from simple nasal infection, smoking or dental disease to more complex and sinister causes such as Parkinson's disease, epilepsy, lesion or cancer.

Nasopharyngeal carcinoma (NPC) is the most common cause of cancer in the upper pharynx and appears to have many causes (such as viral, dietary and genetic factors), and is more prevalent in males of East Asian or African descent. It commonly presents with neck lymphadenopathy as its primary symptom, though it may also present with otitis media, hearing loss, cranial nerve palsy or trismus.

On examination, Ivy presents with opacity on transillumination, nasal congestion and coryzal sounds. She states that her sense of smell is reduced when compared to normal but is still present, and this is consistent with her history of rhinorrhoea and cold-like symptoms.

Throat and mouth

Acting as another primary entry point for pathogens, the throat can be equally affected by infection. An examination may also highlight the need for further specialist assessment and referral, in the presence of abnormal findings. The clinician should look for the following signs and symptoms during assessment:

- **Sore throat** – as a symptom, this can have various underlying causes. The onset of the sore throat can help eliminate particular causes, as a bacterial cause will normally have a sudden onset, whilst a viral cause is more likely to be gradual. However, a sore throat can also have a non-infectious origin (such as environment, mouth breathing, smoking or excessive vocal activity putting a strain on the vocal cords). Thorough questioning around this symptom is therefore warranted.

- **Dysphagia** – as with a sore throat, the onset of dysphagia can help differentiate between a viral or bacterial cause. However, there are numerous possible causes for this symptom and, once again, thorough questioning is warranted, including discussion of associated symptoms.

- **Bleeding gums** – these are most commonly due to an issue with dental hygiene but may also be related to hormonal changes. As a result, this symptom is commonly seen in pregnancy. In female patients of child-bearing age, further questioning may therefore be relevant to consider this as a differential diagnosis if appropriate.

- **Halitosis** – if found, this should warrant further investigation. Assessment and investigations for diabetes mellitus should be considered in the presence of 'sweet' halitosis. Likewise, assessment and investigations for bowel obstruction are warranted in the presence of faecal odour halitosis; and kidney failure should be investigated in the presence of musty or ammonia odour halitosis. Hepatic encephalopathy should be considered for a range of halitosis presentations, such as 'musty', 'sweet' or the smell of freshly cut hay. General dental and oral and throat infections should not be ruled out as possible causes of halitosis, and certain foods and drinks should also be considered as potential underlying causes.

- **Toothache** – this should give rise to consideration of a possible associated abscess.

- **Exudate** – this may signify bacterial infection, especially when it is tonsillar. In this situation, tools such as the CENTOR criteria (Aalbers *et al.* 2011) could be considered for prescription of antibiotics. Antibiotic prescription is not usually necessary for the treatment of pharyngitis, as the condition is predominantly viral in nature and self-limiting, though the patient could consider use of symptomatic relief aids, such as antiseptic lozenges. There is currently no evidence to support the use of vitamin C in treating cold-like symptoms, though increased fluid intake may prove soothing and prevent acute kidney injury as secondary treatment.

- **Uvular deviation** – this may be caused by a worsening peritonsillar abscess and can be easily distinguished from cranial nerve involvement due to the lack of muscle wasting and the presence of inflammatory signs.

On examination, Ivy has mild reddening of her pharynx but no dysphagia or exudate. She has normal uvular presentation and no lymphadenopathy. This is suggestive of viral pharyngitis for which management would include symptomatic relief. She should be seen again if her symptoms worsen (for example, if there is an onset of dysphagia, or she gets a hoarse voice, or fails to improve within one week), as this may be suggestive of glandular fever.

Antibiotics are not indicated at this point but may be considered if the patient presents with a combination of three or more of the following symptoms (Aalbers *et al.* 2011):

- **Presence of tonsillar exudate**
- **Tender anterior cervical lymphadenopathy or lymphadenitis**
- **Fever and absence of cough.**

As Ivy presents with only the absence of cough, it is highly unlikely to be Group A beta-haemolytic streptococcus (GABHS) and is more likely to be viral. It may be worth considering the use of a delayed prescription (post-dated), as many prescriptions are not collected once symptoms begin to improve.

One of the main reasons for patients seeking primary care help regarding sore throats is for reassurance, which should be given and may be reinforced with symptomatic advice regarding antiseptic lozenges or anti-pyretic/anti-inflammatories for mild to moderate pain relief. As with all drug therapies, understanding and confirmation should be sought from the patient to avoid accidental overdose. Non-steroidal anti-inflammatories (NSAIDs) are acceptable in this instance, as Ivy has no contra-indications and is capable of compliance with treatment regimes.

Ivy should also consider contacting primary care services if she experiences worsening symptoms. All advice should be clearly documented and it may also be appropriate to give Ivy an advice leaflet as part of her discharge package.

Conclusion

This chapter has highlighted the importance of the EENT assessment for the primary care practitioner and the management of a potentially complex case (Ivy). Her current working diagnosis is: impounded ear wax causing light-headedness and vertigo symptoms, which have in turn caused the imbalance and worsening falls. She has since developed a viral pharyngitis and is being treated with symptomatic relief, including antiseptic lozenges and NSAIDs.

The differential diagnosis includes glandular fever or developing GABHS, and BPPV which would need to be excluded once the wax has been successfully removed. Ivy will also have a blood sample taken to exclude metabolic causes of her imbalance. If Ivy has not had her eyesight reviewed within the past 12 months, then a referral to an ophthalmologist may also be appropriate.

Ivy has been well informed and involved in the decision-making process, has been given documented advice using a SMART model, and can now be discharged, as we have excluded a number of differential diagnoses following in-depth assessment. Ivy is to be reviewed again within a week, to ensure that the pharyngitis has resolved and that the tympanic membrane is now visible following treatment with ear drops.

LIBRARY, UNIVERSITY OF CHESTER

References

Aalbers, J., O'Brien, K.K., Chan, W.-S., Flk, G.A., Teljeur, C., Dimitrov, D.D. & Fahey, T. (2011). *Predicting streptococcal pharyngitis in adults in primary care: a systematic review of the diagnostic accuracy of symptoms and signs and validation of the Centor score* [Online]. Available from: http://bmcmedicine.biomedcentral.com/articles/10.1186/1741-7015-9-67 (Accessed 5/3/2017).

Baker C. (2015). *Accident and Emergency Statistics* [Online]. Available from: http://researchbriefings.parliament.uk/ResearchBriefing/Summary/SN06964 (Accessed 5/3/2017).

Bickley, L.S. (2013). *Bates' Guide to Physical Examination and History Taking.* 11th edn. London: Lippincott Williams & Wilkins.

Burton, M.C. & Doree, C. (2009). *Ear drops for the removal of ear wax* (Cochrane Review). The Cochrane Library. John Wiley & Sons, Ltd.

Kerber, K.A. & Baloh, R.W. (2011). The evaluation of a patient with dizziness. *Neurology: Clinical Practice.* 1, 24–33.

Glossary

ABC mnemonic Airway, Breathing, Circulation.

ABCDE mnemonic Expansion of the ABC mnemonic: Airway, Breathing, Circulation, Disability and Exposure.

Acromioclavicular Pertaining to the acromion and clavicle.

Acute (Of a disease/condition) Having severe symptoms and a short course.

Adductor pollicis Large triangular muscle that is a powerful adductor of the thumb, and opposes the thumb to the rest of the digits when gripping.

Adnexae Uterine adnexae refers to the ovaries, fallopian tubes and broad ligaments that anchor the uterus.

Aneurysm Dilation of blood vessel wall, often described as 'balloon like'.

Angina Chest pain caused by reduced blood flow through the coronary arteries supplying the heart.

Arcus Greyish ring at the periphery of the cornea.

Arcus senilis Arcus that is likely to be due to age rather than a clinical condition.

Arthritis Inflammation of a joint.

Asbestosis Lung disease caused by inhalation of asbestos fibres.

Asthma Long-term, intermittent, inflammatory respiratory condition characterised by variable and recurring spasms of wheezing, resulting from narrowing and inflammation of the airways.

Atherosclerosis Thickening of the artery wall usually caused by the accumulation of fatty materials such as cholesterol.

Biomechanics Study of the structure and function of biological systems such as humans, animals, plants, organs and cells by means of the methods of mechanics.

Breathlessness Also described as shortness of breath (SOB); the feeling of being out of breath.

Bronchiectasis Widening and distortion of the airways, leading to impaired mucocillary clearance.

Bronchoscopy Using a fibre-optic device to look at the trachea and bronchi.

Bruits Sounds of turbulent blood flow.

Cardiomyopathy Literally 'heart muscle disease'; measurable deterioration of the function of the myocardium for any reason.

Capillary refill Rate at which blood refills empty capillaries.

Cardiovascular disease (CVD) All diseases of the heart and circulation.

Cerebrovascular accident Stroke; rapid loss of brain function due to disturbance in the blood supply to the brain.

Cervical excitation Also known as cervical motion tenderness; pain or sensitivity during vaginal examination when the cervix is moved with the examiner's fingers.

Chlamydia The most common bacterial sexually transmitted infection in the UK, caused by the organism Chlamydia trachomatis.

Cholecystitis Inflammation of the gall bladder, often caused by gallstones.

Chronic (Of a disease/condition) Persisting for a long time.

Chronic airflow obstruction Long-term narrowing of the bronchi, usually caused by a chronic lung condition such as chronic bronchitis.

Clubbing (Hippocratic nails or Hippocratic fingers) Increase in swelling at the distal end of extremities, usually bilateral and painless with no underlying changes to bone structure, eventually causing the nail bed to become convex and extend up nail.

Cochleotoxicity Drug-induced damage to the auditory system.

Coronary heart disease (CHD) Narrowing or blockage of the coronary arteries, usually caused by atherosclerosis.

Crepitus Crackling or crunching sound heard when the ends of two fractured pieces of bone rub against each other.

Cuboid Tarsal bone on the outer side of the foot, articulating in front with the calcaneus and lateral cuneiform, and behind with the fourth and fifth metatarsal bones.

CVA Cerebrovascular accident or stroke.

Cyanosis Blue or purple colouration of the skin and mucous membranes, due to the tissues near the skin surface being deprived of oxygen.

Cyanotic heart disease Type of congenital heart defect.

Deep dyspareunia Deep pain during or after sexual intercourse, felt in the vagina, cervical area and/or lower abdomen.

Diabetes Long-term metabolic condition characterised by insulin deficiency and/or resistance, leading to raised blood glucose levels. Diabetes is divided into types: Type 1, which is insulin dependent and Type 2, which is not insulin dependent but in some cases requires insulin treatment.

Differential diagnosis Process of weighing the probability of one disease against that of other diseases, possibly accounting for a patient's illness.

Diplopia Subjective complaint that involves seeing two images instead of one; 'double vision'.

Dysphagia Difficulty in swallowing.

Dysuria Pain or difficulty passing urine.

Down's Syndrome Also known as Trisomy 21, this is a chromosomal condition caused by the presence of all or part of a third copy of chromosome 21.

Eclampsia Convulsive condition associated with pre-eclampsia, which poses a threat to both maternal and foetal life.

Endocarditis Inflammation of the inner layer of the heart.

Endometriosis An under-diagnosed condition in which endometrial-like tissue is found outside the uterus, causing a range of symptoms such as painful periods, pain during sex and chronic pelvic pain.

End-tidal End of exhalation of the tidal volume.

Epilepsy Chronic neurological condition characterised by seizures.

Erythema Redness of the skin due to congestion of the capillaries.

Evert To turn inside out or outward.

Extra-articular Situated or occurring outside a joint.

Exudate Mass of fluid and cells rich in protein that has seeped out of the vascular supply into areas of inflammation or lesions.

Fatigue Subjective feeling of tiredness.

Fibroids Benign tumours in the myometrial layer of the uterus that can cause heavy menstrual bleeding and infertility.

Fluorescein angiography Injection of a fluorescent dye to allow photography of the blood vessels of the eye.

Fornix Recess around the cervix, formed by the protrusion of the cervix into the vagina.

Friability Fragility of cervical tissue which may bleed on contact.

Fundoscopy Use of an opthalmoscope to view the fundus and other structures of the eye, including vasculature.

Gait pattern manner or style of walking.

Gastritis Inflammation of the lining of the stomach.

General anaesthetic Anaesthetic technique in which anaesthetic agents/drugs are used to induce reversible loss of consciousness.

Genitourinary system The reproductive organs and urinary system.

Gestational hypertension New hypertension presenting after 20 weeks' gestation without significant proteinuria.

Global overview (Of patient assessment) Considering all possible sensory information, used to express scene management and obtaining history during emergency medicine.

Gonorrhoea Second most common bacterial sexually transmitted infection in the UK caused by the organism Neisseria gonorrhoeae.

Gout Form of acute arthritis that causes severe pain and swelling in the joints.

Haemarthrosis Extravasation of blood into a joint or its synovial cavity.

Haemolytic anaemia Form of anaemia due to haemolysis (abnormal breakdown of red blood cells).

Haemoptysis Coughing up blood from the respiratory tract.

Halitosis Common condition causing bad breath or fetor oris.

Heave Heartbeat.

HELLP syndrome Collection of biochemical changes associated with pre-eclampsia, characterised by haemolysis, elevated liver enzymes and low platelet count.

Hemianopia Blindness affecting more than half the field of vision.

Hernia Protrusion of an organ, or the fascia of an organ, through the wall of the cavity that usually contains it.

High Resolution Computer Tomography (HRCT) Non-invasive scan that takes detailed pictures of the relevant part of the body.

Holistic (Of care) Incorporating the physical, psychological, social and emotional when assessing cause and effect of illness on the individual.

Humanistic (Of psychology) Concerning human behaviour.

Hypercholesterolaemia High serum cholesterol level.

Hyperhidrosis Condition characterised by abnormal perspiration.

Hyperopia Hypermetropia or far-sightedness.

Hypertension Medical term for high blood pressure, defined as an elevation from normal range in either the systolic and/or diastolic blood pressure.

Hypothenar Fleshy eminence along the ulnar side of the palm.

Hypothesis Tentative explanation of the clinical diagnosis.

Hypoxia Reduced blood oxygen levels.

Hysterectemy Surgical removal of the uterus (womb).

In-line stabilisation Act or process of limiting movement or making the entire spine incapable of movement.

Interphalangeal Situated between two contiguous phalanges.

Inter-menstrual bleeding Bleeding from the vagina at any time in the menstrual cycle other than normal menstruation.

Intubation Placement of an endotracheal tube into the trachea.

Irlens Syndrome A perceptual processing disorder causing visual stress; also known as Scotopic Sensitivity Syndrome (SSS).

Ischaemia Restriction in blood supply to the tissues.

Kinematics Branch of mechanics dealing with the study of the motion of a body or a system of bodies, without consideration of its mass or the forces acting on it.

Kyphosis Excessive convex curvature of the cervical, thoracic and sacral spine, causing benign to pathological deformity, usually associated with degenerative disorders.

Laryngeal mask airway Airway device with an inflatable cuff, which may be used to maintain the airway during spontaneous ventilation.

Laryngoscopy Procedure that enables visualisation of the vocal cords and glottis; a laryngoscope is used for this purpose.

Lordosis Anterior concavity in the curvature of the lumbar and cervical spine, as viewed from the side.

Lymph nodes Swellings found at intervals along the lymphatic system.

Lymphadenopathy Disease of the lymph nodes.

Lymphoma Malignant tumour of the lymph nodes.

Macrolides Type of naturally occurring product that includes a large macrocyclic lactone ring coupled with one or more deoxy sugars; commonly used as antibiotics with a similar structure to penicillin but safer in penicillin-allergic patients.

Malar flush Cyanotic (blueish) discolouration of the cheeks.

Malaena Tarry-like stool, associated with bleeding from the gastrointestinal tract.

Malaise Vague feeling of discomfort.

Mal de Debarquement Illusion of movement following travel by boat or ship, though may also be precipitated by air and vehicle travel; usually spontaneously resolves within 24 hours after travelling.

Marfan's syndrome Genetic disorder of connective tissue.

Masses Localised enlargements or swellings in a body cavity.

Mastoiditis Inflammation of the mucosal lining of the mastoid bone, usually as a sequela of infection.

Mesothelioma Tumour of the pleura, peritoneum or pericardium caused by past exposure to asbestos.

Metacarpophalangeal Of or relating to the metacarpus and the phalanges of the hand, especially to the articulations between them.

Myopia Near-sightedness through retinal refractory error.

Navicular 1. A comma-shaped bone of the wrist that is located in the first row of carpals. 2. A concave bone of the foot, located between the talus and the metatarsals. Also called the scaphoid.

Nocturia The need to get up during the night to pass urine.

Nystagmus Constant uncontrolled movement of the eye, commonly horizontally, though may also be vertical or circular.

Occult bleeding Escape of blood, as from an injured vessel.

Oedema Excessive build-up of fluid in the tissues.

Oesophagitis Inflammation of the oesophagus most commonly associated with acid reflux.

Onycholysis Loosening or separation of a nail from its bed.

Orthotics Field of knowledge relating to orthopaedic appliances or apparatus used to support, prevent or correct deformities or to improve moveable parts of the body and their use.

Osteoporosis Literally means 'porous bones'; it occurs when bones lose an excessive amount of their protein and mineral content, particularly calcium.

Otitis externa Inflammation of the outer ear (external auditory canal), auricle or both.

Otitis media Group of inflammatory diseases of the middle ear, including acute otitis media and otitis media with effusion.

Ototoxicity Property of being toxic to the ear – commonly the cochlear, auditory nerve or vestibular system; may be reversible, transient or permanent.

Pallor Paleness of the skin.

Palpitations Sensation of rapid, irregular, forceful heartbeats or becoming aware of one's own heartbeat.

Paraesthesia Abnormal sensation, such as burning, prickling, formication, etc.

Paralysis Complete loss of strength in an affected limb or muscle group.

Pathology Structural and functional manifestations of disease.

Pathophysiological Biological manifestation of the disease process.

Pedunculated (of polyps) Attached by a stalk.

Perioperative Relates to the period prior to, during and after surgery.

Peristalsis Series of organised muscular contractions that occur throughout the gastrointestinal tract.

Peritonsular abcess Bacterial infection causing a pus-filled pocket near a tonsil.

Polycythaemia Increase in the blood pack cell volume.

Portal hypertension Abnormally high blood pressure in the hepatic portal vein.

Post-coital bleeding Non-menstrual bleeding that occurs immediately after sexual intercourse.

Pneumonia Inflammation of all or part of the lung, caused by infection.

Pneumothorax Air in the pleural cavity.

PQRST mnemonic Provocative/Palliative, Quality, Radiation, Site, Timing

Pre-eclampsia Condition peculiar to pregnancy, consisting of new hypertension presenting after 20 weeks with significant proteinuria. Severe pre-eclampsia is pre-eclampsia with severe hypertension and/or symptoms, and/or biochemical and/or haematological impairment.

Presbyopia Blurred vision and far-sightedness as a result of the aging process and retinal hardening.

Proprioception Sense of relative position of body parts in space, and strength required to maintain motion, equilibrium or position.

Proteinuria Condition in which there are abnormal quantities of protein in the urine, which may indicate damage to the kidneys. Significant proteinuria is diagnosed when the urinary protein:creatinine ratio is greater than 30mg/mmol or a validated 24-hour urine collection result shows more than 300mg protein.

Psoriatic Of, relating to, or characteristic of the skin disease psoriasis, marked by red, itchy, scaly patches.

Psychophysiological Interaction of the mind and body.

Pulmonary embolus Obstruction of the pulmonary artery or one of its branches usually caused by a blood clot.

Pulsations (of blood) Movements in arteries, caused by the rise and fall in blood pressure during systole and diastole.

Pus Generally viscous, yellowish-white fluid formed in infected tissue, consisting of white blood cells, cellular debris, and necrotic tissue.

Raynaud's disease Condition in which arteries in the hand are unusually reactive and contract when hands are cold.

'Red flags' Reference to patient signs and symptoms associated with serious, potentially life-threatening conditions

Referred pain Pain felt in another part of the body from that where the cause is located.

Regional anaesthesia This anaesthetic technique prevents the patient feeling pain in a large area (region) of the body.

Renal colic Form of abdominal pain typically associated with kidney stones.

Respiratory insufficiency Inability of the lungs to carry out their normal function.

Retina Light-sensitive layer of tissue lining the inside surface of the eye.

Retinosa pigmentosa Genetic condition resulting in progressive degeneration of the retinal photoreceptive rods, causing severe visual impairment and eventual blindness.

Rhabdomyolysis Disintegration of striated muscle fibres with excretion of myoglobin in the urine.

Rheumatic fever Inflammatory disease that can occur after an infection with Group A Streptococcus.

Rheumatoid Of or resembling rheumatism.

Rhinorrhea Filling of the nasal cavity with a significant quantity of mucus fluid.

Sarcoidosis Chronic disorder in which the lymph nodes are usually enlarged and small nodules develop.

Scapulothoracic Pertaining to the scapula and thorax.

Scoliosis Lateral (sideways) deviation/curvature of the spine.

Sequelae Conditions resulting from a previous injury or disease.

Sessile (of polyps) Attached by a base.

Sinusitis Infection of the para-nasal sinuses.

Spider naevi Cutaneous spots caused by dilated arterioles.

Splenomegaly Enlargement of the spleen.

Sternoclavicular Pertaining to the sternum and clavicle.

Striae Irregular areas of skin that look like bands, stripes or lines.

Stridor Noise heard on breathing, when the trachea or larynx are obstructive – louder than a wheeze.

Sub-acromial Pertaining to the area below the acromion.

Subconjunctival haemorrhage Bleeding of the conjunctival and episcleral blood vessels into the subconjunctival space.

Supine Positioned lying down on one's back, with one's front facing upwards.

Supraclavicular Above the clavicle (collar bone).

Supraglottic airway Airway device which may be used to maintain the airway during spontaneous ventilation.

Surgical emphysema Condition in which air escapes into the tissues of the chest and neck from leaks in the lung or oesophagus.

Synaesthesia Neurological phenomenon whereby stimulation of one cognitive or sensory pathway leads to an involuntary and automatic experiences in a second sensory or cognitive pathway.

Syncope The medical term for fainting.

Syphilis Bacterial, sexually transmitted infection caused by the organism Treponema pallidum.

Systemic Pertaining to or affecting the body as a whole.

Temporomandibular Pertaining to the temporal bone and mandible.

Tenoperiostial junction Where tendon attaches to bone.

Thenar The fleshy part of the hand at the base of the thumb.

Thrill (Of the heart) Murmur that is palpable through the chest wall.

Thromboembolism Occlusion of a blood vessel due to a thrombus.

Trismus Inability to fully open the mouth, predominantly through muscular or nerve damage; also known as 'lockjaw'.

Tuberculosis Infectious disease caused by a bacillus called mycobacterium tuberculosis; most commonly affects the lungs.

Ulceration Discontinuity or break in a bodily membrane.

Unilateral Affecting only one side.

Varicose veins Veins that have become enlarged and tortuous.

Vasculitis Varied group of disorders that all share an underlying problem of inflammation of a blood vessel or blood vessels. The inflammation may affect any size blood vessel, anywhere in the body. It may affect either arteries and/or veins.

Ventricular failure Condition in which the lower chamber/s of the heart is/are not functioning efficiently.

Vestibular Relating to the vestibule of the inner ear and a sense of balance.

Wernicke's encephalopathy Neurological symptoms resulting from biochemical lesions of the central nervous system following exhaustion of thiamine and B-vitamin stores.

Wheeze Occurs as a result of narrowing of the airways.

Xanthelasma Yellow lesions above or below the eyes, which may indicate lipid deposits under the skin.

Index